"*Soul Visioning* is a gem of a book, filled with hope and inspiration on how to experience the deepest, richest parts of ourselves. This book can transform your life and is a must-read for everyone."

—Dr. Eileen Borris,
author of *Finding Forgiveness* and
past president, Society for the Study of Peace, Conflict
and Violence for the American Psychological Association

"*Soul Visioning* takes you beyond the usual bounds of therapy to help you access spiritual strengths that not only facilitate the release of limiting patterns, but also deepen your connection with your Higher Self to enrich your life."

—Daniel J. Benor, MD,
author of *Seven Minutes to Natural Pain Release*

Soul Visioning

About the Author

Susan Wisehart, MS, LMFT, NCSP (Illinois) is a holistic psychotherapist, licensed marriage and family therapist, nationally certified school psychologist, and certified hypnotherapist with over
thirty years of professional experience. She received certification
in life-between-lives regression from Michael Newton, PhD, author of *Journey of Souls*. Wisehart also trained with psychiatrist
Brian Weiss, MD, author of *Many Lives, Many Masters*, and in
England with Jungian analyst Roger Woolger, PhD, author of
Other Lives, Other Selves. In her private practice, Susan uses traditional and nontraditional approaches to help her clients heal
body, mind, and spirit. She also facilitates workshops incorporating many topics including Soul Visioning, soul growth, energy
psychology, past-life and life-between-lives regression, and dream
interpretation.

Soul Visioning™

Clear the Past, Create Your Future

SUSAN WISEHART

Llewellyn Publications
Woodbury, Minnesota

First Edition
Third Printing, 2011

Cover design by Ellen Dahl
Cover image © A&G Reporter/TIPS Images
Interior book design by Joanna Willis

Llewellyn is a registered trademark of Llewellyn Worldwide Ltd.

Soul Visioning is a trademark of Susan Wisehart and may only be used with permission.

Library of Congress Cataloging-in-Publication Data
Wisehart, Susan, 1949–
  Soul visioning : clear the past, create your future / by Susan Wisehart. — 1st ed.
     p. cm.
  Includes bibliographical references. ISBN 978-0-7387-1408-0
  1. Self-actualization (Psychology) 2. Soul. 3. Soul—Psychological aspects.
4. Success. I. Title.
  BF637.S4W57 2008
  131—dc22   2008024241

Llewellyn Worldwide does not participate in, endorse, or have any authority or responsibility concerning private business transactions between our authors and the public.

All mail addressed to the author is forwarded but the publisher cannot, unless specifically instructed by the author, give out an address or phone number.

Any Internet references contained in this work are current at publication time, but the publisher cannot guarantee that a specific location will continue to be maintained. Please refer to the publisher's website for links to authors' websites and other sources.

In some of the personal accounts that appear in this book, names and/or identifying details have been changed.

Llewellyn Publications
A Division of Llewellyn Worldwide Ltd.
2143 Wooddale Drive
Woodbury, MN 55125-2989
www.llewellyn.com

Printed in the United States of America

Publisher's Note

The information in this book is general and educational in nature. Some of the energy therapies and other healing modalities described here (the "Techniques") could be considered experimental, and should not be used on a self-help basis to diagnose, treat, cure, or prevent any disease or psychological disorder. The stories, testimonials, and case studies do not warranty, guarantee, or predict the outcome of the reader's use of this book's information. The author and publisher accept no responsibility or liability for the use or misuse of this book's information, including the Techniques, the guided audio processes on the author's website, or links to other resources. Professional advice should be sought from a qualified health care provider for medical or mental health matters.

Contents

PART TWO:
Healing through Spiritual Regression Therapy

Available at
www.soulvisioning.com/svr

Chapter 3

<u>Worksheet download (print format)</u>

- "Applying Your Soul Ideals"

<u>Audio downloads (also available on CD)</u>

- "Peak Experiences Guided Audio Process"
- "A Soul-Guided Journey to Your Ideal Future"

Chapter 4

<u>Worksheet download (print format)</u>

- "Questionnaire: Payoffs and Limiting Beliefs"

Chapter 6

<u>Audio download (also available on CD)</u>

- "Advanced Forgiveness Meditation"

Acknowledgments

I dedicate this book to my beloved husband and soul mate, Dave Birr, because without his help, *Soul Visioning* would not have been birthed. In my life, he is the constant model of unconditional love, infinite patience, and a partnership committed to service to humanity. Dave contributed many of the ideas for the first part of the book from his decades of spiritual research and teaching. Dave, I thank you from the bottom of my heart.

Thanks also to Carrie Obry at Llewellyn Worldwide Publishing, who sought me out and recognized the potential of this book and message. It is your foresight and vision that allowed *Soul Visioning* to garner wind for its sails. You are an earth angel disguised as an editor. My appreciation also goes to Mindy Keskinen, Llewellyn New Titles editor, who polished the words of this book to a high luster. Thanks to everyone on the Llewellyn team for all of their efforts on my behalf.

A special note of gratitude goes to my own primary editor, Sara Steinberg. Who would have guessed that the ultimate purpose of our twenty-five-year friendship would be the culmination of this book? Thanks for sharing your editing skills and talents, patience, and perseverance through the long months of editing, working many nights into the wee hours to meet deadlines. You are a great soul!

Thanks also to Pam Parsons for her numerous editing contributions and her depth of knowledge of the subject matter of this book. I could not have had any greater cheerleader.

I have deep gratitude to Carole Childers for her constant encouragement and for "being there every step of the way." Carol Barnett, Sue Briesch, Helen Moore, Elizabeth Razny, Leslie Roberts, and Catherine Chiesa acted as midwives through all the stages of development of this book. They gave me inspiration, support, and laughter when I most needed it. Thanks to all the wise women in my life.

Thanks to Roz Fowler and Marguerite McMillan for doing a fantastic job transcribing the many hours of interviews and sessions. I am also indebted to Dr. Therese Evans, Beth Sabor, Elaine Morales, Jim Sances, Dr. Barbara Terao, and to Nathaniel Birr (my indispensable assistant) for reading the manuscript and providing valuable insights and feedback. Kathryn Andries gave me valuable book advice along the way. I could not have a better publicist than Bob Sandidge, who embodies and lives the message of *Soul Visioning*.

My love goes to all of those who took this journey with me and generously took the time to share their stories of transformation. Your contributions are priceless.

Sincere thanks to Diane Willis, president of the Chicago chapter of the International Association for Near-Death Studies (IANDS), who believed in me and gave me many opportunities to speak and give voice to this important message. Also, heartfelt gratitude goes to Toni Romano, Outreach Director of the Association for Research and Enlightenment (ARE), for her unfailing support over the years. I am indebted to Nancy Marder of the Infinity Foundation for her long history of sponsoring our workshops and classes. My appreciation goes to Mary Montgomery for helping me to be "discovered." Dr. Wilson and Naomi Young were wise sages in my early years, who proved that when the student is ready, the teachers appear. Kudos to Dr. Ken Wapnick for his decades of mentoring, teaching, and friendship, which helped me to stay focused on my true spiritual path.

I do appreciate all of the "teachers" in my life (in body and in Spirit), both positive and challenging. They were tremendous mirrors who brought the lessons I needed to learn, which provided me the foundation to write this book. Many of the players in my drama this time around taught me deep compassion and a strong desire to help people discover the joy of their true identity as a soul.

Introduction
From Pain to Peace

One of the inspirations for this book was a sixty-five-year-old homeless woman named Mary Margaret. When I met her, she had lost not only her job but her health, her money, her family, and her dignity. She was desperate to change her life and highly motivated to do whatever it took to get out of the mess she was in. Mary Margaret took a courageous healing journey with me and turned her life around. Her soul's vision has brought her the career of her dreams, meaningful relationships, and most of all, a deep sense of peace with herself.[1]

Mary Margaret is just one of the courageous people you will meet in this book, people who have reconciled with the past through forgiveness, cleared their unconscious obstacles to following their higher guidance, connected with their inner abundance, and created a soul-guided life of joy, passion, and purpose. What enabled these people to transform their lives when so many others have tried just as hard to do the same but without success? What made the difference? That is what this book is about!

How to change your life. How to manifest what you want. How to release your blocks. How to grow personally and spiritually. *Been there, done that!* you say, and I believe you. *I've studied and practiced so many self-help methods that I could teach them by heart! I've done them all, and yet I'm still stuck!* I've been there myself, and I hear this all the time from my clients.

If you're like many of the people I see in my practice, you could start your own library with all the self-improvement, motivational, and spiritual growth books you've collected. Many clients come to me having already tried numerous approaches to personal and spiritual growth. We're talking years of workshops, therapies, classes, trainings, and consultations. If you've "done it all" too, then maybe these comments will sound familiar:

> *I try to meditate, think positive thoughts, raise my vibrations, but it is too difficult.*
>
> *I try listening to my inner wisdom, but I just can't hear it.*
>
> *Sometimes I think I hear inner guidance, but I'm not sure whether it's my Higher Self or just my own ego.*
>
> *After everything I've done, I keep repeating the same old patterns.*
>
> *I still haven't been able to (love myself, find my passion, get out of debt, discover my soul purpose for this incarnation, attract my soul mate, create a satisfying career, manifest a healthy body, release my fears, forgive myself and others . . .)*

Most books and trainings that teach us how to manifest what we want in life are missing two things, in my view. First, they ask us to use the small portion of our mind that is conscious—about 5 percent of its capacity—to change the limiting core beliefs and patterns that are fueled by the 95 percent that is unconscious![2] That unconscious programming, from our past lives and this life, sabotages our best efforts to create the life we want.

Second, they assume that using our ego mind, we can create what we really want! But what about accessing our soul? The ego can manifest material wealth to try to fill up a sense of inner lack, but only the soul can provide lasting peace of mind.

I believe the root cause of our pain is that we perceive ourselves as separated from our Divine Source, Spirit, our Higher Self. We have forgotten that we are eternal spiritual beings with a soul. We are hungry for deeper answers to our questions, hungry for spiritual solutions that we haven't known how to find. We have used our ego mind to create our life. No wonder our results have been limited. Only by remembering the abundance of our Spirit, as we fulfill our soul's purpose, can we create the life we truly desire.

After over thirty years as a psychotherapist using traditional and nontraditional approaches as well as insights gained from my own life, I have begun to understand what works and what doesn't. These professional and personal factors strongly motivate me to help people get "unstuck." In most cases, I have found, we are thrown off balance by our unconscious cellular memories, past traumas, programmed beliefs from childhood, or past-life experiences. Our ego voices tell us: *No matter what you do, it isn't good enough. Happiness never lasts. You don't deserve to succeed. You're guilty. You're sinful* . . . or whatever other limiting comments come to mind.

Recently, new therapies have become available that help us more readily let go of the unconscious baggage we've carried from our past. These approaches are user-friendly, and in many cases can be learned and practiced without the help of a professional. Over decades of practice and thousands of clients, I have discovered which methods work best and quickest to help people resolve their internal barriers, heal, and realize their true identity as a soul. I'm not promising quick fixes, but I am saying there are faster roads to healing. You still must do the inner work, but these approaches pave the way.

Soul Visioning™, the seven-step process you will experience in this book, integrates the best of hypnotherapy, the developing field of energy psychology (sometimes called "acupuncture for the emotions but without the needles"), forgiveness processes, and soul work; it also includes guided "audio journeys" (available through my website as a free

MP3 download or for purchase on CD). You will learn an amazingly simple tool to clear the unconscious, sabotaging beliefs and patterns that hold you back. When these resistances are resolved, you can better envision and create your ideal future from *higher soul guidance,* the part of the mind that is intuitive, wise, compassionate, creative, and inspired.

In addition, you will learn about other life-changing soul-based processes such as past-life regression (PLR) and another recent approach, life-between-lives regression (LBL). These methods often work when others don't, because they go to the roots of the issues we have carried over from previous incarnations. You will also read several one- to ten-year follow-up interviews with people who have done this work with me—people whose stories report some amazing results.

Reading this book is much like attending one of my Soul Visioning workshops. Most people who wholeheartedly participate in this process are amazed at how deeply joined they feel to their soul's vision. They feel empowered and inspired. Many say they see and feel, for the first time, how luminous and joyous their life can be when guided by their soul.

This book teaches you to create—in holographic time, where all possibilities exist—your ideal future in the areas of health, career/work, personal/spiritual growth, relationships, and finances. The Soul Visioning process will help you identify where you are blocked and provides tools to clear those unconscious self-limitations. It helps open the channel to your own soul intuition and guidance.

Along the way, I share some personal journeys, my own as well as those of others. Through Soul Visioning and practicing forgiveness of myself and others, I have found it possible to remember the Divine within me and to experience deep peace. By removing the blocks in my unconscious mind and following the guidance of my soul, I have been able to create a life of profound meaning and purpose.

This is my deepest, most heartfelt motivation for writing this book—to share what I have learned and to help pioneer further work in this field. Above all, I want to pass on these life-changing tools to all who wish to heal themselves by manifesting from their soul. May *Soul Visioning* bring hope and inspiration to all who are ready to remember their true spiritual identity.

How to Use This Book

This book offers you an experience that is as close as possible to participation in a Soul Visioning workshop—a seven-step process that leads you to your true spiritual identity. It also introduces you to two spiritual regression techniques that can greatly enhance your journey, and it offers some forward-looking tips on expressing your soul in your daily life. Let's briefly review this sequence.

Our Path through This Book

Part One of this book introduces the philosophy behind Soul Visioning. It discusses the nature of the soul, the main obstacles to its expression, and how the relationship between soul and personality affects our ability to manifest the soul's vision. It also guides you to the actual experience of your own Divine Self, which will illuminate and transform your life, and gives you revolutionary tools for clearing your unconscious resistance to your soul guidance.

As you progress through Part One, you will experience all seven steps of Soul Visioning. Each step helps you connect more deeply with your soul's ideals and vision for your life, and each step builds on the previous one. To get the most out of this progression, I recommend that you complete each chapter in full without reading ahead. Rather than merely reading these words for inspiration, participate fully in all the self-exploration exercises, guided audio experiences, worksheets, and other spiritual-growth tools and techniques found here. Just as you would set aside time to attend a class or workshop, let your reading of this book be as experiential as possible. Give yourself this gift. If you get stuck at any point, you may be encountering unconscious resistance. Make note of this, but keep going ahead with the steps. (You may be able to clear this resistance using one of the tools you will find in Part One, or in the "Living Your Vision" section at the end.) Go easy on yourself, and know that you are worth the effort!

Part Two introduces you to the soul-based methods of past-life regression (PLR) and life-between-lives regression (LBL), which go to the root of deeply held repeating patterns carried from one lifetime to the next. Many people have found these spiritual regression approaches helpful when other methods haven't worked. PLR helps you to directly reexperience events from your former lives. LBL is an unforgettable journey to the soul realm between lives, where your Council of Elders and guides can offer assistance with your soul's progress, lessons, and purpose. These journeys can be profoundly healing, as you'll see in this book's case studies and follow-up interviews, held one to ten years later. (I am grateful to the people who generously shared their stories with me and gave me permission to publish them in this book. Although I have changed their names and some identifying details, their stories are intact.)

Because PLR and LBL therapies call for the assistance of trained professionals, the Resources section at the end of this book can help you locate professional organizations and practitioners.

If you truly desire to connect with your soul's vision and guidance as a natural, ongoing, and evolving part of your life, then pay special attention to the final section of this book, "Living Your Vision: Daily Choices to Express Your Soul." Here you'll find a variety of suggestions for building on and enriching your connection with your soul. Experiment, let your creativity flow, and enjoy the journey!

Preparation: Guided Inner Journeys

This book includes several guided processes: chapter 3's "Peak Experiences Guided Audio Process" and "Soul-Guided Journey to Your Ideal Future," and chapter 6's optional "Advanced Forgiveness Guided Audio Meditation." To make the most of them, I recommend you obtain the audio versions of these meditations *before* beginning chapter 3. These spoken recordings are set to relaxing music and paced to bring about a deeply restful state. From the website *www.soulvisioning.com/svr* you can download free MP3 files or purchase them on CD. (Although this book includes the scripts for these meditations, merely reading the words to yourself is less effective than being guided through them.)

For these sessions, plan to set aside some time when you can be alone without distractions (all phones turned off!), in a quiet, comfortable place where you can sit or lie down. You will want to be reasonably relaxed but alert, not drowsy. Listen to the words in a relaxed state, eyes closed. You may want to have a pen and paper within reach.

Please try to approach these guided journeys without expectations. There is no "right" way to experience an inner session, and you can repeat them as many times as you'd like. Each session will deepen your connection with your soul. What you feel and what you perceive will unfold according to your own unique needs and ways of learning, in that moment. Simply ask your soul to guide your experience, and it will be so.

Preparation: Worksheets

Some of this book's self-exploration exercises are written ones, based on worksheets designed to deepen your connection with your soul. You can photocopy the sample worksheets in the book, or you can download free copies at *www.soulvisioning.com/svr*. (See page 293 for a list of all of this book's website resources.)

Some Commonsense Cautions

Before we begin, please note that this book should not be used as an independent "self-help" resource for the treatment of such conditions as major depression, severe anxiety, psychosis, severe trauma, substance abuse, and bipolar or dissociative disorders. These conditions are best addressed by a qualified mental health professional. If you are already working with a therapist, I advise that you consult with that person before using the material in this book. In addition, you understand that if you choose to use any of the techniques or guided processes, it is possible that emotional or physical sensations or additional unresolved memories may surface or continue to surface, indicating other issues may need to be addressed.

I wish you well as you take an amazing Soul Visioning journey through this book!

Part One

Seven Steps to Connecting with Your Soul's Vision

For those who want to live fully, many "manifestation models" are available today—techniques for achieving or manifesting what we want in life. But I have found that most of these models take us only so far. Why? Largely because when we follow these techniques, our decisions typically come from our ego or personality self instead of our higher soul guidance. When we "hit the wall" of our unconscious blocks and find ourselves still mired in repetitive patterns and addictive behaviors, we may get discouraged and wonder how to take the next step. With this book, we will put our soul in charge. Let's take an overview of our path through Part One.

Chapters 1 and 2 explain the major obstacles that interfere with our ability to create an inspired life, and introduce the philosophy behind Soul Visioning. We will also learn about the process of aligning our personality with the guidance of our soul, a progression of many stages. Understanding the stages of soul growth can help us gain a compassionate and realistic perspective for our journey. If we envision our future with the wisdom of our soul, we will be manifesting from a deep inner abundance that is then reflected in the outer world. When we are in touch with our soul, which is connected to the Divine, we experience who we really are.

Now you are ready to move from the conceptual to the practical application of Soul Visioning. In the next chapters, you will take seven steps to connect more deeply with your soul's ideals and vision for your life. **Chapter 3** leads you on a journey to connect with an actual experience of your soul—your True Self—and to envision your soul's purpose. Then you can better identify the ideals that will act as guiding stars for your life, allowing you to envision the soul-directed life you want. You will take three of the seven Soul Visioning steps in this chapter.

- *Step 1:* The **Peak Experiences Guided Audio Process** connects you with the memory of your soul's presence during peak moments in your life. These memories help you identify your spiritual ideals and prepare you to complete the worksheets you will find in Step 2.

- *Step 2:* These **Soul Visioning Writing Exercises** link your spiritual ideals—your soul qualities—with their expression in areas such as career/work, relationships, health, finances, and personal/spiritual growth. With this preparation, you will answer a key question: What if you could wake up tomorrow and have your life be just the way you want it to be, guided by your soul wisdom? What quality of being would be expressed in your thinking, feeling, and doing?

- *Step 3:* The **Soul-Guided Journey to Your Ideal Future** is a cornerstone experience that deeply connects you to your soul, the part of you that is wise, compassionate, empowered, joyful, and connected to the Divine. With this guidance, you will envision your ideal future in areas of your life such as relationships, health, finances, and spirituality, as if that future were happening right now. We often forget what it is like to *be* in that state of peace, joy, and wholeness. From that expanded state of *beingness*, we can envision a life of true happiness. The purpose is not to fill up a perceived emptiness or to distract from feelings of unworthiness, but to manifest consciously from a place of wholeness.

Chapters 4, 5, and 6 help you identify, forgive, and reprogram your internal "monkey mind" messages—the messages that say, for example,

No matter what you do, it's not good enough or *Happiness never lasts.* These are the limiting core beliefs and programs that block your access to soul guidance. You will also learn some revolutionary techniques to help you get unstuck and clear the unconscious beliefs that sabotage the expression of your soul's purpose. These user-friendly tools are known as energy psychology or meridian therapies.

Many of us need to heal some unconscious blocks to benefit fully from the Soul Visioning journey, as discussed in **chapter 4.**

- *Step 4* focuses on *Identifying Limiting Beliefs and Payoffs.* You can think of payoffs as the reasons why you don't change, even when you desperately want to. Through these unconscious defense mechanisms, you try to protect yourself from something that you fear will be much worse. Addressing these mechanisms is crucial. Remember, you don't consciously know that you have them. So in addition to those "blocks" you already know about, you will discover the unconscious resistances that are holding you back, through self-assessment inventories, observing repeating patterns in your life, and noting resistances that emerge during the Soul Visioning journey.

Chapter 5 includes the next two steps in the process.

- *Step 5:* With the *Energy Psychology Tool Kit* you will learn about easy methods to clear the thoughts, feelings, beliefs, and behaviors that interfere with remembering your essence and following your soul's guidance. You will learn the basics of the WHEE process ("Whole Health—Easily and Effectively")®—one of the easiest techniques for most people to learn and use on their own.

- *Step 6:* The next step is *Installing New Beliefs Using WHEE* to replace the old patterns. Once you have cleared your limiting core beliefs and emotions, you will "install" new, affirming beliefs through a multisensory approach involving visual, auditory, and kinesthetic channels, energetically imprinting the new beliefs into your body-mind.

Chapter 6 illuminates the last of the seven steps of Soul Visioning.

- *Step 7* is about *True Forgiveness,* which removes the blocks to the awareness of our true identity as a soul. Forgiveness, an often misunderstood process, is essential to creating a soul-guided life, because by undoing guilt in the mind, we open a path to connecting more deeply with that guidance. Whenever our mind houses hatred, revengeful thoughts, and pain from the past, it drains our energy and keeps us stuck in toxic emotions. When grievances have been cleared, we can more fully listen to our soul guidance; its vision can express with less resistance. Forgiveness restores our inner peace, unity, and a state of mind that lets us stand in the synchronous flow of Divine Love.

The practical forgiveness exercises in this chapter can help heal our mistaken ego perceptions of who we think we are, and let us unburden the baggage of the past. Meridian therapies, mentioned earlier, accelerate this process of forgiving and letting go. This chapter includes some true stories of forgiveness in action, thanks to my generous clients. Their accounts show the powerful impact that letting go of grievances has brought to their lives and others', often bringing a deep peace.

Chapter 7 presents inspiring real-life accounts of how Soul Visioning can transform lives.

one

The Evolving Relationship between Our Soul and Our Personality

Many of us are asleep at the wheel of life, with the ego self as the driver. We are distracted by the landscape around us; pretty objects catch our attention for a while and then fade. Our ego self says, "Let's stop a while and have a drink. That will be a pleasant diversion." Eventually the anesthetic wears off, and we move on to our next escapade. Perhaps we pick up the attractive passenger on the side of the road, who we hope will convince us of our worth. After the road trip with that romantic partner, the honeymoon wears off and we dump them at the next rest stop. "Let's see, there must be some other adventure we can undertake to bring some meaning to life. Ah yes, there's another good-looking person on the way to nowhere." And on it goes until we either crash, run out of gas, or get tired of the detours of life.

Our job is to wake up and put the soul back in the driver's seat.

Today, there is a wealth of books, seminars, television programs, and Internet sites that focus on how we create our own reality. We are told that by consciously focusing our desire, will, thought, and energy, we can change our life or attract something new into our experience. Some people find these tools inspirational and helpful.

However, I've noticed that many people who practice these methods, including my clients, do well for a while but eventually become stuck, feeling blocked from going further. Some even suffer reversals, lose what they had previously manifested, and may find their situation less satisfying than before. Other people manifest exactly what they set out to create, but wind up disappointed because the result doesn't bring them the happiness or fulfillment they expected. On the other hand, some folks seem to manifest only the bare essentials that they need, seldom gaining anything they desire beyond that. What is keeping most of us from creating the life we say we want?

The answer may lie in looking within, not without. Going beyond this focus on adding something external to our life, there is an emerging literature that emphasizes becoming aware of and expressing our soul nature. This book is about connecting to and expressing our true identity as the key to real joy!

Obstacles to Soul Expression

What stands in the way of joyfully expressing that true identity? Let's look at four common sticking points.

Obstacle 1: The Ego's Agenda

One common problem for those trying to manifest an ideal life is letting the ego take the pilot's seat. Many of the people using current manifestation techniques are learning skills that address the wants and the needs of the personality or ego. This is a key point, because when we put the ego in control of creating our future, we have an impostor in charge.

Now, the ego may learn to manifest a Mercedes or a mansion. (I say *may* learn, because if learning to manifest were as simple and straightforward as mastering the kinds of skills we use to drive, there would be a lot more luxury cars on the road. Many factors can hinder our ability to manifest, including the obstacles we are discussing here.) However, we have observed that even if we get exactly what we want, this alone does not bring us happiness. Eventually we realize that despite having these things, we don't feel content or satisfied. There is always something else to desire, to have, to achieve, until we find ourselves firmly chained to the ego's treadmill of acquisition and achievement.

Our ego wants us on that treadmill; it needs us to believe that we are empty and incomplete, requiring something or someone to make us whole. Its agenda is to anesthetize us and distract us from realizing that *we are already whole*. The ego's strategy is to fill up our perceived lack with material objects and worldly accomplishments. According to the ego, this is its purpose, without which it would cease to exist.

But this strategy is self-defeating. Sooner or later, we realize that it is futile to use external solutions to solve an inner problem. We have been trying to manifest possessions, relationships, and power to fill a void in our life that just can't be filled by worldly success. What has been absent all along is that overwhelming sense of oneness and connection that only comes from remembering our true identity, our soul. No egocentric desire or need can ever satisfy our hunger to reconnect to our Divine nature and live as the soul we are.

This is my life's work and the purpose of this book: to help people realize that we are souls. When we are in touch with our soul, which is part of God (or whatever term you use for the Divine), we experience who we truly are. Our life becomes meaningful, joyous, and abundant when lived from this perspective, and those qualities are then reflected in our outer world.

To help us live a soul-guided life, I have developed a seven-step process called Soul Visioning. As you continue through this book, you will have the opportunity to *experience* this process. Its purpose is not to teach us how to fill up a perceived emptiness or distract ourselves from feeling unworthy, but to enable us to experience our wholeness. Instead of seeking to achieve our personality's version of an ideal life, our goal is to wake up from the dream of separateness from our soul and, finally, to express the Divine Love that we are!

Obstacle 2: Unconscious Programming

One key to this process is an awareness of the power of *unconscious programming* to sabotage our best efforts to create the life we want—a point that seems to be missing from many manifesting techniques. Do any of the following sound familiar?

- *Life has to be a struggle.*

- *No matter what I do, it is not good enough.*

- *Happiness never lasts.*

- *I don't deserve to succeed.*

- *The universe is an unfriendly place.*

- *I cannot be myself, or I'll be rejected.*

- *I must always please in order to have love.*

If you answered yes to any of the above, you have just put your finger on some of your own unconscious beliefs. How much of the mind is unconscious? Estimates vary, but it has been generally agreed upon by many psychologists, including early leaders such as Carl Jung, that the preponderance of the mind is outside of conscious awareness. I use an estimate of 95 percent to illustrate the magnitude of the unconscious relative to the conscious mind. Unnerving, isn't it, to think that our idea of who we are is limited by impulses and forces that lurk in the huge basement of our awareness? Just how successful can we be in manifesting our ideal future (as our conscious mind defines it), when the 95 percent of our mind that is completely unknown to us is also driving our thoughts and decisions? That is like letting a person we have never met, and know little about, make most of the choices about our spouse, career, the place we will live, and how we will raise our children.

Chances are that you have already heard about the power of your unconscious mind. Perhaps you have already tried, or are interested in trying, various approaches to accessing and reprogramming your unconscious mind. Either way, keep reading. This book describes several highly effective new tools that you can employ quickly and easily to release some of your own unconscious programming.

Obstacle 3: Failure to Forgive

A third obstacle to manifesting the life we desire is our failure to forgive others and ourselves. The ego tells us that we are all separate, disconnected beings. It emphasizes duality. It dwells in ideas like "I," "me," "mine," "you," and "competition." It focuses on "getting what's mine" and on being a "winner," not a "loser." This keeps us stuck in a victim mentality, feeling resentment, anger, jealousy, and blame, emotions that drain our creative energy. When we are in this state of mind, we are out of harmony with Divine flow.

The soul *is* love. It enfolds, embraces, and includes, viewing all with compassion and understanding. The soul's vocabulary is filled with words like "we," "us," "community," "brotherhood," "cooperation," and "altruism."

Like attracts like, and when we are in a blaming frame of mind, we create experiences of separation from others. We must become a forgiving presence if we wish to experience oneness.

Obstacle 4: Ignoring Our Inner Guidance

This obstacle to manifesting is quite different from the other three. Although we may be aware of communication from our soul, we may lack the willingness to act on that inner guidance. This is often the case because we don't fully accept or trust our soul. So it is not surprising that some of us simply dismiss or rationalize away our intuitions.

Intuitive messages can be subtle and fleeting, perhaps lasting only an instant. To test their value, we need to practice paying attention and responding "as if" they were true. With time and experience, we will learn the trustworthiness and value of our soul guidance.

We will discuss these ego blocks further in later chapters. The good news, again, is that this book presents revolutionary new tools to more rapidly remove traumas and unconscious core beliefs, helping you overcome these obstacles to a true connection with your soul.

But what do we really mean when we talk about the ego or personality? To overcome the ego's obstacles to manifesting, must we eliminate the ego itself? What are we supposed to do with this "me" that we have known and identified with for so long? Does connecting with our soul imply that we have to go through life without a personality? Not at all!

If our soul wants to express itself in this physical reality, it must do so through a personality vehicle. But our personality first needs to become integrated, meaning that to be effective in life *and* in manifesting, we must balance our physical, emotional, and mental selves.

Our integrated personality then needs to become responsive to our soul. Through a series of stages, the soul's awareness becomes infused into the personality. When this happens, rapid progress can occur, because for the first time, we are truly responsive to our soul and more effective at expressing its fullness in our life.

In just a moment we'll explore these stages, but first let's take a closer look at the personality and its relationship to the soul. Understanding this is fundamental to the Soul Visioning process.

Manifesting and the Role of the Personality

When we attempt to manifest our desires, we may encounter some of these obstacles because we are experiencing the world from the viewpoint of our personality. These obstacles primarily arise from our ego's inability to recognize the soul as our true identity, and to relinquish control to it.

Many of us identify totally with our "personality self" and seldom question or think about it, let alone name it as "ego" or mere "personality." What we think of as our identity—based on gender, family background, culture, race, religion, belief systems, memories, jobs, personal desires, habitual thoughts, and so on—may seem to completely define us. Those of us who are religious may believe that we *have* a soul or spirit, but that is very different from experiencing our life with the full awareness that we *are* a soul.

Having a personality is necessary for us to function in this world. In fact, most diagnostic measures of mental health are based upon how effectively our personality functions within our environment. But identifying exclusively with the personality leads to a very limited view of our true potential. If we expect that the only things possible for us are what our personality self has learned, done, or can imagine, that is all we are likely to experience.

Our personal history and learned beliefs can limit our ability to see and experience truth, causing us to judge anything that *appears* to be different from our everyday experience as undesirable, unachievable, or of no worth. For instance, if we are not open to listening when we receive an inner message, we may ignore that message by labeling it as "just our imagination." The following account from an acquaintance illustrates the crucial value of remaining open to experiences outside the limited worldview of our personality:

> I was helping a neighbor to dig holes and plant trees. I had planted eight trees without any problems when I noticed a few wasps buzzing around. I didn't think much about this, even though I am severely allergic to bees and wasps. All of a sudden, a voice inside my head clearly said, "Calmly walk away." Without stopping to question this, I laid down my tools and unhurriedly walked up the driveway about twenty-five yards. As I did, I was thinking, what am I doing? Then I turned and looked where I had been working seconds before, only to see a wall of wasps, about eight feet wide and eight feet high, right above where I was digging. I found out later that there was a huge ground nest of wasps just where I was about to dig. I cannot begin to explain the emotions I was feeling. Forever will I listen to the inner voice of my soul!

Personality Integration Is Key

Our body, our emotions, and our mind are all vital to our experience here on earth. In the physical realm, it would be hard to interact if we didn't have a physical body. Our emotional body is essential to our capacity to sense and respond to feelings. Without a mental body, we're incapable of thought and reasoning. If our soul wants to express itself here, it needs to do so through these three aspects of our being, preferably as a balanced personality.

Why does the soul have trouble expressing through our personality? An unintegrated personality is usually the problem. Imagine a carriage, a driver, and a horse. The carriage represents the physical body. The driver, who decides which way to go (I'll go this way or I'll go that way), signifies our mind. The driver is supposed to be in control of the horse—our emotional body, which gives us the energy to pull the carriage in a particular direction.

The problem is, they are all separated from each other. The carriage (physical body) is sitting there empty, not moving, because it's not connected to anything. The horse (emotional body) is out grazing somewhere, just running on impulse, doing whatever catches its fancy. The driver (mental body) may have great travel plans, but he or she is off at a bar reminiscing about the past while hefting a few glasses. They're not connected, and they're not integrated.

When we go through personality integration, we link the horse and the driver to the carriage. Now the horse can actually pull the carriage, and the driver can use the reins to direct the horse. What's important is that the emotional, the mental, and the physical are connected and integrated, and they can move together as a unit.

But we've left out a major part of our analogy. What is the purpose of having a carriage? Why not just have a horse and rider? We only need a carriage if there is a passenger! The passenger is the soul. The soul is the one who hires the carriage for the purpose of taking a journey. Many of us ignore the passenger and let the driver go wherever he wants to go, but the soul is quietly whispering directions to the driver.

Have you ever heard an inner voice or had a strong inner feeling? That's your soul trying to talk to the mental body, trying to tell you where to go and what path to take.

Until we integrate the mental body, the emotional body, and the physical body so they can work together in harmony without being at cross-purposes, how can our soul direct the personality? How can the soul work effectively with us if our personality is consumed with mental and emotional conflict?

What keeps our personality from being integrated and responsive to our soul? One factor is early conditioning. Our culture perpetuates certain myths, which are drummed into us by our parents, through school, and through media such as TV or the Internet. The social and familial programming may shape us in ways that are not in harmony with our soul's vision. We may also have unconscious memories from past lives that we carry into this life. Until we change any limiting or unbalanced patterns in our personality, there will be disharmony between our mental and emotional bodies.

Often our body, mind, and emotions are very closely connected, but in dysfunctional ways. For instance, the body reacts rapidly to strong emotions. At a particularly terrifying or stressful moment, our heart begins to race, our hands perspire, and our breathing pauses. Powerful emotions can block our ability to think clearly. In fact, compelling emotions based on limiting unconscious beliefs cause most of the poor choices we make. When emotionally stressed, we may pour milk into the sugar bowl, drive through a red light, or choose the worst possible moment to tell our boss what we really think. Discordant emotions can easily disturb our physical and mental poise.

I am not suggesting that we can heal every one of our dysfunctional patterns. Even if we could, we should not expect ourselves to remain physically and emotionally calm and mentally balanced at all times. Life is filled with challenges at every level of personality development. Situations such as physical illness, emotional traumas, and conflicted relationships further complicate matters.

However, the more harmony between our physical, emotional, and mental urges—the more integrated we are—the greater our ability to be truly effective human beings in our interactions with others and in manifesting our desires. Reducing our internal conflicts frees up tremendous energy, energy that we would otherwise scatter and waste. To manifest on the physical plane, our energy must be focused, not fragmented. Thus an integrated personality increases our relative power to manifest, compared to people who are less integrated. Our personality must have a reasonable degree of integration and balance to be an effective vehicle for soul expression.

Intuition: The Will of the Soul

We need to listen to our inner guidance: our intuition is our soul's Will. Inspiration is the feeling of the soul, and imagination is the way the soul thinks.

How do we recognize the Will of the soul versus the voice of the personality? If we feel genuine joy, that's a clue that our soul is talking to us. Intuition also gives us that "Aha!" feeling of suddenly seeing the solution to a difficult problem.

For example: years ago, I was having a conversation with an intuitive friend, during which I said that someone had approached me about collaborating on projects. My friend made a statement that sent waves of chills from my head to my toes: "If you choose to work with this person, you will help many people." I knew that what that friend said was true. That truth inspired me to make a major life decision that was emotionally difficult. But my soul had communicated with such authority and authenticity that I never wavered in doing what I needed to do. That inner certainty saved me a tremendous amount of agonizing that I would have gone through if I hadn't had a clear sense of following my soul's intuition.

Stages in the Relationship
Between Our Soul and Our Personality

What happens if we receive intuitive soul guidance but our personality is not integrated? If our unconscious conditioning drives us emotionally, it undermines our ability to follow the will of the soul. Our unconscious habit patterns are powerful barriers to following our soul's vision. The problem is that for most human beings, personality desires compete successfully with the soul for our attention.

How can the soul and the personality become collaborators, rather than competitors? It takes time, but through the following five stages, the personality can be increasingly guided by the soul.

Stage 1: The Fragmented and Unconscious Personality

In stage 1, we are not an integrated personality. There is no consistent harmony between our physical responses, our emotional desires, and our mental ideas. We are highly reactive and at the mercy of our mental conditioning and beliefs, as well as outside influences such as other people, events, and even the weather.

We wear a mask designed to display what we want others to see in us. Their expectations, our environment, and our fears dictate our actions. We ricochet around like a billiard ball, responding unconsciously to the pressures of our world. Our emotions shift from sad to happy to annoyed to bored, depending upon which outside influences are prevalent at the moment. In our mind, we blame other people for how we feel. As a result, our happiness seems to be in their hands. We see ourselves not as the cause of our experiences, but as their effect—and often, their victim—because we are unconscious and unaware of our soul.

Stage 2: The Integrated Personality

By this time we have harmonized our physical, emotional, and mental natures to a degree, and we function as an integrated personality. Our sense of identity has shifted from viewing ourselves as a powerless pawn to recognizing our power to direct and change the course of our life. We tell ourselves, "I'm in charge. I'm not part of the herd anymore. I'm making the decisions here."

How can we tell when this vital process of integration has taken place? For one thing, as an integrated personality, we are very effective at acting on and manifesting our ideas in the world. We are able to design a "better mousetrap," or automobile or vaccine or organization. Secure in our abilities, we are self-reliant and confident, knowing that we can make things happen. This characteristic independence is what makes us stand out from the crowd.

The more we achieve, the more highly we regard ourselves, and the outside world generally agrees. We are rewarded with recognition, increased status, financial success, and power. We identify ourselves with these outside accolades, telling ourselves, "I'm a very important person." In fact, most of society's powerful, successful, and well-known people are integrated personalities. Someone who becomes a leader in any arena of life is usually an integrated personality. To achieve at high levels takes the ability to direct and focus the mind, body, and emotions toward a goal, regardless of distractions in the outer world. (However, someone with an integrated personality is not necessarily soul guided, as we will see in stage 5.)

At this stage, we may start asking ourselves, "Who is the 'I' that's making my decisions?" Well, in this case, the "I" that is our personality, not our soul, is still in charge. Our personality's desires and goals are running our life, and about 95 percent of that is unconsciously motivated—hardly a recipe for success of *any* kind.

The personality always has a subtle selfishness. Our relationships, job, home, social and service activities, and hobbies all become the arenas in which our personality achieves and experiences what *it* desires. These desires are valid, but may be limiting. We need to realize that these desires are coming from the personality, not the soul.

Indeed, we may face an obstacle to our further development if the fame, recognition, power, and financial success of our integrated personality prove so seductive that they become our only goals. In that case, our personality then continues to be our entire sense of identity. The integrated personality is supposed to be a channel for soul expression, not the final stage of growth.

Stage 3: The Personality versus the Soul

Here, the soul starts to infuse the integrated personality with higher energy and purpose. The integrated personality becomes aware of the soul's existence and begins to respond to its influence. The more our personality listens to and follows intuition, notices synchronicity in our life, and invokes the soul through meditation or other spiritual practices, the more our interests, abilities, and goals begin to shift. For example, the qualities of our integrated personality typically form the basis for the skills we use in our occupation. However, our soul's agenda evokes different qualities within us, and we find ourselves attracted to new purposes. Our soul invites us to change our priorities and to be guided by its vision of service. When we respond to this invitation, the type of work that we do, or the way we do it, may change.

Resistance to Change

When the integrated personality realizes that the soul wants to use the personality for soul expression, a conflict begins. We—being identified with our personality—are being asked to relinquish the well-defined identity we have worked so hard to create, to exchange it for something that is invisible, intangible, and uncertain. At first our integrated personality, seduced by its own power and what it can do in the world, often fails to respond.

A battle usually ensues as the ego tries to defend and hang on to its own ideas and desires. Attached to a narrow viewpoint and its own beliefs and values, the personality strongly resists the soul's wise vision and abstract values. Our soul is urging us to expand into an ever-higher state of awareness. But this is not easy. The struggle in stage 3 can create tremendous inner turmoil.

Indeed, it took a lot of time and energy for us to build a successful and powerful personality. Now the soul is hinting that we are not who we think we are at all. We are actually something abstract and spiritual that our personality can't understand. For all these reasons, stage 3 can be intensely disturbing and confusing to our personality. The ego may cling desperately to its familiar identity, much like an abused spouse who stays in a painful, destructive situation, preferring the known to the unknown.

If we effectively resist the call of our soul, we may swing toward ever-more-selfish activities, ambitions, and desires. We can display an intense self-absorption and constant need for attention and recognition. "Look at me." "Look at how powerful I am and what I can do."

Although there is no single way in which the personality moves past its resistance and becomes ready for stage 4, certain scenarios seem to propel people into seeking a deeper meaning for their life. In some cases, people have achieved great worldly success but suffer from a chronic "crisis of meaning." They begin to question why they aren't happy, and they feel empty despite their many achievements.

Another catalyst for change in some people is an acute life crisis, such as divorce, illness, financial losses, or the death of a loved one. These spiritual wake-up calls shake us out of our comfortable complacency, and can motivate us to search for deeper meaning.

In other cases, natural life transitions allow us the time and space to focus on deeper questions of purpose. When the major milestones have been reached, such as establishing a career, a family, a home, and relative financial security, we have the time to shift our focus to less mundane concerns. We may ask ourselves some of the same questions we have pondered earlier in our life—Who am I? What am I doing here? Where am I going?—but now these questions pertain not to worldly matters, but to our spiritual purpose.

Each of the above scenarios has the potential to loosen our identification with our personality and open us more fully to the soul.

Look for these profound shifts in consciousness during stage 3 as we move to the soul's perspective.

Perspectives and Priorities:
Contrasting the Personality and the Soul

Personality	Soul
Material	Spiritual
Intelligent	Loving
We wear masks of conformity	We show real authenticity
We prioritize getting	We prioritize giving
We want a payoff	We seek no return
Solar plexus	Heart
Limiting	Expansive
Self-conscious	Group-conscious
Habitual	Creative
Myopic vision	Panoramic vision
Action oriented	Contemplative
We prioritize appearance	We prioritize quality

Stage 4: The Spiritualized Self-Image (Soul Impostor)

When we start to follow the soul's impulses by paying attention and responding to its communication, we enter stage 4. A conscious working partnership between the soul and the integrated personality begins. We have started to awaken. We desire to be a spiritual person, or more accurately, our integrated personality wants to behave like a spiritual person.

The integrated personality says, "I need to do something to make the world a better place, because this is what a spiritual person does." This is an important stage of development, even if it is a wish rather than a reality. Acting as if we already *are* a soul-infused personality (stage 5) may help us to become what we are now only pretending to be.

However, this natural and essential stage in our evolution can be very tricky. Because we are basing our behavior on our personality's *perception* of spirituality, we can fall into the trap of self-delusion—a spiritualized image of our self that I call the "soul impostor."

Concepts of Service:
Contrasting the Personality and the Soul

Spiritualized Self-Image (Soul Impostor)	Soul Vision
We serve when it feeds our self-image	We serve out of an authentic desire to help others
We give in response to others' expectations	We give spontaneously
We seek approval for our efforts	We do not need outer approval
We give with attachment (we want to see results)	We give without attachment (we do not need to see results)
We have a short-term need for spiritual achievement	We are committed to long-term service
We measure effectiveness by manipulating the environment into what we believe is good	We measure success by how fully our soul infuses and expresses its qualities through the personality
We are in a hurry to achieve a quick result	We are patient, flowing with the rhythms of life
We give to benefit a group—often one of personal interest	We give in response to the needs of humanity as a whole
We focus on the quantity of service given	We care about the quality of service given
We see ourself as spiritually superior to others	We see the soul in others

How does this play out? Lurking in the unconscious is a personality-based expectation of reward or recognition for our efforts. We want something back for what we give. This is not a bad thing—we are trying to express a spiritual impulse, such as service to others—yet we are motivated by a self-focused point of view. We look around for circumstances that give us an opportunity to be of service, but primarily where our efforts will be noticed. And so our personality seeks very concrete results that it can point to for credit. We measure our effectiveness by how well we can manipulate the outer environment to create what we believe to be good. We feel an urgency to achieve quick results. We may "keep score" of the hours of service given or the amount of money we contribute, all the while regarding ourselves as spiritually superior to those we serve.

The soul impostor is an evolutionary stage. We're trying to embrace Spirit, but our efforts are being driven by our spiritually idealized self-image, rather than a soul-inspired vision of service.

Stage 5: The Soul-Infused Personality

Eventually, we awaken as the soul-infused personality. What springs from us is a deeply authentic desire to serve, to help, to heal. A spontaneous outpouring of joy, compassion, and benevolence defines who we are. The need for approval disappears. Giving and loving occur without attachment, expectation, or the need to see results or receive recognition of any kind.

Our soul "measures success" by how fully it infuses and expresses its being through the personality—by how constantly, deeply, and purely the soul emanates through us.

We give in response to the needs of the whole, rather than in response to some at the expense of the whole. As a soul-infused personality, we perceive ourself as one with all others. There is no experience of division, separation, or duality. Comprehensive, inclusive, all-embracing, unconditional love is the essence of our soul. The soul is the light that reveals our Spirit and shows us the divinity in everyone.

At stage 5 we become a soul-infused personality, expressing universal love and compassion in service to the Divine.

Manifesting and the Journey to Becoming Soul Infused

Those who have tried other manifesting and prosperity techniques may notice that some of them address personality integration, too. But they generally don't go far enough. They may help us to get from stage 1 to stage 2—from being a fragmented, unconscious personality to being an integrated personality who can function decisively and effectively in the world. This is a necessary step. However, if we stay stuck at stage 2, we won't connect with our Soul Vision (you will have an opportunity to begin to discover your Soul Vision later in this book). The integrated personality has a set of goals and desires it wants to achieve, based on its limited understanding of life. The soul has a much broader perspective and different desires.

From the point of view of a spiritualized personality (stage 4), or, most authentically, from the perspective of a soul-infused personality (stage 5), the measure of a successful life has to do with spiritual service and learning, not with material acquisitions or accomplishments. Material resources and power are simply a means to fulfill soul purposes. Spiritual growth—our own and others'—are what the soul cares about.

Certainly, our personality desires will not suddenly disappear when we become a soul-infused personality. We will still have preferences—we might prefer a red car to a blue car—but we will not be attached to them. And those preferences will be consistent with our Soul Vision.

Cultivating the ability to manifest, then, is a legitimate and useful step in our growth. But as we continue to shift our identity from the integrated personality to the soul, we will start to feel the irresistible embrace of love and understanding. From that place of deep peace, we will begin to remember our True Self as an eternal spiritual being at one with the Divine, which is a transcendent experience. Our greatest desire and purpose for living will be to express from this awareness.

two

Answering the Call of the Soul

As we have seen, there comes a time in our spiritual growth when we realize that we are more than our personality self, and we begin to seek the guidance of our soul. But how do we know which "voice" we are hearing? Wouldn't it be great if distinguishing between the personality and the soul were as easy as looking at our cell phone screen to see who is on the line. *Hello, Personality? You say I should feel what? Decide what? Do what? Personality, I'll have to let you go; I've got another call coming in, and it's from my soul.*

Actually, it's simple to tell the two voices apart, because their qualities are opposites. In this chapter, we will compare some of them, so you can better distinguish just who's calling on *your* line. Stories from my own life, from my clients, and from others will illustrate how we may connect with our soul and shift our awareness, even in the midst of daily life. We'll explore the nature of the soul in preparation for our direct experience of the Soul Visioning process in chapter 3.

Aspects of the Soul: Spirit, Mind, and Will

Before we discuss the qualities of the soul, let's start by looking at three terms used throughout this book. We will refer to three major aspects of the soul as Spirit, Mind, and Will (capitalizing these words whenever we're referring to these aspects of the soul).

Spirit is the pure, unlimited, eternal energy or life force. This life energy is that collective oneness of which we are all a part. We live within this oneness; we exist because of it and can never be separated from it. Spirit is life itself. It is our source.

In chapter 1, we compared our mind (uncapitalized) to a driver who sits on top of a carriage (our body), and decides *I'll go this way* or *I'll go that way*. In that analogy, we were referring to both the conscious and unconscious mind. As an aspect of the soul, however, the Mind is infinitely more expansive, reflecting the nature of its Divine creator. It seeks to manifest the fullness of its creative expression and Divine awareness.

We experience the Mind through our imagination. Our soul communicates in the form of inner images that arise in our dreams, reveries, past-life regressions, and other internal experiences. Just because these images arise from within, rather than from our outer sight, does not mean that they are not true. Even though our personality, with its exclusive focus on the material world, denies the worth and truth of our inner spiritual experiences, our imagination lets us perceive these otherwise invisible spiritual forces at work in our Mind. These inner images may contain profound symbolic insights and truths about the soul.

My husband, Dave, who co-facilitates Soul Visioning workshops with me, relates the following example:

> During a recent group meditation on the future of spiritual consciousness, I had a vision in which I saw the bodies of people turning into glass filled with golden light. The light shone from within them to join the golden light in others. The glass bodies began disappearing with our realization that we were all part of one light. There was a profound feeling of boundaries dissolving to reveal

a deeper reality of love, unity, and transparency. This image and the associated feelings provided me with an inner picture of our spiritual nature.

The Mind holds the knowledge of our perfection. The Soul Visioning process allows us to remember our wholeness and shows us how to express it. We'll look at an example in a minute.

We have defined the Will of the soul as intuition, in the sense that intuition is how the soul directs and guides us. Insights from our soul come in many different ways. Sometimes soul guidance comes to us in little pieces like those of a jigsaw puzzle. Putting together that puzzle may be a slow process; we examine one piece at a time until we see how they fit together. Then suddenly, the overall picture becomes clear—we get that joyful "Aha!" feeling that comes with gaining insight into a situation, knowing the solution to a predicament, or reaching a major life decision.

Dave's Dream Puzzle

Dave shares one of his own "Aha!" experiences.

> I dreamt that I was in the home of a couple who are part of my spiritual group. The wife, Sharon, was having rapid labor pains, and there wasn't enough time to take her to the hospital. I went to find my mother, who is a nurse. I brought her back, but the baby had already been born after only fifteen minutes of labor. Sharon and the baby were both fine. My mom cut the umbilical cord and bathed the baby. I remember that the baby had very large and beautiful blue eyes. My dream ended at that point.
>
> The previous day I had spoken to a spiritual group about the importance of partnering with creative spiritual energies in our work life. As I thought about my dream, I recognized that each element represented a piece of a puzzle. Quickly, they fell into place to form a picture that I knew was a message from my soul. Sharon and her husband represented my connection to these creative forces. My mom and the hospital represented traditional approaches to

work and career. The rapid labor and the infant's blue eyes symbolized the power of these creative spiritual energies to rapidly and easily produce beautiful results. I realized that I needed to be less concerned with following standard procedures in my career and to trust my soul to deliver results aligned with my highest good. The dream was also encouraging me, by a play on words, to "share on" with my spiritual teaching, which was a new activity for me when I had this dream thirty years ago. I wrote a poem that expresses the beauty of this experience.

> *Large, blue, beautiful*
> *Your eyes welcome a new world*
> *With easy blessings.*

Who's on the Line—the Personality or the Soul?

As we explore the differences between the personality and the soul, please keep in mind, again, that we're not talking about eliminating the personality. Our personality isn't a negative thing. On the contrary, we couldn't function within our environment without it. Our personality seeks money, contacts, and power as resources to help make things happen in our outer life; it is the means through which the soul expresses itself in our daily experiences. Meditation is not the only way we make contact with our soul. Bathing a baby, smiling at a stranger, raking leaves—all such activities are opportunities to express the soul.

The soul carries universal forces beyond our understanding and makes them present in our life through our personality. The soul is the source of our true power. Although we can't see it or detect it in a laboratory, we can notice its effects and feel its presence.

A single encounter with a soul-infused person can totally change our life. I will always remember meeting one such person, a well-known spiritual author and lecturer. His loving presence and the inspirational energy he radiated when speaking transformed the consciousness of his audiences and sometimes resulted in the spontaneous healing of long-term health problems.

How *do* we distinguish between the soul and the personality? One way is to examine our intent or motivation. The intent of the soul is to express itself through our every word, thought, and action. The personality is more geared to achieving personal desires in the material world (we will refer to these as *personality desires*).

Another way to discern the difference is to examine our focus. The personality's desire is always for something "out there" that we sense we have to reach for or move toward. The soul is within; it is something we already are. We don't have to work for it or deserve it; all we have to do is recognize and accept it. The personality is known by action; the soul is known by stillness.

Please take a few minutes now to think of a past situation in your life in which you needed guidance. Perhaps you had a decision to make involving your work, a relationship, your health, your personal growth. In this instance, what was your intent, your agenda, your motivation? How did you gain insight into this particular situation? Did you receive guidance by meditating, contemplating your life while on your daily walk, journaling, analyzing dreams, or in other ways?

Think about the answers you received at that time and how they felt to you. What decisions did you make, and what was the outcome? Do you feel you could discern the difference between your personality and your soul?

Perspectives and Priorities Revisited: Comparing the Personality and the Soul

These paired statements describe some of the contrasts between the personality and the soul. Can you think of other examples?

- *Personality* is concerned with and impressed by appearance.
- *Soul* focuses on the quality, the essence, the life that our physical creations express.

- *Personality* excludes, isolates, competes, and separates.
- *Soul* includes, welcomes, embraces, and accepts.

- *Personality* operates from a belief in scarcity.
- *Soul* expresses abundance.

- *Personality*, when integrated, is centered in the solar plexus. It asks, "How can I use my personal power to get what I want?"
- *Soul* is centered in the heart. It asks, "How can I serve?"

- *Personality* is concerned with quickly producing visible results. It asks, "What do I need to do to get as much as I can, as fast as I can?"
- *Soul* expresses unquestioning trust in the timing and perfection of life. It radiates patience, love, and compassion while allowing life to unfold.

- *Personality's* approach to manifesting is, "What can I get from the external world that will make me feel whole and complete?"
- *Soul*, as an expression of Spirit, knows we're all part of the oneness. The soul's approach to manifesting is, "Allow me to reveal the perfection of the unity, wholeness, and love that I am, in service to others."

What Motivates Us to Manifest?

Are you beginning to see a pattern here? When operating from our personality, we have a sense of lack. Therefore, we think about how we can *acquire what we do not have.* This perception of lack leads to the many kinds of techniques that teach us to mentally concentrate on what we want in our life, or to be very emotionally devoted to (passionate about) the object of our desire, so that we will draw it to us.

But these approaches have true power only when guided by our soul's vision for our life. This is the key issue, the puzzle piece that is missing for most people who fail to create a happy, deeply satisfying life. Our integrated personality may use all the techniques of manifesting, but it ignores the infinite energy, wisdom, and resources of the soul. Instead of connecting to the soul's vision and allowing that vision to unfold, our integrated personality uses manifesting techniques for self-gratification—literally attempting to manipulate life circumstances to suit our personality desires. Essentially, the personality perceives that it must work very hard to achieve something external that the soul already has—wholeness, oneness, unlimited well-being, abundance, and love.

Sometimes personality-driven creating seems to work; sometimes not. One of the limitations (and indicators) of manifesting that is motivated by the personality is that *when we achieve our goal, we're still not happy*. A series of recent surveys evaluating life satisfaction found no appreciable difference in happiness between people who said they were above-average in achieving various desires, and people who described themselves as average in this regard.[1] Yet our personality tries to convince us that if we just had a lot more money, a lot more power, a lot more status, or a better relationship, we'd be happier.

The personality's view of what will make us happy is gratification of its desires. But as we know only too well, personality gratification is only temporary; it doesn't last. Real joy comes from connecting to and expressing our soul's vision. The soul is our only source of lasting joy and a deeper sense of our true identity, which is love.

The soul-infused personality approaches manifesting quite differently, asking, "How can I more fully release and express my divinity and the essence of wholeness through my life? How can I serve, share, and radiate my spiritual energy?" Indeed, there's a flow of energy from the soul into the physical. One formula for understanding creation puts it this way (in the words of Edgar Cayce): "The spirit is the life, the mind is the builder, and the physical is the result."[2]

Manifesting our soul vision is not about some spectacular demonstration in the outer world or even a dramatic inner spiritual experience. It's about how fully we express our soul's spiritual qualities every day of our life. Letting our inner light shine is our opportunity to be a channel of blessings.

Who Is the Genie?

Remember the tale of the magic lamp? In some versions of this traditional Arabian story, a person finds a magic lamp, rubs it, and a genie is released. In gratitude to his liberator, the genie grants him three wishes. The granting of wishes in this fable is a metaphor for manifesting; the story contains a deep psychological truth and an important secret. The will has the ability to control the mind, and with it, we can manifest whatever we want. Trapped inside of all of us is our will—our genie. Once activated, our will can be extremely powerful. But is it the will of the soul or of the personality?

Do you remember what happens to the character in the story? His first two wishes are granted, but they get him into so much trouble that he has to use his last wish to resolve the situation. This symbolizes what happens when we use the personality's mind and will to grant our own "three wishes." Unaware of the soul's vision, our personality seeks to fulfill its desires. Inevitably, we find ourselves mired in the unintended effects of getting just what we asked for. If we had just relied on the lamp of the soul all along, the results would have been truly magnificent.

The power of the personality compared to the energy of the soul is like the light reflected off the moon as compared to the radiance of the sun. Just as primitive man believed that all the planets, the stars, and the sun revolved around the earth, we—when operating as a personality—believe that the whole world revolves around us. In truth, all of the planets in our solar system revolve around the sun (Sol/soul). The personality, similarly, is *supposed* to revolve around—be in service to—the soul. The power of the soul is wholeness, radiating life energy and light.

You can easily see how this manifests in the world. When people view life only from their own point of view—when they see the weather, the political situation, the economy, or other people's behavior only as it impacts them personally—they will seldom share the same goals with others. Can you see how the nature of personality perceptions creates our experiences of differences, separation, loneliness, and suffering?

The quality of energy that we will feel when we express the soul's energy, on the other hand, is connection and joy. This is a reliable indicator that we are in touch with our soul. If we're following our soul's vision, we will feel deep joy welling up from within us, regardless of our external circumstances. We will feel a presence, a sense of harmony and oneness. New energy will flow from within us. We will discover abilities that we didn't know we had.

When we allow the intuition or Will of the soul to guide us, synchronicity will happen in our life. In a seemingly effortless way, situations and circumstances will fall into place.

The Call of the Soul: My Own Story

I had been a school psychologist for a number of years. Although I had seniority, benefits, and a secure job, my soul was restless. I began to feel that my soul was urging me to go into private practice. Many people told me I was crazy to let this stability go and take on such a risk. Despite the doubting voices inside and outside of me, my soul was calling, "This is what you came here to do." I had to reassure my worried personality, which complained, "You're jumping into the deep end here. Do you know what you're doing?"

But I clearly heard the deep inner calling from my soul. I responded to that calling, but not recklessly or in haste. Taking things step by step, I went back to school, got more training, and prepared to pursue this new path. With the personality cooperating with my soul, everything was synchronous. Doors began to open. The resources I needed were there when I needed them.

Through the years, as I continued to listen to my soul, I moved through further career stages. You could say that my work was, and still is, a platform for my own evolution. There was a time, for instance, when I began to shift away from a more traditional therapy practice to a holistic practice that encompassed mind, body, and Spirit. Once again, the fearful voice of my personality said, "It's not safe to do this." "This is not traditional therapy." "I'm stepping out of the box." "I will be punished

for this by losing my credibility, and I won't be able to make a living."
On the contrary, my holistically oriented practice has brought me deep
satisfaction and fulfillment, and those fears have proved unfounded.

When my soul guidance began to inspire me to write this book and
reach out to a larger audience, it brought up, once again, some long-
buried fears. Through the Soul Visioning process that you will learn in
this book, I discovered that there are parts of my personality that want
to stay safe, that do not want to step out on a much wider stage. In
fact, I learned that I have experienced several lifetimes in which I was
persecuted for speaking my truth. For example, in a lifetime as a nun
in Europe during the Inquisition, I was burned at the stake for challenging the religious authorities of the day.

I had to heal these fears so that I could express my soul purpose in
this life. Before I could fulfill my soul's vision, I had to clear my own
limiting core beliefs, past life and present. I had to change my mind
about what I deserve. My personality self would have had me believe
that I am limited—separate from and not deserving of love. That illu-
sory belief would have played itself out on the stage of life as scarcity,
sacrifice, and suffering. In other words, I had to be willing to listen to
my soul and step past my fearful unconscious memories. When I did,
my practice became more abundant, flowing, and deeply satisfying.

Discovering Your Soul's Passion

The soul's vision starts from a point of irrepressible passion for a gift
it wants to share, to radiate from its inner being. To discover the passion of our soul, we can ask, *What gives me joy? When do I feel most
alive? When do I feel most creative?* For many of us, we come closest to
this oneness, wholeness, and joy when we feel unselfish love for a child
or another loved one—even a pet—or when we spend time in nature.

When the soul is truly expressing itself, we may sense a natural flow
to the events in our life. We feel our connection and oneness with all
that happens around us. We may experience ourselves as an endlessly
expanding being of light, without boundaries, bursting with life. Our

sense of time shifts from the hustle of the personality's worldly concerns to the peace and abundance of eternity.

When we're attuned to the voice of the soul and its desire to serve, we will use our opportunities to manifest its vision. *We do not have to figure out our soul's vision and control it with our personality*. Rather, the key is to let go, connect with our intuition, and hearken to the Will of our soul. The soul can speak in very subtle but powerful ways. To discover how it operates in our life, we need only pay attention to when our small decisions have had a profound, constructive life impact.

We don't fully know the end of our spiritual journey in advance. But our soul knows when our direction is correct. Every time I have followed my soul guidance, it has been absolutely the right thing to do, and it has brought great joy and harmony into my life. So when your own soul takes you in a direction that brings up fears within your personality and doubting responses from others, be kind to yourself and be patient with the process.

While there's no "caller ID" system to tell us when we're getting input from our personality or from our soul, we've learned that joy is a great indicator that our soul is on the line.

Soul Qualities

Now let's deepen our understanding of five qualities that distinguish our soul from our personality: optimism, willingness to serve, intuition, humility, and impersonality/nonattachment.

Soul Quality: Optimism

An important soul quality, optimism is an antidote to the pessimism of the personality. Doubt and fear literally drain the energy from our energy field and replace it with what can feel like a thick gray fog, which prevents us from seeing or experiencing anything clearly. Doubt keeps us from moving forward, and fear is paralyzing.

If we get stuck in fear, it can be very difficult to follow our soul guidance. Intense fear may delude our personality into feeling incapable of taking the next step. Our soul, on the other hand, draws from its inexhaustible fountain of love and abundance and its connection to an unlimited source of power. It never abandons us, and like a lighthouse in the fog, it shines a beacon to help us navigate home again.

Suppose that we are facing some external challenge or problem. Optimism helps us draw on the soul's wisdom and love. Optimism lets us express the best of our soul qualities in response to circumstances. This shifts our interpretation of the situation to a higher point of view that infuses our response with love and understanding.

One of my elderly clients experienced the gift of optimism at a most difficult time in her life. She had lost her job, she was without family, her health was poor, and her sole means of support was a Social Security pittance that didn't even cover the cost of her food. She came to my office one day in a panic. Her anxiety was manifesting in her body through irritable bowel syndrome and allergies.

When we explored the root of her fears, it led back to childhood memories. She came from a wealthy family that put great value on work, money, and achievement. She learned at a young age that she was valuable only when she was working and accomplishing something. Now, laid off from her job, she felt inadequate and desperate to gain back her validation as a person.

I suggested that perhaps there was a very important lesson to be learned from these earlier experiences, and from her current circumstances. As painful as her situation was, it gave her the opportunity to remember who she really is—a "treasured child of God" whose worth is established by the Divine. (I used language that is meaningful to her.)

Of course we need to earn a living and function in the material world, I told her, but our worth does not come from that. It comes from our essence as a spiritual being, which most of us have forgotten. The truth of what I was saying resonated deeply with her, and tears welled up in her eyes.

The next day, she called to say that she felt at peace. She had shifted from an anxious state of mind to one of optimism rooted in the recognition of her true worth. From this centered place within her, rather than from her ego "driving her to distraction," this woman could now allow her soul to guide her to a more positive interpretation of her circumstances.

Soul Quality: Willingness to Serve

Self-preservation is an instinct of the personality. The will of the personality is forceful and self-directed. Service, however, is an instinct of the soul. Sharing and giving is what the soul desires to do. The Will of the soul, its true nature, is the *willingness* to experience self-transcendence and to serve the growth of others. (For example, I know a couple who demonstrated this soul-inspired willingness to serve by hosting a group in their home, providing a loving space for sharing and encouraging spiritual growth.)

The soul is not concerned with getting recognition for its service. It is about infusing the power of love, compassion, and understanding through us into our relationships with other people, into our service, into everything we do, whether to sweep a floor or design a skyscraper. In any situation, we can express our soul vision by radiating the energy and qualities of our soul.

Considering the motivation for our service, we might ask, "What is the spiritual impact of my interaction with others?" Our soul radiance, when unimpeded by personality goals and desires, creates an energy that inspires others to connect with their own soul. To evaluate the spiritual effect of our interactions, we ask, "How does the other person feel as a result of my soul expression? Was it hopeful and helpful to that person's growth?"

Expression of our soul being and qualities is the most profound form of service we can offer. When we let our own soul's light shine, we encourage others to do the same. The most valuable gift that we can give anyone is to fully express our soul nature. *The essence of manifesting is embodying our soul's vision* by constantly radiating our love and light.

In our desire to be spiritual, we limit our spiritual growth if we think that we need only to reach higher and higher states of awareness without sharing our soul. Being aware of and understanding our soul's vision and purpose is just the first step. The next step is the ability and willingness to act on this vision and bring it into manifestation. What happens if we surrender to the vision of our soul, but we haven't developed the courage to express it? Then we become an impotent visionary! We sit around hypnotized by our vision, but are unable to live it. We need to experience our soul awareness and Will to serve together, so that when we discover our soul vision, we spontaneously express it. The real beauty of the soul is revealed when we share it by serving the growth of others.

Soul Quality: Intuition

When faced with a problem, the personality typically responds by gathering information. The integrated personality uses the intellect to perceive, learn, dissect, and analyze information, and then to draw conclusions. Now, there's nothing wrong with using one's intellect. It definitely comes in handy when managing our finances! But whereas the personality *gathers* information, intuition presents information holistically as an experience of *knowing*. Suddenly, in a flash of insight, perhaps after we wake from a dream or while we take a shower, the solution to a problem that we have been pondering pops into our mind. We know it in every fiber of our being. As we've said, the Will of the soul often creates these "Aha!" experiences. Our soul communicates through intuition, which acts as a window to the spiritual world.

Some time ago, for instance, I worked with a colleague for several years on various projects. At a crucial time, this person declined to support a project grant application I needed to submit. After meditating, I intuitively realized that at some level my colleague did not trust me. I chose to share more of my soul awareness, and this transformed our relationship to one of deeper respect and trust.

The integrated personality deliberately evaluates the information it receives from the outside world and then develops a plan, whereas a personality that is not yet integrated may simply accept the conclusions of others. Intuition, on the other hand, can be sudden and comprehensive. Our intuition actually perceives oneness. By heeding it consistently, we become progressively more sensitive and responsive to its messages.

In the following account, a colleague of mine shares her story about the unexpected blessings that followed when she used intuition to help her college-bound daughter.

> In preparation for my daughter's choice of the colleges she would apply to, my husband and I traveled with her to twenty-three colleges in New England and the Midwest. Not one suited her! She wanted to study both art and English. But every school that we visited either specialized in one or the other, or required students to declare only one major.
>
> In the meantime, we were invited to a presentation at a local hotel for a college that we had not visited. Hardly an hour had passed at that presentation before I simply knew that my daughter would be going there. I knew it through my entire being. There was no thought, no analysis, and frankly, no emotion. There was not even a feeling of relief, that finally we could stop worrying—simply the knowledge that this was where she would be going.
>
> Now, this didn't mean that we did not engage in all the steps—the actual visit to the school, submission of essays and applications, and so on. Rather, as we went through the process, it became clearer and clearer that this was going to be the choice.
>
> The conclusion? Not only did she attend this particular school, but she got a $13,000 annual scholarship. She also met the man she eventually married, eight years after she graduated. One year after they married, her husband won a fellowship to teach at the very same school, requiring them to move halfway across the country to the place where they had met. Within two months, they had their first house and their first child! Now that's what I mean by intuition!

Soul Visioning is fundamentally about cultivating our intuition. Some of the ways to do this are through meditation, working with dreams, having reveries, practicing forgiveness, and taking time to walk in nature while listening to our inner voice. We'll discuss intuition in more detail later in this book.

Soul Quality: Humility

When we recognize that we can use the will of our integrated personality to manifest our desires, we may also discover that we can easily influence others with our powerful personality and the force of our opinions and desires. Being strong-willed is not necessarily undesirable; it can give us the determination to persevere through personal and professional obstacles. However, the temptation exists to identify with our manipulative personality, and to use the strength of its will to influence and manipulate others for our own purposes, rather than to use this power in service to others.

Humility is a powerful antidote to a strong personality. By realizing that our personality does not, and cannot, know everything, we cultivate receptivity to soul communication. When our personality becomes the servant of our soul, we shift from using the will of the personality, with its divisive and selfish motives, to activating the Will of the soul, with its inclusiveness and willingness to serve.

For example, if we sincerely want to meditate regularly, we will also need a daily willingness to set aside our personality urgings and to humbly and attentively listen for the voice of our soul. Eventually, with practice, life becomes a living meditation as we become mindful of the "still small voice" of the soul that guides us, moment to moment.

Soul Qualities: Impersonality and Nonattachment

These are the means by which the soul gives without asking for anything in return. Giving and sharing are spontaneous actions that spring from the soul's knowledge of abundance and wholeness. The soul has no "you owe me" thoughts—and be aware, "you owe me" thinking can be very subtle. For example, if we see someone suffering, we may respond by giving them healing energy or money or help of some other kind, but we may not feel comfortable until we see some outer evidence that they have been positively affected. Our personality can become attached to the outcome of our actions.

True service is a spontaneous effect of soul contact. When we're really connected to our soul, we cannot stop the flow of energy, love, and service to others, any more than a flower can fail to offer its fragrance. This is our very nature. It is who we are.

In her own words, a friend of mine recounts an event in which she experienced the spontaneous nature of true service:

> I was staying at the home of my niece after a birthday party. A number of family members were present. I had not seen my niece for several years, and after a short time, I could easily see that she had a drug problem. However, her husband and two young sons seemed to be functioning fairly well. She had a strong support system, including full-time help as well as parents who were supportive and loving grandparents.
>
> However, a sister-in-law who was known for her ability to create conflict and cause friction chose to make some very hurtful comments to my niece while a guest in her house. Things quickly escalated out of control, from shouting to screaming and even to physical violence, frightening everyone, especially the children.
>
> My niece was violently angry and out of control. For some reason, I was overcome with a sense of peace and a full heart, and felt compelled to walk right up to her with outstretched arms and an open heart. To my amazement, that was exactly what she needed and she fell into my arms. All those who were shouting at her suddenly calmed and began to imitate my behavior, talking to her in soothing and comforting voices while showering her with love and understanding. I do not know how this happened or what came over me, but I was so filled with love and appreciation, and wondered at the power of such a simple act to bring such instant peace.

Recognizing the Presence of the Soul

The question we've been focusing on is, "How can I know when I am experiencing the presence of the soul?" We'll feel a sense of spiritual peace and contentment. We will feel tremendous love and connection to others.

The following incident, shared by the same woman, describes another unmistakable experience of the power of the soul's love. As you will see, her behavior in this instance, too, was spontaneous and outside the realm of her personality's usual reactions.

> I was attending a trade show, sharing a hotel room with a female employee and two other women. One day I was so busy working at my booth, I was unaware that one of my employees had been seriously ill for most of the day. Apparently, someone had slipped a drug into her drink the night before, and she was feverish, fainting, and vomiting. She was lying in our room, surrounded by several people, when I arrived there that evening.
>
> I sent for one of the healers who were attending the trade show. When he arrived, the strangest thing occurred. I felt like the area of my heart, in my back, opened up into a huge funnel. I could feel love pouring through my back, through me, and toward my very sick friend. I felt completely suffused with love, and I knew exactly why she was sick and what she needed.
>
> When she was a child, her mentally ill father and biker mother were unable to take care of themselves, never mind her. From a very young age, she had become their caretaker. I told her that I knew that the only way that she felt entitled to the love and care that she deserved was to become desperately ill. I was so aware of her need and felt completely capable of giving her that care and love. I held her all night until she recovered. That feeling of intense love lasted for three weeks and was one of the most memorable experiences in my life. During that entire time, I never needed to use my mind for anything, but knew all things only through my heart.

The personality is a separate sense of identity, one that is finite, limited, and narrow. The soul is expansive and limitless. While the personality often displays unconsciousness toward suffering in the world, the soul has heightened sensitivity toward others. But it responds to suffering with an awareness that carries joy, compassion, and love.

Awakening to Soul Vocation

The soul will also awaken us to our soul vocation, the calling to express what we really are. The soul serves by sharing its being, not by personality-driven activity. The form of our vocation is an opportunity and an environment in which we can serve by infusing our work with our soul beingness. The radiance of the soul is needed everywhere, in all walks of life and in all professions. Our vocation is where we can radiate our light because of our own particular talents and gifts.

Dave's Decision

My husband, Dave, whom you met earlier, shares a story of such an awakening.

> I was having a good time in graduate school. Not your typical graduate student, I took whatever courses appealed to me: psychology, management, engineering, philosophy, and political science. I wasn't working that hard, but I was having fun exploring various fields. After three years in grad school, I received a job offer, due to some volunteer work as an environmental educator. I had to decide whether to accept the job offer or stay in school.
>
> During that time I had a dream that I was in Hawaii. I was enjoying the relaxed environment, but there was a plane leaving for the mainland. I considered getting on the plane, but I was reluctant because no movies were being shown. Leaving Hawaii didn't appear to be an entertaining option. But something bothered me about Hawaii, too. In the dream I noticed that all around me, people were sleeping.

When I woke up, I realized this dream was showing me a picture of my current consciousness. For me, graduate school was like being on vacation, but most of my potentials were sleeping. I was having a good time, but I wasn't fully using my abilities. Taking a plane to the mainland represented the opportunity to take a job. I could stay on vacation with my sleeping potentials, or travel to the mainland—the working world.

Guided by this dream, I took the job, which helped me to develop many skills and launched me on a very successful career. Being open to my soul's point of view, and then doing what was most in harmony with my own growth toward wholeness, was the key to living my soul vision.

When connected to our soul, we feel an inner certainty of spiritual truth. Intuition is the compass of our soul's vision, and keeps us in harmony with it.

The Experience of Soul

The more we connect to our soul, the more we will have experiences like these:

- We will have a sense of aliveness, wonder, awe, and energy that feels like it comes from beyond ourselves.

- Other people will benefit spiritually through their contact with us. We will be a radiant light unto others.

- We will be more frequently and deeply aware of the presence of the Divine in our life, experiencing unity and wholeness instead of feeling separation and lack.

- We will feel spiritual peace and contentment.

- Synchronicity, the feeling of the flow of events, will become part of our everyday experience.

- We will have a deep awareness of the sacredness and unity of all life.

- Greater creativity will emerge as an expression of our unique gifts.

- A deep sense of joy will pervade our life.

- We will gain a profound sense of the purpose and meaning of our life and a fuller appreciation and understanding of others' soul purpose.

- We will experience heightened awareness of our higher calling and our true service vocation.

- We will desire to give selflessly without any thought of return.

Expressing the Soul in Daily Life

The presence of the soul lies not in some far-off dimension, but in our everyday expression of qualities of being that empower, align, connect, uplift, and liberate all life. We nourish others every moment when we remember to be fully present and open, appreciating and cherishing their soul beingness. That is what happens in Soul Visioning—we allow our spiritual energy to emerge fully. The soul strives to unfold its fundamental identity, to be true to itself. We measure the success of Soul Visioning by how fully our soul infuses the personality with its energy. The more we experience our soul, the more we participate in its connection with the Divine. We learn how to recognize its energy and channel it into our daily life.

A person who consistently radiates a spirit of lovingness and synthesis is far more valuable to others than someone who simply seeks to have a "spiritual experience." Love is actually the source of all our abilities, and the more love we express, the greater the abilities that emerge from within us. Our primary purpose for connecting with the soul is to channel that spiritual energy of love to other people.

It is essential that we develop our sensitivity to the flow of Spirit and the ability to discern—with our own soul attunement, wisdom, and Will—the choices that align with that flow. To perform small actions

The Joy of Soul Contact

Here Dave describes some of his own moments of soul connection.

I was teaching a meditation class at a church many years ago. I have done a lot of teaching over the last thirty years, but while I was teaching this particular class, I felt my soul flowing through me very strongly with incredible energy and joy. I always enjoy teaching, but that experience was an overwhelming feeling of bliss.

I find that soul contact doesn't necessarily express itself in something visible; rather, there is a quality of feeling and energy that we experience. Sometimes we become so absorbed in moments of soul connection that time seems to stop. I remember hiking on the island of Iona, off the western coast of Scotland, when I became fully focused in the moment. The waves in the ocean and the clouds in the sky both stopped moving as I experienced the stillness of the eternal now.

well (no matter how insignificant they may seem to our personality) and fill them with the quality of soul—that is more valuable than attempting great projects with enthusiasm, but without sufficient love to be spiritually effective. The value comes from the quality of our effort, our motivation, and our Spirit.

Even little acts of kindness, when unselfishly motivated, can have a significant impact in our daily life. When the soul is flowing through us, we spontaneously and effortlessly extend our love to others, whether being patient with a rude clerk, offering a smile to someone who needs uplifting, or helping a neighbor. We can even be mystics in a traffic jam, forgiving rather than cursing the driver who cuts us off. These are automatic impulses when guided by the soul, based on a deep knowing that our interests are not separate. When we love another, we love ourselves. There is no difference.

The Power of a Peaceful Presence

Like most people, I have said hurtful things to others plenty of times when I have been stressed or fatigued. Yet even the most everyday instances of this can have a far-reaching impact.

For example, a server in a restaurant made a mistake on my order one day, and although I could have chosen to forgive and extend kindness, I chose instead to attack the person and make their day more difficult. The negative emotions I expressed took a toll not only on the server and on me, but probably on many other people as well. Who knows how much stress I contributed to the life of that waiter, who then could have passed that negativity on to other customers, who then might have passed it on to their families.

However, the more I choose the soul's perspective and connect with my own intuition and my own peace, the more my everyday experiences shift. One day when I went into a sandwich shop for lunch, I consciously set the intent to have a peaceful experience there, instead of my usual feeling of impatience while waiting in line. That day, somebody in front of me in the line was having difficulty and was taking a long time to order. I had to get back to work soon, and most likely other customers did, too. An atmosphere of irritation pervaded that whole restaurant.

In that moment, I shifted out of my personality's perception and its usual impulse to judge, and entered the soul experience of oneness with others. Instead of getting irritated and adding to the general frustration, I felt a deep sense of peace, centeredness, connection, and compassion for all of us there. My consciousness expanded. I felt everybody's emotions. I blessed everyone there and smiled.

And it seemed to have an instant impact in the restaurant; everything seemed to shift. A crying child calmed down. The person working behind the counter smiled back at customers. That's being in the flow. That's being connected with Spirit.

The contrast between what happened in the sandwich shop, when I saw myself joined with everyone, and the other restaurant experience, when I saw myself as separate, taught me some valuable lessons. When I attack others, I attack myself. In those moments when my ego gets the best of me, I have learned just to observe my attack thoughts without judgment, and to forgive myself for having them. This helps me to shift my attention back to the choice of what I want. Do I want peace or fear?

· · · · · · · · · · · ·

Now that you have had a basic introduction to Soul Visioning, let's get right into your own process.

Just ahead, you will embark on the seven-step path to connect with your soul, start to clear your inner blockages, and affirm your soul's vision. You will begin to identify your life's ideals and purposes, linking them with the expression of your soul's vision in areas such as work, relationships, health, finances, and spiritual growth. You will also take a Soul Visioning "audio journey" connecting you to your soul self. This process will deeply imprint your soul's vision into the unconscious mind and body.

three

Connect to Your Soul, Discover Your Ideal Future

Our ultimate aim in life is to realize our true identity as a soul. The most important wisdom any of us can have is to know our soul's purpose. The essence of our life's path is to remember and express that purpose, making choices in accord with that spiritual ideal.

Not everything we define as material success is soul success; unless our success is founded on spiritual ideals, it will fade. We may think that our goals should be to get the best education, find a job with the highest status or pay, marry the right person, create the perfect family, and the list goes on. There is nothing wrong with having all of these things, but unless our ideal serves humanity, we are falling short of our potential. To serve humanity, we can seek to be a channel of blessings to everyone we meet. So rather than using our conscious mind to program our unconscious mind, we must invite our Mind—capital M—to express its highest purpose by guiding both our conscious and unconscious mind.

Perhaps our spiritual ideal is to be so full of love, wisdom, and joy that our very presence is like a pure, refreshing stream to others. When we are able to see and remember what is good and beautiful in others, even when their actions suggest they have forgotten their True Self, our heart becomes the altar on which we offer them their innocence. By consistently expressing the purity of our purpose in all our relationships, we strengthen that quality in our own mind and heart.

Many of us endlessly search outside ourselves for happiness, hoping that the perfect partner, situation, or possession will come along to fill us up and "complete" us. Our true nature is love, but we have forgotten that we are spiritual beings. Yet from a higher perspective, our real purpose is to remember who we are, to know that we are more than bodies that get sick and perish. While we are focused on the physical dimension, we can use this "classroom" to undo the erroneous belief that we are separate, sinful, and undeserving of love. When we go beyond that illusion to experience our identity as an immortal soul—a soul that is perfect, complete, and one with the Divine—everything can flow from that understanding.

When we connect with our soul qualities, we have a deep sense of peace, joy, radiance, wisdom, and well-being. What do I mean by soul qualities? If you take some water from the ocean and place it in several containers of various sizes, shapes, and colors, the water takes the form of the vessel into which it is poured. The ocean is like undifferentiated Spirit, and the containers are like our individual identities. We each contain the essence of Spirit, but the form is varied. We each express Spirit through a unique blend of our soul gifts and our personality traits.

Feeling stuck or empty is one indication that we are out of touch with our soul. When we fully manifest our true nature, how will we feel? We will wake up inspired, enthusiastically sharing with people, experiencing the joy of service, with a sense of gratitude for our opportunities. Synchronicities will occur more frequently as we choose to allow our ideal to inspire our life. Our ideal provides us with spiritual energy and motivation; by applying this ideal, we mobilize our soul energy. We are a channel for this purpose in our everyday life, through our attitudes, emotions, and actions. We continually share the spiritual energy of our soul with everyone we meet.

"You must be the change you want to see in the world," Mahatma Gandhi said. I would add that *living our soul's ideal is the path to becoming the change we want to see in the world!* We become the carrier of that spiritual quality, radiating its energy and vibration. Self-observation and daily application of our ideal must be our first priority. Our soul purpose and the sincerity of our love have much more to do with the quality of what we create than any personality-based technique of manifestation.

Just as a radio station broadcasts signals that can be picked up with a receiver, we are all broadcasting at the soul level, sending out our frequency to be picked up by the unconscious mind of every one of our fellow human beings. This means that there are no hidden thoughts or feelings. Energetically, our own personal thoughts and feelings can either harm or heal. But we can choose what we want to broadcast, and we can all try to radiate only from our soul.

Bottom line: we must learn that our worth is established by God, the Divine, or whatever label we wish to give it, not by what we do, accomplish, or possess. Many of my clients tell me they feel they have failed in life because they didn't accomplish anything "great" or fulfill some grand life purpose. I remind them that one's greatest purpose is to experience wholeness as a spiritual being, and to express that love every day, whether by extending kindness and patience when waiting in line at the grocery store, being peaceful in a traffic jam, or practicing forgiveness of oneself and others.

It is important to keep in mind that this process occurs over time for most of us. To remember our soul, we must "undo" some deeply programmed beliefs and patterns. We are like a diamond in the rough. Our Spirit is perfect, whole, and complete. To access it on a consistent basis, we must forgive the layers of erroneous belief that hide the beauty of that identity. So we need to be gentle, patient, and kind with ourselves on our healing journey of awakening. We are loved unconditionally by the Divine.

A spiritual teacher of mine once said that our job is not to be without an ego, but to forgive ourselves for having one. This really took the pressure off the perfectionist part of me, the part that was bemoaning all the mistakes I was making. Mistakes call for correction, not condemnation.

Soul Visioning Step 1
Peak Experiences Guided Audio Process

Have you ever had experiences when you felt your soul's presence? When the light of your soul peeked through? Your memories of these peak (peek!) experiences can reveal when the soul's essence entered your conscious awareness. We all have had these moments, however fleeting. Perhaps you may recall the beauty and the peace of being in nature, or a time of creative inspiration when the energy just flowed through you.

Reviewing your life for such memories will inspire you and can help you discover your soul ideal or purpose. For example, when my husband Dave did the exercise that you are about to do, he recalled a night when he was nine years old. He was lying on the grass at a local park, watching the stars. He had gazed at the stars before, drawn by their beauty and a sense of wonder. But this particular night, he recalled after finishing the exercise, *There was a moment when I experienced my oneness with the universe and felt a sense of cosmic connectedness. I remembered that experience, and it came to me that one of the qualities of my soul that has reverberated throughout my life is joyous oneness.*

How has Dave expressed this spiritual ideal? For example, during his college years he was elected president of the Residential College of Philosophy and Religion—even though he was an engineering major—because of his joy in studying the oneness of truth expressed in diverse spiritual traditions. He now enjoys teaching and sharing these spiritual truths in classes, workshops, and retreats.

While doing this "Peak Experiences" exercise, a woman who is a healer recalled a moment from her past. She was doing energy healing work on another person when she experienced herself as a soul whose nature was love and whose expression of that love was the transfer of healing energy. Upon remembering what she had felt at that moment, she realized that sharing her loving being as a healer was a major spiritual purpose of her life.

Joyous oneness, spiritual healing, awareness, understanding, love, service, wholeness, balance, and purity are just a few examples of soul qualities or ideals. The following guided audio session is designed to help you reclaim some of your own peak spiritual experiences. (**Note: To access the tools you'll need to get the most out of it, see "Preparation: Guided Inner Journeys" on page 9.**) Soon afterward, continue to the writing exercise that follows it.

PEAK EXPERIENCES GUIDED AUDIO PROCESS: SCRIPT

Sit or lie comfortably now. Close your eyes and just observe the flowing in and the flowing out of your breath. You don't need to try to change the rate or depth of your breathing. Just be present and observe the rhythm of breathing in your body . . .

Be present to the intention of your soul and feel its guiding presence, allowing yourself to trust its wisdom and love . . .

Imagine a timeline on which your whole life appears before you. Starting today, slowly move back through yesterday . . . last week . . . last month . . . last year. Go back to the beginning of this current lifetime, where your whole life is before you on this timeline . . .

As you lightly scan that timeline, gradually looking forward now . . . notice that just a few experiences stand out . . . They have a certain luminosity because these were peak spiritual events in your life, moments when you caught a glimpse of something different about life . . . These were very positive occasions, times when you were in touch with life in a more authentic, deep, and meaningful way than in your regular daily routine . . .

Remember these experiences, and try to relive just two or three of them right now . . . As you move back into the feelings of these peak spiritual moments, be still . . . Let a word or a phrase come to your mind that describes the essence of those feelings, those moments . . . With that word or phrase now in mind, begin to bring your attention back to your breathing, to the natural rhythm of your body . . . Let your breathing bring your attention back to your body, and when you're ready, open your eyes.

Soul Visioning Step 2
Writing Exercise A:
Determining Your Soul Ideals

If you haven't already done so, now choose a word or phrase that captures the quality of the peak experiences you recalled in the previous exercise, and write it down. Take as much time as you need. This word or phrase will remind you of the soul quality that most inspires you. It should reflect your best conscious understanding, at this time, of your soul's *ideal, purpose,* or *quality.* (We'll use these three words interchangeably because they stand for similar concepts.)

For example, I recalled this peak spiritual state: I was driving in my car one day, thinking of my beloved husband-to-be. I suddenly felt a love that I had never experienced before: a tenderness and caring so profound and unconditional that it was overwhelming! Every level of my being was singing in response to his reflecting my soul to me. I felt cherished and joyful. I felt that all my boundaries had dissolved into the oneness of my spiritual home. A phrase to remind me of this peak state, which became an ideal for me, is *unconditional love.*

Did you recall more than one peak experience? If so, you may have come up with two or more words or phrases, each revealing a different soul quality, purpose, or ideal. That's fine, but for the moment, choose *just one.* Working with multiple ideals at the same time dilutes our focus. Concentrating on just one amplifies our power in expressing it. The specific ideal you begin with may be less crucial than the process of accessing and expressing it in your daily life. And once you have mastered one soul ideal, it may be time to focus on another. (In part B of this exercise, you will choose one quality and learn how to express it in various life areas.) Should you need a bit of help, here's another approach: think of the two or three people you most admire. Write down their most inspirational qualities: they can be a clue to your own soul ideals. Or you can refer to the following list.

Sample Soul Ideals
HEALTH

Balance	Freedom	Vitality
Energy	Stamina	Wellness
Flexibility	Strength	

RELATIONSHIPS

Commitment	Honesty	Non-judgment
Common soul vision/	Humor	Openness
purpose	Intimacy	Respect
Connection	Love	Trust
Friendship	Mutual reciprocity	Understanding

CAREER/WORK

Cooperation	Fulfillment	Inspiration
Creativity	Gratitude	Purpose
Enjoyment	Growth	Rewards
Excitement	Harmony	Service

FINANCES

Flow	Generosity	Sharing
Freedom	Gratitude	

SPIRITUALITY

Balance	Forgiveness	Peace
Bliss	Joy	Understanding
Compassion	Love	Wholeness
Enlightenment	Oneness	Wisdom
Fearlessness		

PERSONAL GROWTH

Autonomy	Exploration	Objectivity
Clarity	Fearlessness	Openness
Compassion	Freedom	Patience
Creativity	Harmony	Self-acceptance
Efficiency	Humility	

Soul Visioning Step 2

Writing Exercise B:
Applying Your Soul Ideals

In this exercise, if you haven't already done so, you will choose your most meaningful soul ideal, purpose, or quality. Then you will link this ideal with its actual expression in various aspects of your life, such as health, career/work, personal/spiritual growth, relationships, and finances. How will you express this ideal in your thinking, feeling, and doing? Before we begin, let's make sure that you've come up with a soul *ideal*, rather than a goal.

Ideals versus Goals: What's the Difference?

Applying internal soul ideals is about how we live our daily life, which is quite different from focusing on manifesting or achieving goals. Ideals are personal, internal standards or criteria by which we measure our motives, attitudes, and behavior. Our soul ideal is our highest purpose, and we can use that purpose to guide us as we evaluate our desires and set our goals. These ideals are clear, constructive, and growth-producing. They inspire us to be our best and highest selves.

We may tend to think in terms of *manifesting goals*, but our soul calls us to *live our soul's ideals*. Like a star, our ideal guides us; we know we can't touch that star, but it inspires us with its beauty. An ideal is a quality that our soul aspires to express in our life. When faced with a decision, we ask, "What is motivating me? Is what's spurring me on only an ego desire, or is it harmonious with my soul's ideal?"

A typical goal, for example, might be "I want to be healthy." An ideal, on the other hand, is the *purpose* for which we want to be healthy. What would be a soul purpose for attaining better health? What are we going to use our body for? The quality of our motivation can differ profoundly as we seek to achieve our goals. If our desire to be healthy is inspired by our soul ideal of giving ourselves in loving service, that is very different from, say, an ego desire to be attractive so we can get a partner to take care of us. Thus, taking health as an example, our underlying spiritual ideal might be joyous service or respectful caring.

Worksheet Examples: From Ideals to Attitudes to Actions

Before you get started with the "Applying Your Soul Ideals" worksheets, let's go through a few examples. On the five sample worksheets on pages 72–76, you'll see *love* as an example of a soul ideal, and the worksheets have been filled in to show how one might proceed from ideals to attitudes to actions.

To give you some hands-on practice, suppose that in the "Peak Experiences" session you realized that one of your soul's ideals is *healing*. Using a downloaded worksheet or one of your own, write *healing* in the left-hand column, as it is a spiritual purpose, ideal, or quality.

Next, look at the middle column, the mental/emotional. What attitudes, thoughts, or feelings could you cultivate to express this purpose? Write them here. For example, if you want to extend healing to another person, one attitude might be appreciation of his or her soul nature. By acknowledging that person's spiritual gifts, their qualities that bless others, you may help them remember their wholeness. Regardless of their personality's behavior or attitudes, your appreciation of their spiritual perfection helps them become more aware of their own soul. You might also include in this column such things as kindness, humility, harmony, consistency, persistence, hope, truth, patience, gentleness, and love. Just a few are enough: write them down and focus sincerely on them.

Now look at the right-hand column, the physical: what actions might you take to actualize your soul purpose? Perhaps you could share your knowledge by writing an article on healing. You could meditate for ten minutes every day to connect to your healing soul presence. Or you could learn one of the many healing modalities, such as acupressure or massage, then offer it as a gift to your friends or family.

Most people will find some ego resistance to actually writing down their ideals, because it makes them responsible for expressing their soul. But once you experience applying your ideals in your daily life, you will discover that this seemingly simple exercise has the power to transform your life.

Now, let's look at a third example of a soul ideal. What attitudes and emotions could you hold that would help express the soul quality of *joy*? Some might be delight, humor, appreciation, gratitude, kindness, understanding, openness, mercy, generosity, and sharing. If you choose to hold any of these thoughts and feelings in your mental and emotional body, they could help express the fullness of joy.

What physical actions could manifest this quality? To link the emotion of delight with a physical action, you might really immerse yourself in playing with your pet. How about being willing to listen with all your attention, doing nothing else, to music that makes you feel light-hearted or joyful? To open yourself to experiencing kindness, practice random acts of kindness. What about telling the five most important people in your life what you appreciate most about them? You could respond to people with the kindest interpretation of their behavior, and read books to deepen your understanding of joy. In this way, you start with joy as a higher purpose, allow it to express as specific attitudes in your mental and emotional nature, and then help give it form through specific personal actions.

Focus on Varied Life Areas

Focusing on several areas of our life can provide opportunities to apply our ideals (that is, areas such as relationships, career/work, health, personal/spiritual growth, and finances). To express *joy* in the area of *relationships*, for instance, we might choose attitudes of appreciation, acceptance, encouragement, empathy, flexibility, respect, equality, humor, or honesty. Each of these attitudes can inspire specific actions. Sharing and processing dreams together with our partner promotes honesty and acceptance. Writing notes and cards describing what we appreciate about them is encouraging. Consulting with our significant other about major decisions inspires mutual respect and equality.

To express our soul purpose of *joy* in the *health* area, we could choose attitudes such as purity, wholeness, balance, caring, vitality, or respect. As part of caring for our body, we could decide to schedule a monthly massage and do daily stretching. To express our respect, we might choose to get at least seven hours of sleep each night. To promote purity, we could eat organic foods and drink pure water.

"Applying Your Soul Ideals" Worksheet Instructions

Before you begin these worksheets, please complete:

- The "Peak Experiences Guided Audio Process" on page 62

- "Writing Exercise A: Determining Your Soul Ideals" on page 64, generating a word or phrase that expresses your soul purpose at this time.

Remember, to access the tools you'll need to get the most out of the writing exercise, please see "How to Use This Book" on page 7.

Now you're ready to use the blank "Applying Your Soul Ideals" worksheets to work with your own soul's purpose. Make your own versions based on the samples in this book, or download printable, ready-to-fill-in worksheets at *www.soulvisioning.com/sv.*

Column 1 is for the soul's purpose or ideal that you want to radiate in your life: you chose this ideal in the previous exercise. Remember, an ideal is something we *grow toward* expressing more perfectly. If we were already perfectly expressing it, it would not be an ideal for us. Column 2 is for the attitudes, thoughts, and feelings you choose to express that ideal, and column 3 is for the physical actions you will take to manifest it.

For each worksheet, you will focus on one area of your life, making more copies of the sheet if needed. For instance, see the sample worksheet on page 72: "Relationships." You may find it more useful to fill out separate worksheets on each of your most significant relationships—perhaps your life partner, family members, friends, and community members. Of course, you can also cover those areas of your life that you feel need the most attention. Maybe you want to focus on childrearing; continuing education; service to your community, country, or world; or your upcoming retirement. The life areas shown are only suggestions, so if you wish to focus on other areas, please do so. These exercises can have a major impact, so make them your own.

Now we'll begin the soul-guided process of using these worksheets. *As you do so, please go within and hold the intent that your soul, rather than your ego, will be the source of the insights you receive.*

First, imagine the attitudes and emotions that would express your spiritual purpose in five areas of your life: relationships, career/work, health, personal/spiritual growth, and finances. (Add more areas, if you wish.) These will form the foundation of your plan for living your soul's vision.

Using the five worksheets on pages 72–76 as models, select six to eight attitudes, thoughts, or feelings for starters. If you're honest with yourself, you can probably identify a few of them quite easily. For each of these, write down one or more corresponding physical behaviors or actions that would help you "live" your soul ideal.

Are you feeling stuck? Remember, it's normal for our ego to resist making specific commitments like this to our spiritual growth. Applying our ideal is one way of making that resistance more conscious so that we can deal with it more effectively. We can nonjudgmentally acknowledge how we may be falling short, and then get back to our real focus: living our soul's ideal.

Follow your own intuition in developing your soul ideals and applying them to your life. Be honest with yourself and write down only those ideals, thoughts and emotions, and physical actions that you are willing to make an effort to express. And choose your words carefully; they should stimulate your heart and soul.

Remember, it is worth giving your full attention and time to this important step in your growth. (As you progress through the many areas of your life, you may find it helpful to occasionally revisit this exercise.) Completing these worksheets is essential to prepare you for **Soul Visioning Step 3: "A Soul-Guided Journey to Your Ideal Future,"** a cornerstone of the process.

Soul Visioning
APPLYING YOUR SOUL IDEALS

Life Area: RELATIONSHIPS
(Consider primary, family, friends, and community relationships)

Soul Ideal *(Name one ideal, quality, or purpose)*	Mental/Emotional *(Attitudes, thoughts, and feelings that express that ideal)*	Physical *(Behaviors and activities that express that ideal)*
LOVE	Compassion	Listen with patience and empathy.
	Joy	At least weekly, do something together we both/all enjoy.
	Honesty	Share dreams, desires, and goals together on a weekly basis.
	Encouraging	Remind the other(s) of their achievements and successes at least once a week.
	Accepting	Consciously focus on seeing the Divine in the other(s) every day.
	Equality	Fairly divide responsibilities for tasks.
	Respect	Balance our time and energy commitments outside the relationship with those inside.
	Appreciation	Daily, express your gratitude to your partner.
	Intimacy	Share emotional and physical affection.
	Trust	Engage in honest, open communication.
	Forgiving	Be a love finder rather than a fault finder.
	Humor	Laugh together.

Soul Visioning
APPLYING YOUR SOUL IDEALS

Life Area: CAREER/WORK

Soul Ideal (Name one ideal, quality, or purpose)	Mental/Emotional (Attitudes, thoughts, and feelings that express that ideal)	Physical (Behaviors and activities that express that ideal)
LOVE	Fulfilled	Work with like-minded people.
	Grateful	Focus on the strengths of my coworkers.
	Exciting	Learn something new every week about the service I provide.
	Cooperation	Consider everyone's point of view when planning our joint work.
	Harmony	Maximize the areas of agreement in my relationships with coworkers, and minimize differences.
	Honesty	Clearly communicate my needs and priorities in a respectful way.
	Generosity	Freely share my knowledge and experience with coworkers.
	Passion	Do Soul Visioning for guidance in making decisions.
	Inspired	Use my talents and gifts to be of service.

Soul Visioning
APPLYING YOUR SOUL IDEALS

Life Area: HEALTH

Soul Ideal *(Name one ideal, quality, or purpose)*	Mental/Emotional *(Attitudes, thoughts, and feelings that express that ideal)*	Physical *(Behaviors and activities that express that ideal)*
LOVE	Energetic	Exercise vigorously for at least 30 minutes three times a week.
	Purity	Eliminate white flour and white sugar from diet.
	Balance	Get a massage at least once a month.
	Flexibility	Do 10 minutes of stretching every morning. Practice yoga.
	Strength	Do weight-training exercises for 15 minutes two times a week.
	Stamina	Get at least 7½ hours of sleep every night.

Soul Visioning

APPLYING YOUR SOUL IDEALS

Life Area: PERSONAL/SPIRITUAL GROWTH

Soul Ideal (Name one ideal, quality, or purpose)	Mental/Emotional (Attitudes, thoughts, and feelings that express that ideal)	Physical (Behaviors and activities that express that ideal)
LOVE	Guidance	Seek, listen to, and follow the guidance of my Higher Self on a consistent basis.
	Kindness	Be gentle with self as well as with others in every interaction.
	Consistency	Meditate for 10 minutes every morning to strengthen my intuitive awareness.
	Peace	Read inspirational spiritual material every day.
	Awakening	Share my intuitive awareness with others to encourage their awakening.
	Hope	Look for opportunities to use my intuitive awareness to improve every situation.
	Patience	Take the time to fully understand challenging situations before responding.
	Forgiveness	Practice forgiveness of self and others.
	Growth	Take classes or workshops.
	Mindfulness	Practice non-judgment.
	Self-Healing	Use WHEE or other methods to clear limiting beliefs, attitudes, emotions.

Soul Visioning
APPLYING YOUR SOUL IDEALS

Life Area: FINANCES

Soul Ideal (Name one ideal, quality, or purpose)	Mental/Emotional (Attitudes, thoughts, and feelings that express that ideal)	Physical (Behaviors and activities that express that ideal)
LOVE	Abundance	Keep a gratitude journal listing all the gifts of time, energy, and attention that I have received from other people.
	Generosity	Look for opportunities to share my resources more completely with others (such as donating money or volunteering time).
	Worthiness	Take time to participate in recreational activities that I enjoy.
	Stewardship	Share resources wisely to support groups that nurture my spiritual growth.
	Freedom	Manage my resources responsibly.
	Flow	Look for opportunities to meet my needs in ways other than financial resources.

Living Our Ideals

Daily Ideal Application Journal

Would you be willing to remind yourself of your soul ideal every day, and measure your daily goals, decisions, desires, and choices against that ideal? Another effective and practical way to train your mind to express your soul purpose is to keep a daily journal. Here you record what you are thinking, feeling, and doing to express your spiritual purpose, and any related experiences. You just might find that this is the best type of journal you could keep to support your personal growth.

To use our earlier example, suppose our ideal or spiritual purpose is *joy*. Do we always choose to radiate that energy? Not likely—that's why it's an ideal. But it is something that we can work toward. We *can* improve. We *can* get better at applying it. That's the whole point of our soul ideal: to inspire us toward greater manifestation of that quality of being.

Applying ideals requires using our Will to direct our choices. Ideals are like training wheels to stabilize the focus of our conscious mind. Working with our ideals is a process, because with our application comes greater awareness and understanding.

These questions may help you better use your Daily Ideal Application Journal:

- How frequently was I aware of my soul's purpose?

- How often were my actions inspired by my ideal?

- What energized me when I was applying my ideal?

- How was it challenging for me to apply my ideal?

- What was the most significant thing I learned?

- What could I do differently to apply my ideal?

Guidelines for Living Our Ideal

- The soul ideal is the standard by which our personality's will is aligned with the soul

- An ideal is a constant reminder of our spiritual purpose, which can be expressed in any circumstance. Our ideal should awaken a high sense of purpose in our consciousness.

- We can use our ideal to stimulate our soul expression.

- Applying our soul ideal in daily life deepens our awareness and understanding of our soul nature.

- We need to visualize, feel, and know our ideal so vividly in our imagination that it inspires us to surrender to our soul purpose.

- We can use our ideal to select new patterns to replace our old, limiting patterns.

- An ideal can never be completely attained, so it acts as a perpetual motivator.

- Rather than condemning ourselves for not living up to our ideal, we should focus on constructively using our spiritual purpose to inspire positive action.

- Written ideals help us to focus on definite criteria to guide our choices. They must be practical.

- It is helpful to keep a journal about our daily applications of our soul ideal.

Advanced Methods for Applying Ideals

One of the keys to spiritual growth is consistent focus on our soul ideal. This practice accelerates the infusion of soul energy and light into the mind, emotions, and behaviors of the personality. We can use our ideals to invoke soul awareness in our consciousness.

Ideals are the source of our courage and integrity because they become our personal soul standards. They're not coming from outside us—from another person, our religion, or our community demanding that we follow *their* values. Rather, our ideal is our own soul standard for the quality of *our* purpose and motivation. The fact that it is *our* personal internal standard is what makes it so powerful. With experience, our understanding and ability to apply our ideals will grow.

Remember, the journey from the unintegrated personality to the soul-infused personality is a path to our core Self, leading to a deep abiding faith in our own inner wisdom. The more we are guided by our intuitive soul nature, the more constructive and the more powerful are the results we create in any area of our life.

Meditation is an effective method by which we can experience soul awareness. By meditating on our spiritual purpose in the morning, we will find that in addition to inspiration and energy, we may get specific constructive guidance. Meditate first to get in touch with your soul purpose, then for inspiration on how to apply and express your ideal that day.

Another approach to invoke soul awareness is to consciously choose to cultivate an ideal, quality, or purpose to replace a limiting mental pattern. For example, my husband Dave recognized that he had a pattern of rigid self-control, which inhibited his ability to surrender to the flow of his soul. "To express my soul purpose of joyous loving, I had to learn to let go and trust my intuition," says Dave. "To cultivate an attitude of receptivity to spiritual flow, I decided to take a course in spiritual healing. Through this training, I learned to release my conscious control and allow intuition to guide the flow of healing energy. I also practiced floating in water as a way of relaxing, trusting, and letting go of the need for control."

How Ideals Guide Our Growth

At the earliest stages of our spiritual growth, before we discover our soul ideal, we start out as an *unconscious incompetent*. In other words, we don't know what we're doing, and we are so unconscious that we don't even know that we are incompetent! We are not consciously aware of our ideal.

Over time, we move to a stage that psychologists call *conscious incompetence*. At this stage, we have become aware of our soul ideal, and it helps us realize, "I'm spiritually incompetent. I'm not fully living up to or expressing my higher purpose. My attitudes, emotions, and behaviors are not congruent with my soul's vision. But at least I'm aware of it, and I wouldn't be aware of it without a conscious understanding of my spiritual ideal."

Later, we get to a stage of relative accomplishment, termed *conscious competence*. By practicing and applying our ideal, we discover that we are consistently making better, more loving choices. We are able to do this because we are aware, in the moment, of our soul's purpose.

The final stage is *unconscious competence:* we have trained our unconscious mind to express our spiritual purpose automatically and naturally, without the need for us to consciously think about it. Our soul's purpose has simply become a quality of our being, a light that never stops shining. This does not happen overnight. It is a result of our growth into the full, conscious awareness of our higher nature.

Manifesting from our soul's vision, rather than taking a personality-based approach, makes a real difference in our life! Since we are transcending our limited, conscious mind, this brings very expansive results. Our soul ideals produce the fruits of the Spirit in our life, which include peace, harmony, hope, patience, and kindness. Focusing in our imagination on our soul ideals acts as a bridge to connect us to our intuitive soul energy, to guide and empower our life. The process I call Soul Visioning can help us to cross that bridge.

Soul Visioning Step 3
A Soul-Guided Journey to Your Ideal Future

Now that you know your spiritual purpose, and have some ideas about what your soul wants to express in major areas of your life, it's time to take a journey into your ideal future. During this guided journey, you'll envision this future life as if it is actually happening right now. As we know, this is *holographic time*, where all experiences—past, present, and future—exist simultaneously. When we access the realm of the eternal soul, there are no limits. In this expanded state of consciousness, we can more easily connect to our soul guidance; our True Self intuitively guides the unfolding of our vision for our life.

In this meditation, you will first reach a deeply relaxed state. Then you will be guided into a garden setting, or you can choose your own favorite place: for example, a beach, a mountain, or a meadow. You can make this place just the way you want it. This is your sacred space, a peaceful, safe, healing sanctuary in which you invite your *ideal Future Self* to be with you. This ideal Future Self is the part of you that is whole, complete, compassionate, wise, empowered, and connected to the Divine, and has access to your soul guidance. This True Self merges with you and becomes your guide into your ideal future: a time of your choosing, anywhere between one and five years from now. With higher soul guidance, you can envision your future just the way you want it—in your career/work, relationships, health, finances, personal/spiritual growth, or any other areas. You may want to focus on just one or two areas at a time.

The key is to *tap into the good feeling* of your ideal future. Using all of your senses, immerse yourself in the experience. This will prepare you to answer some "What if?" questions:

- What if I could wake up tomorrow and have my life be just the way I want it to be, with the guidance of my higher soul wisdom? If I could live my soul's highest desire, what would that look and feel like?

- What would I do if I knew I couldn't fail?

- What will I see in my future that will let me know I have achieved my soul's vision?

- What will I hear people saying about me? What will I be saying about myself?

- How will I feel? Have I ever felt that way at any time in my life?

Suggestions for Envisioning Your Future

You may not know exactly what your ideal career or work would be, for example. Don't focus on the details yet; start with the ideal qualities and feelings you seek in this work. For instance, you wake up in the morning and feel passionate about your work; you work in a harmonious environment with like-minded people who are being of service to others; you feel gratitude toward and from those you serve.

The same advice applies to your ideal relationship(s). Even if you can't fill in all the blanks, you can envision a conscious partnership with someone who shares a common purpose with you, a partnership based on mutual respect, humor, love, passion, and the willingness to forgive and grow spiritually together. What would you be doing and feeling together? The more you feel it and believe that you deserve it, the more likely it will begin to manifest in your world.

Envisioning a life of abundance comes not from thinking "I'm going to win the lottery," but from knowing that abundance is already within you. When we remember our true spiritual nature, the outer world reflects that wholeness. So when envisioning your ideal future, there is a feeling of well-being, that everything you need is provided.

In the area of your ideal future health, you could envision yourself *feeling* how good it is to live in a vital, energetic, and strong body. You have a balanced lifestyle that shows you care for yourself. The intent is to use this body in a loving way, under the direction of your soul.

In the area of personal/spiritual growth, your ideal life is in the synchronous flow of Divine Love. You feel peace, joy, and purpose in your life. You are aware that you are one with everyone. You practice forgiveness and mindfulness, moment to moment. You are empowered and confident, trusting your intuition to guide your soul's vision.

Identifying Resistances to the Soul's Vision

In Soul Visioning workshops or private sessions, during the "Soul-Guided Journey to Your Ideal Future," I ask, "Is any part of you holding you back or saying no to your soul's vision?" Most people have some limiting beliefs that emerge in response to that question. For example, their "judge and critic" voice says, "Don't even hope for it—it will never happen!" or "You don't deserve it."

So whatever comes up for you, make a mental note of it, because that is what we will work on to forgive and reprogram when you return from this journey. In the next chapters you will be using many tools to help you change your mind and your beliefs about yourself.

Anchoring the Soul's Vision

At the end of the journey, when you are feeling the awe of being in your ideal future, I will suggest that you take a picture of that scene as you want to remember it, then put a picture frame around it. I will then ask what color your picture frame is. You will take that color and run it throughout your body, everywhere it will go. At the same time, I will ask you to form a circle with your index finger and your thumb, making an "OK" sign. These are anchoring techniques. They install the good feeling deep within your unconscious body-mind, so that when you call up the scene in the picture frame or use the OK sign, you will be taken back to that sublime feeling you created during your Soul Visioning journey.

How Soul Visioning Awakened a "Conductor of Light"

Before we embark on our journey into your own ideal future, I want to share Bob's story with you. Bob is a media and public relations consultant for whom I facilitated a Soul Visioning guided journey. During his session, the energy in the room was very high, filled with awe and sacredness. A year later, I talked again with Bob to find out how connecting with his soul had made a difference in his life. Excerpts from that interview follow.

SUSAN: *What do you recall most vividly about your Soul Visioning experience?*

BOB: There was strong imagery, powerful images of my role, the sense of myself. I was conducting something like an orchestra, except the orchestra was creating light. There were different lights coming from the people, and people began handing the lights back to the people behind them, and on and on. There was this fountain of light moving backwards, like visual and kinesthetic music without the sound. I was enabling it in some way, helping this process to happen. I felt transparent, like I was not as totally solid as I might feel in the physical realm. I felt light coming through me.

During our conversation, Bob seemed to emanate a glow, a peaceful radiance. His smile seemed to recognize his True Self and purpose. The feeling was contagious, because I can still feel it to this day.

S: *What benefits did the Soul Visioning journey provide you over the past year? Were there tangible results?*

B: In terms of my relationships, I have more patience and serenity in working with other people, looking more for the light in other people and helping them to bring that up. So it's not just "get the business done." It's more like a process—taking my time, playing the role of the conductor, setting the tempo, reminding the other members when to come in—more of an orchestration.

S: *You're orchestrating a lot of different people's services, bringing teams of people together so that they work in harmony. You support their vision, their life's work, or their project. What strikes me is that the quality of consciousness you bring to your work has been enhanced by experiencing your soul's vision.*

B: There is a surety that I didn't have before. I'm clearer with what's going on in my relationships and with groups that I belong to. I interact with people in a more conscious way. Whenever there is doubt about what's going on, this imagery keeps coming back and showing me, "It's OK, what you are doing."

S: *What kind of doubts has this helped you to overcome?*

B: Oftentimes working with groups, pulling the "orchestra" together, not everybody plays in harmony. Sometimes people get impatient or want to throw somebody out of the band. In the past, I might have just thought, "That's the way it goes." But Soul Visioning gave me a sense of perspective that all of the players are needed to create this harmony. I am the director, and it's my job to help people figure out how to harmonize. Now I see things in a more patient way. This is my role, not just to make the music work, but to help the players harmonize interpersonally.

Bob went on to say that the Soul Visioning experience had imprinted on a cellular level with him, such that it had stayed with him and validated his purpose for being here.

Bob: The imagery and the vision are so powerful that this really informs me all of the time. I'm very aware of standing in that conductor position ... passing on the light to others, awakening the light in others so that they can pass it on.

Prepare for Your Guided Journey

Listening to and following the guided journey below is well worth your time and effort; it is a key component of the Soul Visioning process. Remember, your soul is creating this ideal future. You are not psychically "reading" what will "happen" in your future. The difference is that your soul—not your ego—is in charge of consciously directing your life. When your soul is in charge of your future, it brings a deep state of joy, meaning, and purpose.

Remember: to access the tools you'll need to get the most out of this session, see "Preparation: Guided Inner Journeys" on page 9.

Soul-Guided Journey to Your Ideal Future: Script

Take a couple of deep breaths . . . Breathe in peace and exhale any tension that you might be holding. Focus on your breathing . . . letting go more and more with each breath . . . Feel how good it feels to just relax and let go . . . Allow the quietness of Spirit to be present with you.

And now I invite you to imagine a bright white light coming down from above . . . a beam of shimmering, iridescent white light coming down from above and entering the crown of your head with the unlimited light of love. This is the universal light of love energy . . . It enters your head and fills your body to overflowing . . . The light now surrounds your heart with light and love, and expands to totally surround your body with an aura of protection, peace, and harmony. You are relaxed and at ease with yourself and the world and everyone in it . . . And any outside noises that you hear only help you to go even deeper into relaxation . . . If any outside thoughts should come into your mind, simply brush them aside.

And in this wonderfully relaxed state, I invite you to imagine a beautiful staircase of five steps with hand railings. As you step down, one step at a time, each step will light up with a luminous golden light that fills every cell of your being. . . 5 . . . 4 . . . 3 . . . 2 . . . and 1 . . . at the bottom of the stairs.

And ahead of you, notice a door, a beautiful golden door, and I invite you to open the door to a garden of peace and safety, a sanctuary of healing, a sacred space. This could be a garden that you have visited, or one that you want to visit, or one that you imagine in your mind . . . Enter this garden . . . Immerse yourself with all of your senses ... Notice the beauty that surrounds you. Smell the fragrances of nature, feel a gentle breeze against your face ... Perhaps you hear birds singing joyfully in the background, welcoming you ... This is your sanctuary of respite and healing. You can add or take anything away ... Perhaps there are benches on which to sit, and fountains. Just enjoy being here, making it just the way you want it ... Feel how good it feels to be here. So relaxed ... so comfortable.

And now if you are willing, invite into your garden your Ideal Self from your future ... That part of you that is unconditionally loving, wise, compassionate, joyful, empowered, and connected to the Divine ... How does it feel to be in the presence of your ideal Future Self? (Pause.)

Look into the eyes of your Future Self, and what do you see in those eyes? (Pause.) What does your Future Self want to communicate to you? What words of inspiration and encouragement does your Future Self want to say to you? Be open to receiving this message ...

This Future Self will be your guide into your ideal future. From this deeply relaxed place, I invite you to go out into your ideal future. And under higher soul wisdom, envision your ideal future. Be there now as if it is happening in this moment ... What are you doing and feeling in this ideal future?

Let yourself envision your ideal future relationships. Feel how wonderful it is to experience the joy of being in meaningful, deeply connected, fulfilling relationships ... You feel a sense of trust, unconditional love, and respect in your primary, intimate relationship. (Long pause.)

And now moving into your ideal future work or career ... Feel the excitement of waking up in the morning and looking forward to doing your life's passion ... Being in a harmonious environment with people who are cooperative ... creative people who have a common vision ... being appreciated by those you help. (Long pause.)

Experience all of your financial needs being met, and feel the abundance of the universe fully supporting you . . . Your inner abundance is reflected in your outer world. (Long pause.)

In your ideal future, you experience a vibrant, energetic, healthy body that supports you in all that you do . . . You experience a balanced lifestyle of healthy habits. (Long pause.)

You feel confident, empowered, and self-accepting, and trust your inner wisdom and intuition.

You experience a deep connection with Source, God, Higher Self, and your oneness with everyone . . . You are filled with joy and wonder . . . You are in the right place, at the right time, with the right people. You are in the synchronous flow of your Divine destiny . . . All is being manifested effortlessly, comfortably, easily, under the direction of your soul. You feel a deep sense of trust that all will be provided.

Now ask, is there any part of you saying no or holding you back . . . What is that part saying? . . . Where did this belief come from—this life, or a past life? . . . Know that when you return, you will be given tools to change these beliefs, and that you have the ability to change your script and heal these resistances.

Now reconnect with your ideal future again. How can you expand it to make it even more awesome? You are in holographic time where all possibilities exist simultaneously, where all is possible. (Pause.)

Now take a snapshot of your ideal future, showing a scene that will remind you of what you have created, just the way you want to remember it and feel it . . . Put a picture frame around the picture . . . Take the color or colors from the picture frame and run that all throughout your body, like a waterfall of beautiful color, running over you and through you to every cell of your being . . . Now put your index finger together with your thumb to make a circle.

Now return to the garden, knowing that you and your ideal Future Self are one . . . Feel a deep sense of relaxation and comfort. Know that you have connected with your destiny. Know that you will continue this process, connecting every day by envisioning and feeling the good feeling of your ideal future . . . Are there any further words of encouragement from your Future Self to bring back with you? (Pause.)

When you are ready, coming back out of the garden . . . through the door . . . to the staircase of five steps. Coming back to waking awareness on the count of five.

1 . . . Feel the life blood returning to your body

2 . . . Coming out

3 . . . Wiggling your fingers and toes

4 . . . Reenergized

5 . . . Back in the room, open your eyes, refreshed, feeling wonderful in every way.

Welcome back. Take a moment to process and savor your experience. Write down the highlights now, while you remember them.

Also write down some notes about any resistances, limiting beliefs, or feelings that may be holding you back from your ideal future. For example, was part of you doubting or skeptical? What did that part of you say? We will pinpoint those blockages and counterproductive core beliefs in chapter 4. Then we will forgive, release, and reprogram, using the revolutionary tools in chapters 5 and 6.

You might also return to your worksheets and add any new thoughts, feelings, or guidance for taking the next steps in one or more areas of your life. Ask yourself, "What is the next step I can take to fulfill my soul's vision?"

If this journey process was difficult for you, don't be discouraged. Some people need practice in learning to relax and follow guided instructions. Remember, too, that not everybody "sees" images. If you are not visually dominant, you might have sensed the journey more on a feeling level, as a "knowing." However the experience presented itself, that was the right way for you.

Look between the lines. Did an unconscious blockage stop you from even feeling worthy of entering the garden? If so, then you have a limiting belief to identify so that you can change your mind about what you deserve. In the next chapters, you will address some of these issues.

four

What's Really
Holding You Back?

When Lisa was a child in school, she had an undiagnosed learning disability. Even though she was above average in intelligence, some of her teachers repeatedly criticized her, causing her to doubt her abilities. She didn't get much validation at home or anywhere else in her life, either. Since "I am stupid" was the core belief Lisa internalized in childhood, she was an underachiever for most of her life, with very little confidence in her abilities.

Let's look at another family. Vanda's alcoholic mother left her children, and her siblings were put up for adoption. Her father kept Vanda, but she always felt that she had to earn her keep, or she, too, would be abandoned. Her core beliefs became "I am bad and people will leave me" and "I must be perfect to be loved." She developed a pattern of "people pleasing," catering to others, fearing she'd be rejected if she acknowledged her own worth and needs. In adulthood, Vanda picked men who treated her poorly: she didn't feel she deserved to be loved.

What do I mean by *core beliefs*? During childhood, we begin to develop positive and negative beliefs based on our life experiences. Traumatic issues like divorce or alcoholism may impact our early years. Or we may grow up in seemingly less dramatic circumstances, yet we have parents who are emotionally unavailable to meet our needs. Some of us experience losses (as when Vanda lost her mother and siblings), while others are criticized, emotionally abandoned, or overwhelmed by internal and external stresses. (This is not to blame parents, who often carry their own baggage from the past. It is to acknowledge the impact that these experiences have on a child.)

We develop beliefs and coping strategies to survive these situations. Sometimes we instill and reinforce harmful core beliefs by telling ourselves, "I'm stupid" (or ugly, unlovable, inadequate, and so on). We then develop strategies to cope, such as overachieving *(I'll prove I'm lovable)*, perfectionism *(If I'm perfect, I won't be rejected)*, or "people pleasing" *(If I meet your needs, you'll love me)*. Although these defenses can help us survive challenging circumstances as a child, they can hold us back when they persist into adulthood.

How do detrimental beliefs, emotions, and behaviors develop in the first place? In my view, the original mistaken, limiting belief is spiritual: we believe we are separate from Source (Love, God, the Divine), and we feel guilty about that. Most of us aren't aware we have this erroneous belief because we've buried it beneath our awareness. In reality, of course, we aren't separate from the Divine; we are eternal spiritual beings of Love.

For most of us, it is too big a leap to recognize our original error—our guilt over believing we are separate—so it is better to focus on where we are right now in day-to-day life. The way that this mistaken idea plays out in our life is highly individual. We arrange many dramas, scripts, and players in our chosen "classrooms" here on earth. As individuals, we often manifest "blocks" at a young age, when we feel vulnerable and unable to cope with life's stresses. Barriers can also emerge in a repeating pattern from lifetime to lifetime. (We will discuss past lives in chapters 8 and 9.)

Our so-called blocks can be obvious, or they can operate at an unconscious level. Take divorce, for example. Children often feel that they caused their parents' divorce, and take responsibility for it. Even though the adult part of us says, "It's over—what's the big deal?" our inner child may harbor guilty beliefs and have unhealed wounds and unmet needs that are still running the show in our unconscious mind.[1] It is important to bring those thought patterns to conscious awareness so that they can be acknowledged with compassion, cleared, and re-programmed.

As we have noted, about 95 percent of our mind is unconscious, so we have "programs" running in our mind that are outside of conscious awareness. Many of those programs are essential to maintaining our physical bodies: we don't have to think about how to digest our food or how often to breathe; they are involuntary. Many skills that we've mastered also become useful unconscious programs. From showering to typing to shifting gears on a bike to playing a musical instrument, we perform an amazing number of tasks without needing the conscious mind to direct our physical movements.

But not all these unconscious programs are beneficial. To use an analogy, our computer might be humming along (picture a smiley face on the monitor), but all the while, programs running in the background could be interfering with the optimal functioning of the system. As the above examples of Lisa and Vanda so clearly show, our unconscious mind can house sabotaging programs of its own—troublesome habitual thoughts and feelings that can block our path. Ignoring the self-defeating aspects of our unconscious mind is like forgetting about trash accumulating in our basement: out of sight equals out of mind. Forgetting about it does not eliminate the odor or the trash itself. Someday we will have to deal with it, one way or another.

Dealing with our own "trash"—including some new, more effective methods for doing so—is the subject of the next few chapters. First, we have to uncover and identify it. Some of it will be obvious to us, lying on top of or just beneath the surface. These patterns or challenges in our life are so evident that nobody has to point them out to us. We're consciously aware of our surface issues, such as extreme procrastination or persistent, troublesome problems involving money, relationships, or career. However, we may have to dig down to uncover deeper layers. We're looking for patterns of self-sabotaging beliefs, emotions, and behaviors.

Soul Visioning Step 4
Identifying Limiting Beliefs and Payoffs

There are many ways to identify and access what's really holding us back, and these methods will help you take this crucial next step. (To get the most out of this section, please see "Preparation: Worksheets" on page 9.) Try any or all six of these methods:

1. Think back to the chapter 3 exercise where you envisioned your ideal future. What resistances and limiting beliefs did you become aware of? Did you write them down? Identify those detrimental feelings and thoughts again: perhaps yours include "Happiness never lasts" or "No matter what I do, it isn't good enough." We will use these as starting points for clearing, using the tools that follow in chapter 5.

2. Most people have some obvious life challenges. Others carry painful memories that still hold a charge for them. Any of these are material we can use to get to our core beliefs. If we have an unhappy relationship history, for instance, we can ask what conclusions we draw about ourselves as a result. What self-defeating things do we tell ourselves (statements such as "Nobody could ever love me")?

3. Review the "Examples of Positive Core Beliefs" (pages 105–113) in the areas of health, career/work, self-esteem, personal growth, spirituality, relationships, and finances. If you feel a strong resistant reaction to any of the positive statements, put a check mark next to it. It may be a clue that there is a blockage in that life area. (I know one woman who reviewed the lists and burst into tears: she felt that very few of the statements applied to her,

and she hadn't realized how unconscious her poor self-concept was.) Or review these affirmations and rate them on a scale of zero to 10. Zero means you don't believe it at all; 10 means you strongly believe it. The ones you rate between zero and 3 are good candidates for reprocessing.

4. To uncover more beliefs, try working with the sample list of limiting core beliefs on pages 114–115. Once again, put check marks by any that you react to strongly, or rate them on a scale of zero to 10. In this case, the statements that you strongly believe are ones you may want to reprocess, using the methods you will learn in the next chapter. You might also look again at the sample lists of positive core beliefs (pages 105–113) to see which ones you do *not* fully embrace. Usually there is a limiting belief around that.

5. Fill out the "Payoffs and Limiting Beliefs" questionnaire (pages 116–117) to see where your unconscious defenses may perceive it as "unsafe" to heal your mind. For example, to question 8 ("What am I afraid of losing if I succeed?"), you might answer, "If I get healthier, people will expect too much of me." In other words, you might have a reason *not* to improve or heal: you believe that if you do, something worse will happen.

Here's an example: Shauna had fibromyalgia. She knew all the steps she needed to take to heal—diet, fitness walking, stress management, and so on—but she wasn't doing any of them. She was sabotaging herself, but she didn't know why. When we got to the root cause of what was stopping her, it turned out there was a payoff for her in staying sick. Shauna believed that if she got well, her family would expect a lot from her, and she feared she couldn't measure up to her family's and community's expectations.

"I haven't learned how to say no, and I'm afraid I'm going to get back into working too hard and trying to please everyone again," she said. "My disability protects me from having to face adult responsibilities." That insight cleared the way for Shauna to work on transforming those old patterns. She learned to speak up for herself, set appropriate boundaries with other people, and enhance her self-worth. Once she had healthy coping skills, she could move forward to create the life she wanted without self-sabotage.

Another example of payoff might be holding on to excess weight. If a woman wants to lose weight but doesn't despite her best efforts, she may have an unconscious fear that men might hit on her, or that other people in her life would be jealous, or that others will expect too much of her. In any of these cases, the payoff for not losing weight is perceived protection from undesired consequences.

6. By observing your daily life, you can discover repeating patterns and themes that reveal your unconscious self-defeating agendas. Pay attention to the players and the script in the drama of your own life. For an example from my own life, read "Potholes in Paradise."

Potholes in Paradise: Discovering My Own Limiting Beliefs

Join me now on my sojourn in Hawaii. I have come to the island of Kauai planning to have a wonderful time writing this book by the ocean. Gentle sea breezes caress my face as I sit writing on the balcony of my hotel room.

Suddenly a putrid odor invades my sacred space. I look up to see a truck, then I hear clanging as the workmen unload metal rods to set up a tent for a luau that night. This can't be happening. How can I write with these distractions? I was in the flow, and *poof,* it's gone! I request a more private room with an oceanfront. Nothing is available for several days. I feel myself sinking into anger and disappointment.

Taking a break, I drive to the northern part of the island. I am in a rented Mustang convertible with the top down, heading up the coast on this balmy summer day. To my left is the majesty of the mountains, layered in a lush, forest-green carpet with waterfalls traversing the mountainsides. On my right, a vista of turquoise-blue ocean stretches as far as I can see. Every turn brings a breathtaking new view.

I decide to revisit a sacred site. Parking will be scarce there. No problem, though: I'm confident in my ability to manifest a parking space. I proceed to my cherished spot and voilà, a parking space appears. But oh no, it's right in the middle of a mud-filled pothole! I have to take my shoes off and step into the mucky water. So much for creating what I want.

Then it strikes me. How is it that I'm writing a book about creating the life we want, and I get THIS? An inner struggle ensues. *Well, if my vibration and thoughts were high enough, I wouldn't have manifested this . . . What am I complaining about? This is heaven on earth.*

When I return to my hotel room, I calm myself down with some energy tapping (more on this later). I tell myself: *Even though I am upset, I deeply and completely love, forgive, and accept myself.*

More centered now, I meditate and ask my Higher Self for help in finding the underlying cause of what I realize is a repeating pattern: I get a room on the ocean, but it is in a location with many distractions. I get a parking space, but it is in a muddy pothole. But why is this triggering such deep feelings of disappointment? Why am I concentrating on the one mud hole on a beautiful tropical island?

I know this must relate to my unconscious beliefs about myself. Do I only deserve so much and no more? Could I believe that I don't even deserve to be happy? Then I remember my childhood, and my mother saying, "We are missionaries and our reward is in heaven," her words implying that we were servants, sacrificing and suffering for the greater good. The more we suffer here, the more we are rewarded in heaven. I become much more aware of that unconscious programming, my martyr script.

Going even deeper now, my ego's agenda really hits home. Believing myself unworthy to enjoy the paradise that is Hawaii, my ego looks for and creates situations that are consistent with my belief in sacrifice and suffering. The problem is not that I didn't get the hotel room I wanted; it is that I unconsciously believe I don't deserve it. If I don't deserve the joy of paradise, then my ego mind sets out to prove that, by demonstrating it in my outer world. I am attracted to situations that prove my unworthiness. Thus I focus on potholes, rather than the beauty all around me and in me. Then my ego can say, "See? If you were worthy, this wouldn't be happening."

Another part of my mind has been watching this inner drama and understands its lesson. What a gift: this is an opportunity to see my unconscious beliefs played out on the stage of life. Fortunately, I have done enough of my own healing work that I am now experiencing glitches rather than serious challenges.

After further contemplation, I realize that in my preoccupation with the mud puddle mishap, I overlooked something. In the past, because of my fear of heights, I had been reluctant to drive the island's mountain roads, bounded by sheer cliffs and steep drop-offs. But this day, I drove with confidence. I was so focused on the landscape's beauty that I forgot to be scared!

What is the lesson here? When things don't go my ego's way, I can make myself miserable, or I can choose something else. No matter what enters my awareness, I have an opportunity to choose peace or fear. Love or hate. In this case, I am grateful that I can decide how to see this situation and what to do about it. Nothing can rob me of my peace. I immediately think of the fun that the people will have under that luau tent tonight, enjoying the food, music, and native dancers. I bless the workers and say "aloha" as they perform their duties. I return to my writing with a peaceful mind.

Day Two in Paradise

I am driving the convertible south toward Poipu, anticipating a wonderful trip. That end of the island is usually drier and warmer. I drive through an incredible tunnel of overgrown vines and bent trees arching over the road. I seem to be transitioning from one world to another; my life, too, is entering a new phase with the writing of this book.

Unexpectedly, the air becomes cooler. Misty, gray clouds gather. Sprinkles of rain start falling. Once again, I have a choice. I can bemoan my "fate," or I can welcome the precipitation that is so needed on this island right now. Instead of raining on my parade, the shower becomes a welcome source of nourishment for a thirsty land. I have an attitude of gratitude.

This day brings new realizations. Every moment, I can choose how I see the world and everyone in it. I can look at the world through my ego eyes or perceive it through my Higher Mind. The goal is to heal my mind of its false perceptions of who I am and what I deserve. It is not necessarily easy, given that this ego-based world reinforces a fictitious view of who we are and what happiness is.

The ego says that we can only be happy when we have a bigger house, more money, a life full of trinkets, the perfect partner, or a better body. I can attract and create all of those things, but they will not bring me peace and happiness. They will not heal my mind of its belief in my separation from Source, from Love. Having these things numbs me for a while, but in the end, the anesthetic wears off and I feel emptiness and inadequacy again. I then seek out other distractions—maybe a special relationship, food, shopping? Until I recognize where the real problem is, I will remain asleep, unaware, distracted, and anesthetized. Until I heal the root of my problem, the pattern will continue, much as in the movie *Groundhog Day*. Wherever I am, every day I wake up in paradise and keep falling in mud holes. They find me everywhere I go! The joke is on me. The holes are in my head.

We are the writers of our own scripts. We are the painters of our own landscapes. The question is, which part of our mind is creating, ego or Spirit? With Soul Visioning, we create our life under the guidance of higher soul wisdom, the part of our mind that is wise and knows what will truly make us happy.

Day Three in Paradise

I am in the flow, writing easily. But alas, fatigue sets in. What should I do? A trip to Waimea Canyon might be inspiring. Yet something is holding me back.

Suddenly a thought enters my mind. I want a lomi lomi, a traditional Hawaiian form of massage. I don't have an appointment, but I go down to the hotel spa and, amazingly, a practitioner is available right away. As the masseuse—I'll call her Melinda—begins a wonderful treatment, she asks why I am on Kauai. I tell her about my book project. Something about her inspires trust, so I share that I sometimes wonder whether anyone will read it. "Oh, you must write this book," she says. "My husband and I went through an experience where we manifested incredible things very quickly, including a large amount of money. But we couldn't hold on to it, because we had not dealt with our unconscious programming. I would love to read a book like yours. It is needed." I feel deep gratitude toward this woman. As I tell her more, she knows exactly what I'm talking about and encourages me to keep writing. I get just what I need, when I need it.

Yet this is only the beginning. I'd been hoping to visit some of Kauai's more hidden, sacred places, but hadn't had any luck finding them. Now Melinda tells me about some of the island's energy spots that are not listed in the guidebooks, offering to show me where they are. So after my massage, we travel together to a beautiful cave and hike within to a pool of crystal-clear fresh water. I feel like I am in a mystical womb of enchantment. I sit dumbfounded as she shares amazing stories about herself and her past lives on the island. I feel a deep connection; I sense that I knew her long ago and that we have come together again to encourage each other's journey. We develop a friendship that has lasted to this day.

This was a momentous day for me. I was given an important lesson on manifesting, on what can happen when I change my mind from thoughts of judgment and fear to ones of peace and love. Having calmed my mind over the previous two days, which prepared me to listen to my intuition, I allowed a fantastic experience to happen and a new friendship to begin. Had I done what I originally planned, instead of following my inner guidance, I would have missed this opportunity. It was a reminder that I can choose to follow my ego's agenda, which results in chaos and pain, or my Higher Self's plan for me, which brings joy and fulfillment.

Over these three days, as I observed my recurring patterns, I glimpsed what was in my unconscious mind, projected onto the screen of my life. This awareness let me get to the root of some limiting beliefs that were sabotaging me. Now I could begin to forgive myself for having them and allow myself to experience the joy of my True Self.

You Can Change Your Mind

I hope that these stories from my own journey encourage you to care enough about yourself to do this work, to discover what is holding you back. I, too, have had to clear my own past-life and childhood issues, cellular memories, and limiting beliefs in order to experience my true identity as a spiritual being. The more I practice forgiveness of myself and others and undo my unconscious programming, the happier I am. The more I feel my soul's abundance, the more my outer world reflects it. By clearing these blocks, I have allowed a wonderful soul mate to come into my life. I have a deeply satisfying career helping others to heal, and now a book that is an expression of my highest soul's desire.

Not that there aren't challenges in my life, but I am more at peace, regardless of outer circumstances. I can more consistently view with equanimity whatever turns up, whether it is a mud hole or a majestic mountain scene. If I am thrown off balance, I now return more quickly to my peaceful center. This is not magic! Healing is a life-long process. But with persistent practice we become happier, more peaceful, more aware, more awakened to our Essence. Some days it is two steps forward and one step back. Other days it is one step forward and two steps back. How long the journey takes is up to us.

The Smiley Face on the Screen of My Mind

I'd like to share one more personal story, one that showed me again how everyday recurring situations can reveal the unconscious programs that run like software in the background of our mind. These repeating life patterns, no matter how mundane they seem on first glance, can expose a deep, burdensome core belief.

For several weeks, I had noticed that I was getting poor service in restaurants and shops. Ordinarily this wouldn't be a big deal, but it was happening consistently and pushing my buttons big time. I was getting annoyed and couldn't seem to let it go. One morning at a local coffee shop that also sold CDs, a disk caught my eye. I love some kinds of reggae music, having grown up in Miami. Finding a reggae CD I'd been looking for, I was about to pay the cashier when a friend greeted me. I asked the clerk to put the disk aside while I chatted. A few minutes later, when I went to pay for it, the clerk said he was sorry, but he had sold it. He looked for another copy, but there were no more. I made it clear that I was not pleased and left the store.

Sitting in my car, I realized that this was part of that recent pattern. Why did I keep experiencing clerks and waiters who made mistakes with my requests? To center myself, I used an energy balancing method called the WHEE technique (which we will learn in chapter 5). When I was calm, I asked my Higher Self to help me understand what was going on. An image came to me: a computer screen on which a seemingly happy "smiley face" was singing lyrics from a reggae tune, "It's all right . . . let's get together . . . and feel all right." But I was aware that an invisible software program was running in the background: a belief in my unconscious mind that I am a victim and will be unfairly treated. With this belief running the show, it is no wonder that I was creating dramas that validated my unconscious beliefs about the world and myself.

When I looked deeper into this insight, I saw that below the victim script was a belief that I am guilty and undeserving of good things. Whew! Of course, this was all unconscious, and the smiley face of my conscious mind kept saying, "Everything is fine." Like scenes from a play, the events in my life were showing me that my ego had a hidden agenda. By observing those patterns, I could begin to get a glimmer of what was going on below the surface.

My personality self orchestrated this whole scene, based on a false belief about myself. My "shadow" self was creating evidence to support my belief that the world is unjust, that bad things are always someone else's fault, that I am a victim and will be treated as such—all the result of my unconscious guilt. And the law of attraction calls in the actors who unconsciously want to participate in these dramas. Possibly the clerk stepped in and played his part, unknowingly wanting to be punished by my displeasure, because of *his* limiting beliefs. Hence we play out our mutual dance of victimhood. None of this is conscious to us at the time.

I further realized that I needed to change my perception of who I am and what I deserve, to keep reprogramming my own unconscious software, guided by the master programmer, my soul. When I viewed it from that perspective, I could see that my programming was based on a false premise. The truth is, I am not separate from Source/God/the Divine. I am not guilty, and I can choose how I see myself and others. Most of us are unaware that we have these deeply buried core beliefs. But the good news is that by stepping back and observing them without judgment, we can begin to undo these misperceptions.

Through the practice of forgiveness, which we will explore in chapter 6, we can see the innocence of those on whom we project our guilt. Every person in my life who pushes my buttons, such as the clerk who sold my cherished CD to someone else, provides me with a "screen" on which I can project compassion rather than condemnation. By extending goodwill to them, I offer it to myself. Of course, this is an ongoing process until I can consistently stay aware of my choices and my mind is healed.

On a deeper level, the root of our problem is a spiritual one. We need to undo the beliefs that we are disconnected from our Divine

Source and that we are guilty and sinful. Separation from our Creator is an illusion. In reality we are one with the Creator, innocent, whole, and complete, but we have forgotten who we really are as eternal, loving spiritual beings. We have forgotten our perfection. As we noted earlier, we are like a beautiful diamond in the rough. At our core we are perfect, but we have to blow the dark soot away to remember it. The layers of soot are our ego notions that we are incomplete and separate from Source. The traumatic memories and limiting beliefs that we carry with us from this life and previous lives keep us stuck in self-defeating, recurring patterns. The good news is that our unconscious sense of separation and unworthiness is a case of mistaken identity. Our perfection is always there; we've just forgotten it. When we undo the false beliefs in our mind and clear our distressing memories, what remains is our essence as a soul.

How do we go about undoing our self-sabotaging, habitual beliefs? Well, first we have to identify them—not judge them—then forgive them and reprogram the unconscious mind. Some of the layers we may clean off quickly, but as we get to the core beliefs, it can take longer. From a soul perspective, some people take many lifetimes to learn certain lessons. But the fact that you are reading this book and have the willingness to change your mind suggests that you are ready to get unstuck, wake up, and embrace a soul-guided life of joy and purpose!

Your Next Step Awaits

You have identified some undesirable beliefs, emotions, or behaviors, using insights gained from Soul Visioning step 4. Perhaps you noted any resistances you experienced during the "Soul-Guided Journey to Your Ideal Future," or used the "Examples of Positive Core Beliefs," the "Questionnaire on Payoffs and Limiting Beliefs," or the "Examples of Limiting Core Beliefs." You may have also uncovered self-defeating patterns by observing your daily life. Now we will take the next step. In chapter 5, we will learn some revolutionary methods for reprogramming and clearing those blocks.

Soul Visioning
Examples of Positive Core Beliefs

Life Area: HEALTH

1. My body is a powerful vehicle for expressing my soul's purpose.
2. My body is vibrant and healthy.
3. I unconditionally love and accept my body.
4. My mind, body, and Spirit are in perfect balance.
5. I am responsive to my bodily signals.
6. I enjoy caring for my body through relaxation, exercise, and healthy eating habits.
7. I give my body the rest it needs.
8. I am strong and in perfect condition.
9. I am full of energy and vitality.
10. I maintain a healthy weight.
11. I make decisions daily that add to my good health.
12. My body has an inner wisdom that can heal itself.
13. I am consistent in caring for my body.
14. I am worth caring for my health.
15. My positive thoughts and feelings create a healthy body.
16. All the systems of my body work together perfectly.
17. I schedule time to care for my body.
18. My body has stamina and resilience.
19. My body easily heals and rejuvenates itself.

Soul Visioning
Examples of Positive Core Beliefs

Life Area: SELF-ESTEEM

1. I am loved and lovable.
2. I love myself unconditionally.
3. I take full responsibility for my self-esteem.
4. I value and honor myself.
5. I enjoy being me.
6. I treat myself with respect.
7. I deserve to be happy.
8. I enjoy a loving relationship with myself.
9. I like the person I see in the mirror every day.
10. I accept myself completely for who I am.
11. I give recognition and encouragement to myself.
12. I am confident and self-assured.
13. I unconditionally love all parts of myself, including the imperfect parts.
14. I radiate positive, enthusiastic energy.
15. I am a happy person.
16. I take good care of myself.
17. I trust myself.
18. I feel deep inner peace and serenity with who I am.
19. I am an eternal spiritual being of love.
20. I have much to share with others.
21. I am able to receive love.
22. I am getting more powerful every day.

23. I approve of myself without having to please others.

24. I am joyous, happy, and free.

25. I am light-hearted and fun-loving.

26. I am wise, intuitive, compassionate, and one with the Divine.

27. All of my false images of myself from the past are forgiven and released.

Soul Visioning
Examples of Positive Core Beliefs

Life Area: PERSONAL GROWTH

1. I trust my inner wisdom and intuition.

2. I am true to myself.

3. I accept my ability to create the life I desire with higher soul wisdom.

4. I use my power, talents, and gifts for good.

5. My power has all positive outcomes for me.

6. My ability to understand and acknowledge truth is the basis of my personal power.

7. I am committed to manifesting my life purpose from my Higher Self.

8. I act on the guidance of my soul wisdom.

9. I am responsible for myself.

10. I accept myself even when I make mistakes.

11. I can set appropriate limits and boundaries when needed.

12. I can speak up for myself and effectively communicate my needs.

13. I am an empowered spiritual being, Divinely guided in all that I do.

14. I accept myself and others accept me.

15. I recognize that real power comes from within.

16. I am capable and competent.

17. Love is the source of my power.

18. I am a powerful being of manifesting light.

19. I fully accept and express my power of creation.

20. My power comes from following my inner guidance.

Soul Visioning
Examples of Positive Core Beliefs

Life Area: SPIRITUALITY

1. I am one with Divine Love.
2. Divine Love is guiding me in all I do.
3. The source of my contentment and joy is within me.
4. The peace of God/Source/the Divine is with me always.
5. I remember that giving is receiving.
6. I willingly forgive others, knowing that they are a mirror of myself.
7. In stillness, I remember the Divine within.
8. My true nature is Love.
9. I awaken others to their connection to the Divine within them.
10. I manifest my soul purpose in every moment.
11. I am a channel of blessing to everyone I meet.
12. I radiate peace and light.
13. I perceive the spiritual truth in all situations.
14. I surrender to my purpose, which is to remember my oneness with Divine Love.
15. I forgive myself for every time I thought I harmed anyone.
16. I am responsible for my reactions to every experience in my life.
17. I make time to nurture my spiritual awareness.
18. I practice forgiveness, patience, and acceptance to correct my errors.
19. I practice moment-to-moment mindfulness.
20. I enjoy sharing in a spiritual community.

Soul Visioning
Examples of Positive Core Beliefs

Life Area: FINANCES

1. The universe has an infinite supply of resources.
2. My outer world reflects the abundance and wholeness within me.
3. Everything that I need to manifest my soul's vision is available to me.
4. I am prosperous.
5. I am abundant.
6. I am precious and have gifts to share with everyone.
7. I forgive any fear or guilt around money issues.
8. I let go any barriers to remembering my true identity as a spiritual being.
9. I experience the abundant love of God/Source/the Divine within me.
10. I allow my Higher Self to guide my financial decisions.
11. It is OK to have more money than I need.
12. I enjoy my achievements.
13. I manifest Divine Love in all aspects of my life.
14. I easily attract unlimited resources.
15. I make money easily and effortlessly.
16. I forgive my belief in scarcity and struggle.
17. I am willing and able to give and share.
18. I am willing and able to receive.
19. I give money all the meaning it has for me.

20. I create more abundance for myself as I help others become more abundant.

21. My joy and gratitude create more abundance for me.

22. I am open to opportunities to be a channel of blessings to others.

23. I use my resources wisely.

24. I always have enough energy, time, wisdom, and money to accomplish all my desires.

25. Prosperity and happiness are my Divine birthright.

26. My worth is established by God/Source/the Divine, so my worth is unlimited.

27. Everything I want is already within me and I gratefully accept it.

Soul Visioning
Examples of Positive Core Beliefs

Life Area: CAREER/WORK

1. I am passionate about the work that I do.
2. I work in a positive, harmonious, and supportive environment.
3. I enjoy working with like-minded people with a common vision.
4. I use my talents and gifts to be of service.
5. I freely share my knowledge and experience with my coworkers.
6. My work is enjoyable and fulfilling and I am appreciated.
7. I am well compensated for my services.
8. I am honest in my business ventures.
9. My soul's vision for my career path manifests effortlessly.
10. I follow my soul's guidance when making decisions.
11. My work and personal life are in perfect balance.
12. My clients/customers/students/audience are grateful for what I offer, and I am grateful to them.
13. I am challenged and inspired in my work.
14. I clearly and respectfully communicate my needs and priorities.
15. I maximize the areas of agreement in my relationships with co-workers, and minimize differences.
16. I practice forgiveness of myself and others when mistakes are made.
17. I am successful and financially prosperous.
18. I am inspired and challenged by my work.
19. My opinion is valued.
20. I enjoy learning new skills and knowledge to be of greater service.

Soul Visioning
Examples of Positive Core Beliefs

Life Area: RELATIONSHIPS

1. I am sensitive and responsive to my partner's growth needs.
2. I am worthy of a committed, intimate, and inspired relationship.
3. My relationships encourage me to be and express my True Self.
4. I support my partner in manifesting their soul's vision.
5. I make time for my relationships.
6. I nurture my relationships.
7. I create harmony and cooperation in my relationships.
8. I communicate with kindness and authenticity.
9. I perceive the wholeness in my partner.
10. I communicate what is in my heart with honesty and integrity.
11. I experience mutual appreciation in my relationships.
12. I experience joy, fun, and playfulness in my relationships.
13. I flow with being close and I flow with being separate.
14. I give and receive unconditional love in my relationships.
15. I experience joy in physical intimacy.
16. I share my inner world with my partner.
17. I am honest and trustworthy in relationships.
18. I support and nurture my partner's highest well-being in the relationship.
19. I experience courtesy and respect in my relationships.
20. I create an atmosphere of safety to resolve disagreements.
21. I willingly forgive myself and my partner.
22. I understand the spiritual purpose of my relationships.

Soul Visioning
Examples of Limiting Core Beliefs

1. I am not lovable.

2. I am undeserving of love.

3. Love will smother me.

4. Love will go away.

5. I will inevitably be abandoned by those I love and want love from.

6. I will not be listened to or acknowledged.

7. Other people and forces control my life.

8. I am unable to get what I want and need in life.

9. Love is dangerous.

10. I expect the worst to happen.

11. Happiness never lasts.

12. I will never measure up.

13. People will not like me as I am.

14. I don't deserve to be happy.

15. I don't deserve to have a happy and loving relationship.

16. I will inevitably be rejected.

17. People will betray me.

18. I don't deserve closeness.

19. I want to die.

20. I do not know who I am.

21. I hate myself.

22. No matter what I do, it is not good enough.

23. I cannot be myself, or I'll be rejected.

24. I blame myself and others for my difficulties.

25. I must always please in order to have love.

26. I will be left out.

27. I am afraid of success.

28. I am afraid of failure.

29. I am not enough.

30. I can't . . .

31. Life has to be a struggle.

32. Relationships must be a struggle.

33. I will never measure up.

34. I will be controlled or overpowered by others.

35. I must do what everyone else wants me to do.

36. I don't deserve a happy life or relationship.

37. I want things to stay the way they are.

38. I am unfairly treated.

39. I cannot be assertive with people who are special to me.

40. I am separate from, and unimportant to, God/Source/the Divine.

41. If I accept love, I'll have to pay for it.

42. I will always be an outsider.

43. I don't have much of value to give.

44. Surrender means I will be controlled.

45. I deserve to be unhappy.

Do I repeatedly feel like I am _____?
(These emotions are often symptoms of negative core beliefs.)

unloved	mistreated	abandoned
rejected	not acknowledged	angry
ignored	attacked	anxious or fearful
depleted	judged	selfish
deprived	controlled	unloving
lonely	powerless	withholding

Soul Visioning
Questionnaire: Payoffs and Limiting Beliefs

Sometimes we resist change because there is a secondary gain or pay-off for staying the same. Answer these questions to better understand how your attachment to these payoffs can sabotage your growth.

1. What do I get to avoid?

_____

_____

_____

2. Who do I get to punish with my struggling behavior?

_____

_____

3. What emotion am I not willing to release, or who am I not willing to forgive?

_____

_____

_____

4. What guarantee am I holding out for?

_____

_____

_____

5. Am I manipulating with self-pity to get what I want?

_____

116

6. Am I afraid to take responsibility for my own life? What will be expected of me?

_____

_____

_____

7. Am I feeling better than or less than other people?

_____

_____

8. What am I afraid of losing if I succeed?

_____

_____

_____

9. What are my attitudes toward successful, rich, powerful men and women?

_____

_____

_____

10. How do I plan to sabotage myself?

_____

_____

11. If I am successful, the consequences are:

_____

_____

117

five

New Methods to Clear Your Path

Here are the tools you've been waiting for! It's time to drop some of that baggage you've carried from the past. You'll use some exciting new methods that will help you quickly and easily reprogram your self-defeating patterns. You'll reprocess and "clear" those old, mistaken ideas about who you are, the ideas holding you back from fully expressing your soul's highest desire.

As a psychotherapist for over thirty years, I find these developments thrilling and gratifying. What used to take *years* of talk therapy to clear blockages, traumas, cellular memories, and limiting beliefs now takes only *minutes* in some cases. Of course, some issues take longer to heal, depending on their severity. But these new user-friendly tools help many people to resolve some of their own challenges without the aid of a therapist. The more easily we can resolve our issues, undo our ego barriers, and awaken to our true spiritual identity, the sooner we will live a soul-inspired life of joy. We then embody the soul's expression to create a life of happiness and purpose. We literally become the change that we want to see in the world!

What are some of these new tools? Many are based on the emerging field of energy psychology (EP), which has been endorsed by Norm Shealy, MD, PhD; Deepak Chopra, MD; Candace Pert, MD; and other authorities. Professional organizations such as the Association for Comprehensive Energy Psychology (ACEP) train therapists in EP and conduct research to test these revolutionary methods. Amazing results have been reported by laypeople as well as professionals. Many of these techniques were used with people traumatized by the Kosovo war, the 9/11 attacks, and Hurricane Katrina.

An outgrowth of Chinese medicine, these therapies have been called "acupuncture for the emotions, but without the needles," as noted earlier. Also known as meridian therapies, these new mind/body methods are being increasingly used by lay and professional people to swiftly heal unconscious limiting beliefs, cellular memories, and self-defeating patterns from this life and past lives. Meridians are the veins and arteries of the body's energy system. Blocked energy can be restored by stimulating certain spots on the meridians known as acupuncture points. In energy psychology, rather than using acupuncture needles, we tap with the fingers on the meridian points in a particular sequence, or we use pressure points to release blockages in the body's energy system.

Soul Visioning Step 5
Your Energy Psychology Tool Kit

In this chapter we will explore three of the many energy psychology systems: the Emotional Freedom Techniques (EFT), the Tapas Acupressure Technique® (TAT), and an approach known as WHEE®, which stands for "Whole Health—Easily and Effectively." All three are highly recommended, but here we will focus primarily on the WHEE method because it is one of the easiest to learn and therefore is highly likely to be used over the long term. Feel free to go by your personal preferences, remembering that these approaches can also work differently depending on the person. For more information, refer to the Resources section at the back of this book, and to the ACEP website for details on emerging research on these methods.

A Word of Caution

Energy psychology methods are not designed to work with severe mental disorders without the involvement of a qualified mental health professional. While they can be most helpful with day-to-day challenges, they are not suitable as self-help resources for the treatment of mental disorders such as major depression, severe anxiety, and bipolar, dissociative, or psychotic disorders. If you are already working with a therapist, it is advisable to consult with them before trying EP processes. In general, WHEE and other EP systems can greatly ease self-defeating thought patterns, behaviors, and counterproductive emotions such as anxiety, anger, grief, guilt, jealousy, fear, self-judgment, worry, sadness, and shame.

Emotional Freedom Techniques (EFT)

Emotional Freedom Techniques, one of the most popular meridian therapies, was developed by Gary Craig, a Stanford-trained engineer who streamlined the work of clinical psychologist Roger Callahan, PhD, the originator of Thought Field Therapy (TFT). The premise of EFT is that emotional and physical pain sometimes result from disruption in the body's flow of energy. Restoring the natural flow leads to emotional and physical relief. EFT, in addition to restoring the energetic flow in the body, is theorized to shift the "fight, flight, or freeze" instincts of the primitive brain to the higher cortical centers, where a more helpful response can occur.

EFT can also help free us from certain problematic mental, emotional, and behavioral patterns. Anecdotal reports suggest good results with anxiety, depression, phobias, weight loss, anger, pain management, limiting beliefs, sports performance, and more.

For more information, refer to the Emotional Freedom Techniques website, *www.emofree.com*, for a free how-to manual with illustrations of the EFT procedure. Refer also to the ACEP website for ongoing research, workshops, and conferences (see this book's Resources section).

Emotional Freedom Techniques: Short Version

The following is an adaptation of the short version of EFT.

1. *Identify a problematic thought, feeling, or behavior.* This might be, for example, an intense craving for sugar.

2. *Rate the problem* on a scale of zero to 10 (zero is no distress and 10 is highly distressed).

3. *State the set-up affirmation* (statement of the problem, feeling, or thought). Say the affirmation "Even though I have this [intense craving for sugar], I deeply and completely accept myself" while gently rubbing a particular point on the chest three times in a circular, clockwise direction. This is a lymphatic pressure point (sometimes called the "sore spot") located about three inches below the midpoint of the collarbone.

4. *Perform the tapping sequence with reminder phrase.* Repeat a shortened form of the above statement—such as "this craving for sugar"—while tapping seven times, with two fingers, on the following pressure points in sequence (either side of the body is OK):

   - the inner edge of the eyebrow bone
   - the outside corner of the eye at the temple
   - under the eye (middle of the lower eye-socket bone)
   - under the nose
   - just below the lower lip (middle of the chin)
   - one inch below the collarbone where it meets the diaphragm
   - four inches below the armpit
   - the outside of the fleshy part of either hand

5. *Rate the problem again.* Repeat the above sequence again, and then rate the problem on a scale of zero to ten until the intensity is down to between a zero and one. If the issue is not responding, you may need to identify and address other aspects of the problem, or refer to *www.emofree.com* for more detailed information.

Tapas Acupressure Technique (TAT)

This method was developed by Tapas Fleming, a specialist in acupuncture and Chinese medicine. The Tapas Acupressure Technique® (TAT®) is designed to get energy flowing again and to release trauma, limiting beliefs, allergies, phobias, even physical pain. The person using TAT lightly touches critical acupressure points on the front and back of the head while reciting or thinking about several affirmation statements, following a simple, nine-step procedure. A short, free, how-to manual with complete instructions and accompanying pictures can be downloaded from *www.TATlife.com.*

A brief summary of the process: The person thinks about a specific issue to work on, and then rates it on a scale of zero to 10, with zero indicating no stress and 10 being the most distressing. Then the person uses three fingers of one hand to apply very gentle pressure to three acupressure points on either side of the bridge of the nose and forehead, while the other hand holds the base of the skull. While holding the "pose" position for one minute or less, a specific affirming statement is said at each of the nine steps, such as: "All the origins of this (problem) are healing now," "I forgive everyone who hurt me related to this and wish them love, happiness, and peace," "All the parts of me that got something from this are healing now," and so on.

After being in the TAT pose and doing the steps, most people are delivered to a place of inner freedom, relaxation, and peace. With some sessions, you may feel immediate, significant shifts–a weight that suddenly lifts from your shoulders, or a dramatic easing of stress or pain. Other times, the changes might be much more subtle. One day, you may realize that you simply haven't thought about a problem for weeks, when it used to be on your mind every day. TAT is deceptively simple for the remarkable results it produces.

TAT®, Tapas Acupressure Technique®, and TATLife® are registered trademarks of Tapas Fleming and are being used with permission.

Whole Health—Easily and Effectively (WHEE)

One of the fastest of the many meridian-based therapies, in my view, is the energy psychology technique called Whole Health—Easily and Effectively (WHEE)®. Developed by psychiatrist Daniel J. Benor, MD, this simple and highly effective self-healing method blends a modified protocol of Eye Movement Desensitization and Reprocessing (EMDR) and Emotional Freedom Techniques to resolve sabotaging beliefs, emotions, and behaviors, and to relieve stress. Dr. Benor compares the process to a vacuum cleaning that clears away old psychological debris or "unfinished business."

WHEE is based in part on the well-researched EMDR process; EMDR has been approved by the American Psychological Association.[1] EMDR was created by psychologist Francine Shapiro, PhD, after she noticed that her feelings of depression lifted when she moved her eyes back and forth from left to right. The back and forth movement was also effective with bilateral auditory stimulation, such as playing tones alternately to the left and the right ears. Alternating tapping on the left and right thigh also worked to relieve various symptoms. This left- and right-brain stimulation seems to contribute to a whole-brain response of centering and calming around previously nonproductive thoughts, feelings, and behaviors.

With WHEE, the bilateral stimulation of the left and right brain hemispheres is done by tapping alternate sides of the body. In addition to these EMDR-style benefits, WHEE adds the affirmation statement of EFT: "Even though I have this problem [fill in the blank], I deeply and completely love and accept myself."

What are some advantages of the WHEE method?

- WHEE can be done in a fraction of the time that some other meridian therapies require because there are fewer steps to remember.

- WHEE is effective in clearing a diverse range of issues.

- People are more likely to follow through and use WHEE because it is relatively easy to learn and apply.

- WHEE is empowering as a self-help tool because of its simplicity.

Healing a Phobia in Red Rock Country

Let's look at a practical example of how I used WHEE to help with a fear of heights.

I was visiting the red rock country of Sedona, Arizona. There were many awe-inspiring scenic outlooks and energy vortexes to visit, including my destination this day, Oak Creek Canyon. It was a clear Indian summer day as I took the road that parallels the riverbed canyon. This road was unfamiliar to me, but the spectacular views took my breath away. The autumn colors of gold and red blended perfectly with the bronze backdrop of the mountains.

Now the incline was getting steeper and the drop-offs sharper. I gripped the steering wheel more tightly. My stomach clenched and adrenaline coursed throughout my body. My fear of heights was kicking in. I pulled over at the next turnoff to contemplate my options. Part of me demanded to turn around. But another part of me said, "Don't let fear be your compass."

Then it occurred to me that I could do the WHEE process, which helps release phobias. I hugged myself (one of the WHEE positions) and began the series of alternate tapping on my upper arms, using the affirmation, "Even though I have this fear of heights, I deeply and completely love and accept myself." My anxiety eased and I decided to continue my trip.

Driving on, I realized that this journey was a metaphor for my life. When my climb up the mountain became fearful and difficult, self-doubt crept in. Could I do it? Was I safe? What was ahead? Although my fear had significantly lessened (from a 10 to about a 7), I knew I would have to pull off the road several times before the process was completed. The cliffs were steep and the turns were narrow, but I was determined. Three times I stopped and repeated the tapping and affirmations. Each time I pondered turning back, but something inside me wouldn't let me give up. My decision to move forward turned out to be a good one, because once I moved through the fear, what awaited me was heaven on earth. The air and the traffic thinned out at 5,000 feet. I passed in and out of pine forests, and with each turn, I was greeted with yet another stunning view. Best of all, on my drive back there was no fear, and I could fully enjoy the journey down the mountain.

WHEE Method, Step by Step:
Reprocessing Limiting Core Beliefs

The following is an adaptation of the WHEE format. Remember, if you are seeing a therapist, it's advisable to discuss WHEE in advance. The technique should not be used as a self-help approach in addressing serious mental disorders.

Preparation for the WHEE Process

Be sure that you are well hydrated: drink some water before beginning. Take several deep breaths to ground and center yourself.

Set your intent by saying something like, "I allow my soul (Higher Self) to be in charge of the healing process and I am ready to let go of what no longer serves me." If you can't agree with that statement, you may need to review "Payoffs and Limiting Beliefs" (pages 116–117) to determine the basis for your resistance. Once you have identified the limiting belief, it would be wise to clear this resistance before you attempt to heal other issues. Since you have already identified resistance as your initial problem (WHEE step 1), you can proceed to step 2 and do the entire WHEE process to clear it.

Once you have let go of any resistance to healing, you can start once again at WHEE step 1 and use the entire process to clear other limiting core beliefs. Note: If at any time you are too uncomfortable with anything that comes up for you, stop the process. Some deeper issues are best processed with a professional.

WHEE Step 1: Identify the problem

Choose a limiting belief or payoff that you would like to clear. Start with one that you identified during the "Soul-Guided Journey to Your Ideal Future," or in the chapter 4 worksheet exercises, or in the process of noticing your resistances to any affirmations, or from your daily life patterns. Begin with one that is not too challenging, and intend for your soul to help you with it. The problem or issue you want to change might be:

- an emotional response ("to overcome my fear of heights")

- a physical reaction ("to stay calm when my boss is upset with me")

- a limiting belief ("to let go of the notion that happiness never lasts")

- a behavioral habit ("to stop biting my nails")

WHEE Step 2: Rate the problem

Rate the amount of distress you feel when you think about the problem *right now* on a scale of zero (perfectly calm) to 10 (the most distress possible). (WE'LL USE FEAR OF PUBLIC SPEAKING AS AN EXAMPLE. WHEN I IMAGINE SPEAKING IN FRONT OF A GROUP RIGHT NOW, I RATE MY DISTRESS LEVEL AT ABOUT A 10.)

WHEE Step 3: Tapping and affirmation

Fold your arms in front of you, resting your fingers anywhere on your bicep muscles (upper arms) as if hugging yourself. Pat your left and right biceps alternately with your hands, with about a second between taps. While doing this, say this affirmation aloud or to yourself: "Even though I have a fear of _____ [name your own issue], I deeply love and accept myself." Continue until it feels right to stop, then assess your distress level on a zero-to-10 scale. (Alternative: some people prefer to tap back and forth on their thighs, eyebrow bones, or just under the collarbone. To do it inconspicuously in public, you can tap your feet or even move your tongue back and forth in your mouth. Experiment to find your preference.)

WHEE Step 4: Take some breaths

Stop and take a couple of deep breaths, releasing and letting go.

WHEE Step 5: Reassess the problem

Once again, rate on a zero-to-10 scale the amount of distress that thinking about the problem causes you. (FOR EXAMPLE: I NOW RATE MY FEAR OF PUBLIC SPEAKING AT ABOUT AN 8.)

WHEE Step 6: Repeat the process

Repeat the tapping and affirmation until you get the rating down between zero and 2. If you can do so, go on to the next step (WHEE step 7 follows, under the name "Soul Visioning step 6"). If you cannot, see the "Resistance" sidebar on page 129. (FOR EXAMPLE, I IMAGINE AGAIN THAT I'M SPEAKING IN FRONT OF AN AUDIENCE, AND I RATE THE DISTRESS AT 5 THIS TIME. I SEEM TO BE STUCK AT 5, AND I REALIZE IT'S BECAUSE I'M *MOST* AFRAID OF SPEAKING TO *LARGE* AUDIENCES. SO I FOLLOW THE " RESISTANCE" INSTRUCTIONS ON PAGE 129.)

Resistance:
What if my rating number won't drop?

Try these ideas to help get that number down.

You may need to tweak the affirmation phrase to tailor it to your issue. (FOR EXAMPLE, I REFINE MY STATEMENT TO SAY, "EVEN THOUGH I HAVE A FEAR OF SPEAKING TO *LARGE* AUDIENCES, I DEEPLY LOVE AND ACCEPT MYSELF".)

Or try this simple tip: find a pressure point about three inches below the midpoint of your left collarbone and rub it a few times clockwise, as if a clock were painted on your chest. The exact spot isn't crucial; the technique still works. Optional: repeat the affirmation while you rub. (I RUB THE SPOT A FEW TIMES WHILE SAYING MY AFFIRMATION.)

Then repeat the tapping with the affirmation as before. Recheck the rating to see if it drops. (THIS TIME I SAY THE MORE DEFINED STATEMENT, "EVEN THOUGH I HAVE A FEAR OF SPEAKING TO *LARGE* AUDIENCES, I DEEPLY LOVE AND ACCEPT MYSELF," WHILE TAPPING A FEW MORE ROUNDS. THE NUMBER GOES DOWN TO 1 I CAN NOW GO ON TO INSTALL A NEW BELIEF.)

Remember, complicated, longstanding issues are beyond the scope of a self-help book to resolve. You will need the assistance of a professional to guide you through the process. To find a qualified practitioner, check organizations such as ACEP, found in this book's Resources section.

Soul Visioning Step 6 / WHEE Step 7
Installing New Beliefs Using WHEE

Installing new, desired beliefs (WHEE step 7) is such a landmark that we're giving it the banner of Soul Visioning step 6.

With a distress level now between zero and 2, you are ready to replace the old belief. Installing a new belief is like programming new software into your unconscious body-mind, or anchoring an affirmation. The key is to combine a good *feeling* with the *belief* in what you are saying, while imagining it. With some practice, the belief and feeling should intensify. If they don't, other aspects of this issue need to be cleared.

A. Ask yourself what you would rather believe instead of the limiting belief, feeling, or behavior that you just reprocessed. Form an affirmation statement: see page 131 for guidelines. (FOR EXAMPLE, HAVING CLEARED THE FEAR OF PUBLIC SPEAKING, I FORM THE AFFIRMATION, "I SPEAK IN FRONT OF LARGE AUDIENCES WITH CONFIDENCE AND EASE.")

B. Now rate your belief in this new affirmation on a scale of zero to 10 (zero if you don't believe it at all, 10 if you totally believe it. (I RATE MY BELIEF IN MY AFFIRMATION AT ABOUT A 7.)

C. Imagine yourself responding to a situation in an ideal way. (I SEE MYSELF STANDING IN FRONT OF A LARGE GROUP, SPEAKING WITH CONFIDENCE AND EASE.)

D. *Say it, imagine it, and feel it:* Now combine steps A, B, and C while doing the tapping. (IN MY MIND'S EYE, I STAND IN FRONT OF A LARGE GROUP, FEELING CONFIDENT AND AT EASE, AND I SAY MY AFFIRMATION: "I SPEAK IN FRONT OF LARGE AUDIENCES WITH CONFIDENCE AND EASE.") Do a few rounds of tapping and affirmations. Then rate your belief in the affirmation again. Keep doing this until you rate between an 8 and 10. (THIS TIME I RATE MY BELIEF AT A 9. I CELEBRATE MY NEWFOUND CONFIDENCE.)

If your believability rates below 8, you may have a limiting belief that you can address with tapping. (For example, I say, "Even though it's hard for me to believe that I can speak to a large group with confidence and ease, I deeply love and accept myself.") If it is still hard to believe your affirmation, other issues may need to be resolved. Later chapters address further work for clearing deep-rooted issues.

E. Once you have installed the new belief and feeling, reinforce them, using the same process. (A few days before I am to speak to a large group, I imagine myself in that setting, feeling very confident, doing the WHEE tapping, and saying, "I enjoy speaking in front of large audiences.")

If you replaced a limiting belief with a positive one, reinforce it by saying, feeling, and imagining the desired outcome as if it is happening now. Do this daily for seven days.

Sometimes when you have cleared a self-defeating belief, behavior, or feeling, you may need some other new skills. (For example, I have cleared my fear of speaking to large groups, but I may need to learn effective public speaking skills. That would be a practical next step to take.)

Tips for Formulating Affirmations

- Affirm a want, not a "should" or a "would." (For example, "I am calm and confident speaking to large audiences," rather than "I should be calm ..." or "I would like to be calm ...")

- State what you want in the first person, in positive terms and in the present tense, as if it is already true. ("I am confident and calm speaking to large audiences," rather than "I don't want to be afraid of speaking in front of others.")

- Create a goal that is realistic for you right now. ("I enjoy speaking to like-minded people in large audiences," rather than "I SPEAK AT LIVE, INTERNATIONALLY TELEVISED CONFERENCES.")

- Affirm a goal that inspires you with passion and a sense of challenge. ("I FEEL PASSIONATE ABOUT SPEAKING BEFORE RECEPTIVE LARGE AUDIENCES.")

- Keep it short and direct. ("I ENJOY SPEAKING IN FRONT OF LARGE AUDIENCES.")

Sample Affirmations

I appreciate being in the moment.

I nurture my body in healthy and loving ways.

My sleep is relaxed and refreshing.

I am clear about what I want in a relationship.

It's okay for me to set boundaries in relationships, and I do.

I listen to my inner voice and I confidently act upon what I hear.

The source of my contentment and joy lies inside myself.

I receive and accept money with love and gratitude.

I use time efficiently and creatively.

I am assertive in meeting my own needs.

I give myself permission to do what I love.

I accept my imperfections as opportunities to learn valuable lessons.

I enjoy my own company.

You may also wish to refer to the sample list of positive core beliefs in chapter 4. While you are tapping, say this affirmation: "Even though I _____ [name the issue], I deeply love and accept myself." Continue until it feels right to stop, then take a break to assess your distress level.

WHEE Method Summary

1. *Identify the problem,* keeping it simple. Set your intent to let your soul help you in the process. Drink some water and take several deep breaths.

2. *Rate the problem* on a zero-to-10 scale. What degree of distress do you feel when you think about the problem now?

3. *Tapping and affirmation:* Fold your arms in front of you and pat your right and left biceps alternately with your hands, about a second apart, while saying aloud the affirmation, "Even though I _____ [name the issue], I deeply love and accept myself." Stop when it feels right to do so.

4. *Take a couple of deep breaths,* releasing and letting go.

5. *Reassess the distress level,* on a zero-to-10 scale, that the problem causes you when you think about it *now.*

6. *Repeat the tapping cycle* until the rating drops between 0 and 2 in intensity. (Note: If the number won't drop, rub the spot three inches below the midpoint of your left collarbone clockwise for a few rounds, repeating the affirmation if you wish.)

7. *Install a positive affirmation.* Repeat steps 3 and 4, this time using an affirmation that describes your ideal response to the previously triggering situation. While *feeling* the positive emotion of that response, state what you want to affirm: "I speak in front of any audience with confidence and comfort."

You may wish to summarize these steps on a brief "cheat sheet" to carry with you.

The WHEE Method for Children

With a few modifications, WHEE can be an effective tool for parents to use with their children. Youngsters usually clear their issues faster than adults because they have accumulated fewer layers of trauma. And they often find the self-hugging posture comforting.

First, help the child identify the problem or feeling, and how big it is. Very young children may have trouble rating their distress numerically, so you can ask them to use their hands to show its size to them. For example, ask them to think about the problem or feeling. Have them hold their hands out, palms together, then move their palms apart as wide as they feel their problem is.

Then have the child cross their arms in front, in a self-hug, and pat their upper arms, first right then left, back and forth, while saying a simple statement, such as "Even though I have this _____ [state the problem or feeling], I am OK." Keep the affirmation simple.

One mother used WHEE with her four-year-old after he was traumatized by a microwave fire at his preschool. The fire engines, loud sirens, and alarms had also frightened him. His mother showed him the WHEE tapping and together they tapped and said, "Even though I am scared of the fire, I am OK." She had him use his hands to rate how scared he was, and he was able to lower his distress to very low after a few rounds of tapping. She also had him tap on his fear of the alarms and fire engine noises by saying, "Even though I am scared of the loud sounds, I am OK." Again, after a few rounds, his fear was minimal. When there was another microwave fire at his preschool a few months later, his reaction was not a problem that time.

How wonderful it would be if parents worked with their children daily to clear their hurts and distressing feelings, helping minimize them over the course of their childhood. I know one mother who taps with her child every night at bedtime, to clear his daily stresses. She also uses WHEE to manage her own stress.

WHEE has benefits for every member of the family: use it to its fullest advantage.

six

Forgiveness Is the Key to Happiness

Forgiveness is the seventh step in the process of Soul Visioning. I call it the "F" word, because while forgiving is one of the most important things we can do to heal ourselves, we seem to resist it more than anything else. Whenever our mind harbors resentment, thoughts of revenge, and pain from the past, it drains our energy and blocks our soul awareness. Forgiveness restores our sense of peace, unity, and a state of mind that allows us to remember our true identity, which is love. Our soul's vision can fully express itself in our life only when the past is forgiven and the barriers to love's awareness are cleared.

However, there is a great deal of misunderstanding about forgiveness. *True forgiveness is not possible at the level of the personality.* The ego/personality's version and the soul's version of forgiveness are quite different. We will illuminate those differences in this chapter, so that when your spiritual journey brings you to a fork in the road, you can choose the path of soul-based forgiveness, the path that leads to your soul's vision, and to true peace.

Let's start with an overview of those differences.

Soul Forgiveness is NOT about:

- Condoning, approving of, or accepting hurtful behavior such as abuse, violence, aggression, betrayal, or dishonesty. Sometimes we need to stop another's inappropriate actions that cause pain to us or to others. Forgiveness does not preclude our acting to change a situation or to protect our rights.

- Absolving a person from the consequences of their hurtful behavior. A person who abuses or murders another needs to be arrested. It is compassionate to stop someone from harming themselves or anyone else.

- Reconciling with the offending person. We need not invite them back into our life if they have not changed their behavior. Forgiveness is not about becoming a victim or doormat so we can say how righteous and long-suffering we are. It is OK to set limits with people who violate our boundaries.

- Denying our feelings about an offense or pretending that it didn't occur. Many people want to be seen as nice, righteous, and spiritual. They think that they have forgiven and forgotten, when in fact they have just repressed their true feelings.

- Changing the other person. This is not about striking a bargain with the other person ("If you change, then I will forgive you"). Forgiveness is about changing our own attitude.

- "Giving in" or weakness. Although some people see forgiveness as giving in or being a wimp, it is just the opposite. Forgiveness requires great courage and strength to resist the ego impulse to retaliate. It takes spiritual power and wisdom to show compassion and empathy to those who have made mistakes through identifying with their ego.

Soul Forgiveness IS about:

- A choice that we make with our soul's guidance. We freely decide how we will perceive and respond to painful situations— a choice that becomes easier when we have healed our own traumas, limiting beliefs, and unconscious guilt. With these unconscious triggers, it is hard to consciously stay in the present and let the soul take charge. The more we clear our blockages, the more easily we can make the choice for peace, rather than attack. (Some of this book's tools, such as the WHEE method and other meridian therapies, past-life exploration, and life-between-lives regression, can facilitate soul forgiveness.)

- Courage and strength. These soul qualities help us choose a healthy response to offending behavior.

- Peace of mind. This results when we let go of our attack thoughts, because that stops the attack-defense-attack cycle.

- The knowledge that to forgive another is to forgive ourselves. What we judge in another is often what we unconsciously don't like in ourselves. This is a difficult concept to grasp, because we don't want to own up to our shadow self (our disowned self, our hidden aspects that we dislike). It is much easier to see the speck in someone else's eye than the log in our own. We often project our own sense of guilt onto another person, because it is too painful to acknowledge it in ourselves.

- Loving ourselves enough to practice forgiveness of ourselves and others.

- Knowing that what we need to heal is not the other person, but our own mind.

The Ego/Personality View of Forgiveness

At some time in our life, we have all felt attacked, betrayed, or wronged by someone, or felt that another person is responsible for our suffering. We have judged the person we believe has victimized us, feeling angry at them, and condemning them.

Many of us have also sincerely endeavored, as a personality, to forgive the "guilty party." But this is the *ego's* version of forgiveness: "You caused my hurt and I am a victim and you must be punished . . . but I forgive you." It bears repeating: *At the level of the personality, true forgiveness is not possible.*

To understand why, let's look a little deeper into the personality's perceptions and the role played by our unconscious feelings.

The Ego's Perceptions Are Always Illusions

The ego's limited capacity for perception makes its seeing an illusion. It has little ability to comprehend a true picture of reality, based on its identification with the body and personality. Its perceptual range is limited by space and time. It does not know what will happen next week as a result of its choices, let alone next year, or ten years from now. It does not know how others will be affected by its choices, and is therefore in no position to judge them. To think that it can properly evaluate any situation, based on its extremely limited data, is substituting its illusion for truth.

What do we mean by an illusion? An illusion is a limited, incomplete, and therefore, inaccurate ego perception (which we have selected in preference to the knowledge of the soul, which is provided by our intuition). We can even say that everything we perceive in physical reality is an illusion, to the extent that we evaluate it and try to interpret it with our ego. *Everything we perceive through our personality is an illusion, because our personality can never have a true experience of reality.*

Our error is our attachment to our ego's interpretations of our experience. The personality persuades us that we actually know what is going on. The truth is, our conscious mind does not ever know the full picture. We must learn to question the certainty of our perceptions of others, and give up the idea that we can make an accurate judgment with our personality. This is just being honest about the limitations of our personality's perceptions! We must be willing to admit that our ego's perceptions are illusions that do not provide true knowledge. It requires humility to set aside our perceptions of others and to become open to our soul's vision of them.

The Ego Projects Unconscious Guilt Onto Others

As if we were looking in a mirror, our personality's perceptions of others reflects back to us our own unconscious thoughts. When we condemn someone, we often do not see that we are projecting our unconscious feelings about ourselves onto that person.

My husband Dave shares a forgiveness lesson that he needed to learn.

> I was aware of the anger I felt toward people who did not understand or apply the spiritual truths that I shared with them. My feelings mirrored the anger that I felt toward myself for not fully applying the spiritual truths that I knew. I realized that the roots of this pattern went back to past lives, when people had ignored my warnings with disastrous consequences. It was my personality's illusion that I can, and need to, evaluate the effects of my spiritual sharing on other people. The soul knows the truth, that it is part of a wholeness that does not need anything from others. My intuition whispered softly that I only needed to share my soul.

Consciously, we blame others, perceiving them as responsible for our suffering. Unconsciously, however, we project our guilt onto others in a futile attempt to get rid of it. Our unconscious thoughts and feelings of guilt represent an ego perception of ourselves; we condemn ourselves for perceived failures. So our ego demands punishment for what it views as our sins.

We must learn to look with the eyes of the soul and question our unconscious, limiting ego beliefs and their painful consequences. Through healing and forgiving our mistaken beliefs, traumas, and unconscious unfinished business, our true nature as a soul can fully express itself. When the blocks are removed, what remains is our essence as a soul.

Ego Forgiveness Is an Outer Shift, Not an Inner One

Personality forgiveness is a mask of social acceptability. It makes no inner demand that we shift our perspective to the soul's vision; it simply shifts our outer behavior without changing how we feel in our heart. Ego forgiveness often involves pretending that everything is fine, when unconsciously, we feel angry, hurt, or afraid. The personality offers an illusion of forgiveness, which does not heal our unconscious mind. It maintains the belief that our interests are separate from those we forgive. It may even secretly feel superior to those it "forgives."

Soul Forgiveness

Only at the soul level is true forgiveness possible.

Our soul knows that an "attack" by another arises from their unconscious fearful belief that they are separated from love (not lovable). Our soul can interpret another person's "attack" as a call for love. The soul understands that we are not spiritually separate, and that the purpose for every experience is to remember that our true nature is love.

How we respond to that call for love is not so much about what we do behaviorally, but about our attitude. For example, if someone steals your car, you can take them to court. The attitude with which you do that is the key. You can do it with condemnation or with a compassionate frame of mind. Obviously, the thief does not feel connected with love or their soul when behaving in such a way. For most of us, compassion for a criminal is an advanced form of forgiveness that takes considerable practice to master.

Releasing our attachment to our personality's interpretations is what forgiveness is about. We choose to see past the ego's illusions that we have projected onto others. We need to forgive our projections of guilt onto others and ourselves by recognizing that guilt is an illusion.

Only when we recognize our personality's perceptions as illusions does forgiveness become possible. Forgiveness, then, is about changing our mind—from our ego interpretations to our soul's knowledge of spiritual truth.

Only at the soul level is it possible to recognize that ego illusions are not true. Soul forgiveness recognizes that the soul is our true nature, and that the ego concepts of sin, guilt, and fear of punishment are illusions. It is a soul-based decision to see the real identity of another, not confusing their personality's behavior, fears, and errors with their soul. We will be able to see in this way if we allow our intuition, the Will of the soul, to guide our vision.

Soul Vision Is Required for Forgiveness

Our soul offers true forgiveness. It expands and awakens us to our transcendent nature beyond the personality. The soul knows that only love is eternal; anything else is an illusion. Soul love is giving without need or attachment. That is what our soul desires! Only by expressing the love that we are can we fully experience it.

How do we know when we have chosen forgiveness? Soul forgiveness brings feelings of peace, love, joy, freedom, and contentment, because it returns us to the awareness of our true nature.

A Father Forgiveness Lesson

Charlene has been on a transformational path for at least fifteen years. The catalyst for her seeking a spiritual path was her divorce from her husband of thirty-two years. She had been a stay-at-home mom, raising three children. He had left her for another woman. Charlene was devastated, shocked, angry, and bitter towards her ex-husband. To make matters worse, her children were divided in their allegiance to their mother and father. For many years, it was just too painful for her to attend family gatherings to which her former husband and his girlfriend were invited. Her self-esteem was battered and she was barely keeping her head above water emotionally. "I literally had to hang on to the walls of my house," Charlene recalls, "because it felt like the foundation was ripped out from under me."

However, the gift of this overwhelming experience was that it forced Charlene to look inward and seek healing. It seems that crisis, pain, and loss are the impetus for many people to choose a spiritual path. Although it need not be that way, that is how most of us learn. When we exhaust our own ego resources and hit bottom, we ask the important questions, such as Who am I? Why am I here? Where am I going?

Charlene sought out a spiritual study group that focused on practicing forgiveness in relationships, and began to focus diligently on undoing her ego perceptions of herself. It was especially important that she not skip steps in the healing process. She had to own her feelings of resentment and anger.

A mistake that some spiritual thought systems make is to deny and/or to spiritualize negative emotion. The general idea is this: "Let's just stay in the light and not focus on the dark feelings." However, attempting to forgive without acknowledging what we really feel is like living with a skunk under our house, but pretending everything is fine. Eventually the stench overpowers the house. When authentic feelings are acknowledged and processed, we then can change the perspective from which we view those feelings. We can stay stuck at the level of our personality's perceptions, or we can open to the vision of our soul. Listening to and following our soul's guidance is the key to true forgiveness.

It took Charlene many years to discover her inner spiritual strength, which prepared her to work on true spiritual forgiveness of her former husband. Charlene began to see how she had contributed to the relationship problems in her marriage. She realized that she had repeated a pattern from her childhood.

> In effect, it was like I married my dad, who was emotionally unavailable and distant. I desperately wanted attention and love, but my husband didn't know how to give it any more than my father did. I had the insight that I never really loved myself, so how could I feel like I deserved the love of others? Through my spiritual stud-

ies, I began to see myself as perfect, unconditionally loved, whole, and complete, from the perspective of the soul. I was not the miserable, sinful person that my religious upbringing had taught me I was.

Charlene's most significant forgiveness lesson involved her father. I asked her to talk about him, and what changes she noticed in herself as she worked on forgiveness and healing their relationship.

For the most part, I was afraid of my father while growing up. He had a volatile temper, especially with my younger siblings. So our relationship was not close. My father was an old-fashioned guy, and work was number one for him. He wasn't affectionate or demonstrative. I never had the sense that I wanted to reach out to him or to change things to improve our relationship.

I didn't feel that I was part of my family, either; I didn't feel accepted. When I went to family gatherings, I always hoped that this time, I would make a connection with somebody. But always when I left, there was just that let-down feeling that I had been left out again.

Then came a year when my parents arrived to help me celebrate my birthday. My father said that he thought when we get to heaven, we were going to be surprised at who would be there and who wouldn't. I argued with him, and told him that we would all be there. Well, that stopped the conversation cold. My opinion fell on deaf ears. I remember feeling very frustrated after that.

Then came Father's Day of the same year, a couple of months later, and I was invited to go out with the family for lunch. Before I went, I decided to do a meditation to calm and center myself. I asked the Holy Spirit to be with me that day. After lunch, the family gathered at my parents' house.

We were sitting at the table and my dad again said, "I think we're all going to be surprised when we get to heaven, at who will be there and who won't." From deep inside I asked myself, "What should I do, what should I say?" One part of me said, "Let it go." And another part said, "If this is not right, I should say something."

Finally I heard, "It doesn't matter, let it go." I heard a voice inside me say, "See his Spirit." At that point, I suddenly saw my father's Spirit rise in front of him, and in that moment, I felt my own Spirit and my father's Spirit cross the table and join in the middle. I had an incredible experience of understanding what "oneness" is.

I went home that evening, feeling like I was floating on air. Nothing truly mattered except that I finally had a sense of belonging, not because somebody had said anything in particular to me, but because I finally knew what "oneness" was all about. The feeling lasted for about three days. I would have incredible moments of deep stillness. It was as if I was in a trance for a few minutes, and that feeling of being so calm and peaceful would flood over me.

I have looked back at that experience and learned so many things. Initially, I learned that I'm not responsible for changing anybody, or for correcting anybody else's mistakes except my own. Mine is the only mind that I can change. I am the only one that I need to correct, and that's okay. And wherever my dad is in his thinking, that is okay.

When my dad got sick with esophageal cancer, it changed my relationship with him even more. I had to care for my father as if he were an infant—changing diapers, cleaning him, trying to get him to eat some soft foods. Part of me hoped that because he knew he was so sick, we might have some conversations. But that never developed. My father didn't change all that much.

For my part, I was just more accepting about what was. I finally realized that I could not impose my spirituality on him, but I could embrace what I believed, knowing what was true for me. I learned that, "The holiest of all the spots on earth is where an ancient hatred has become a present love."[1] What a thrill for me to experience that with my father. I let go of a lot of my expectations. I realized that the ability to love and forgive is always inside of me. No longer would I constantly search for love and validation from the outside. I found that peace inside of me.

Soul Visioning Step 7
True Forgiveness

This step has two parts: a practice to use on an ongoing basis and a let-ter-writing exercise that can also be used repeatedly as needed. (You'll also learn an optional advanced guided audio meditation, one that you can approach whenever you're ready for it.) Let's look first at the ongoing practice: a simple but powerful prayer.

Forgiveness Practice
The Forgiveness Prayer

I love you, I forgive you, and I thank you
for the opportunity to heal my perceptions of you.

I say this prayer with the help of my soul's Mind when someone or something upsets me. This simple prayer is based on the idea that ev-eryone acts as a mirror for how we feel about ourselves. The power of this prayer is its recognition that the healing is really about healing our-selves. Whatever upsets us in another person is often a part of us that we need to heal. We often see the problem as "out there," but in reality, the problem is in our own mind. I try to have an attitude of gratitude for those who push my buttons, because I know that they are giving me a chance to see myself differently.

When we say, "I love you, I forgive you, and I thank you for the op-portunity to heal my perceptions of you," we are really saying this to ourselves. When I say, "I forgive you," I mean that I am forgiving my own projections onto you that you are mirroring back to me, which I did not previously see in myself. In that sense, someone who upsets me becomes my best teacher, revealing what I was not ready to own in myself.

Remember, this does *not* mean condoning or excusing inappropri-ate behavior, or even reconciling with another person. It merely ac-knowledges that we have a choice about how we see the other person and, therefore, ourselves. We can set behavioral limits for others and stop another from violating our boundaries, but what is important is the attitude with which we do that. If we condemn another, we keep ourselves locked inside the prison of our own hatred and resentment. To condemn another person is like taking poison and expecting the other person to die. On the other hand, if we have compassion and empathy for another, we learn compassion for ourselves. Everyone is a screen onto which we project our beliefs and attitudes. We can see the world through the personality's lens or with the soul's vision.

As we noted, the ego's version of forgiveness says, "You caused my hurt and I am a victim and you must be punished . . . but I forgive you." The soul's form of forgiveness says, "You are my brother/sister and *our interests are not separate*." Our mutual goal in this world is to remember who we really are as spiritual beings, to remember that we are more than an ego/personality that feels separate from Source. We are all in this classroom to learn who we really are. Therefore, when I attack or condemn another person, I remind them that they are guilty and anything but a soul. When I look beyond their behavior and remember that they are a spiritual being, we are both blessed.

The offending person's behavior is either coming from love or fear. This does not mean that we can skip steps and deny our hurt and anger. We must own what our personality is feeling without judgment until we can shift our identification to the soul. When we reach that realization, we can choose to see the situation differently. In the later stages of forgiveness, we can have compassion and empathy for the other person.

A Mother Heals Her Fearful Projections: The Forgiveness Prayer in Action

When I met her, Victoria was beside herself with worry about her suicidal, bipolar (manic-depressive) daughter. Her oldest child, now a young adult, is very bright but has suffered from depression most of her life. She had a history of self-injury and social isolation. She received professional treatment at a young age, and was functional until she had an accident in high school. She had never recovered her mental health, despite medication, extensive therapy, and repeated hospitalizations, including treatment at the Mayo Clinic. Her parents had provided her with the best of available treatment since she was very young.

To have a chronically ill child who often threatens suicide is obviously very difficult for a parent. Victoria was looking for a way to deal with her own anxiety over her daughter's emotional problems. I suggested that there might be another way for her to see her daughter. I taught Victoria to say the Forgiveness Prayer for her daughter, while keeping in mind that the prayer was really for herself. The more she could accept the perfection in her daughter, the more she could accept her own perfection as a soul.

I interviewed Victoria about eight months after I saw her as a client, to find out how the prayer had worked for her.

SUSAN: *What benefits, if any, did you experience from using the Forgiveness Prayer?*

VICTORIA: It reinforced the truth that we are all the same, and we are all one. The idea is that the shortcomings I see in others are the shortcomings I see in myself. The prayer also helped me to see my life in a more meaningful way than before, when I would think, "Oh, this is my lot in life. This is all it's going to be." My outlook now is not resignation; it's more of an acceptance.

S: *How do you now see your daughter, after using the prayer?*

V: Before, I think I was looking at how to fix her. This prayer's perspective is that there is nothing to fix. If there is something to fix, it is within [me]. It reinforces the idea that you can't change anybody else; you can only change yourself. I feel that my expectations changed. I completely replaced [my expectations] with love, acceptance, and appreciation for a perfection that I never knew was there, the perfection that is her soul.

S: *What alleviated your fear that your daughter might take her life?*

V: At first, I had the intellectual acceptance that I cannot stop this. I enlarged upon that, to embrace the idea that this is her life and I have *my* life. I need to live my life as best as I can. My worrying about her is not going to solve anything or prevent anything, if it's to happen. It serves no one to be in that place of fear. I have replaced that fear with acceptance that she has this mental health challenge, but it doesn't change the truth of who she really is as a perfect, immortal soul.

S: *You can see beyond her body to the perfection of her soul, which is the truth about her.*

V: I think I made my peace with that, if you ever can make your peace with that. I certainly made a decision not to monitor her. Occasionally we'll talk about it, but I don't ask, "Are you going to be OK tonight?" I'm not going to live my life that way. I'm not going to let fear rule my life. The difference is, I'm not turning my back on her.

S: *You're detaching but you're not abandoning?*

V: Exactly. In fact, I am embracing at a different level.

About one year after this interview, Victoria reported that her daughter's depression had decreased, she was no longer suicidal, and she had even taken three college classes. Her mother said, "Since we last talked, she has become very committed to fitness, rides her bike ten to fifteen miles a day, works out with a trainer, etc. This summer she is taking a jewelry-making class. Her progress is remarkable."

Now that Victoria can embrace her daughter, see beyond her flaws, and remember her wholeness and perfection, she can also better accept and allow her own flaws with unconditional love. Victoria is doing wonderful work as an instructor and advocate with the National Alliance on Mental Illness (NAMI). Through education and advocacy, she is a champion for improving the lives of people who suffer from brain disorders.

Forgiveness Exercise
A Forgiveness Letter from the Soul

In this exercise, you will experience soul forgiveness as a process. Only by starting with your personality self can you grow to forgiveness from the soul self.

Step 1: Write a grievance letter from your personality self (a letter you will not mail).

You are going to write a letter to someone (alive or deceased) with whom you hold a grievance.[2] It can be to another person, to yourself, to God, to a group or an organization—to anyone or anything you haven't forgiven. Imagine that you can say whatever you like, and that the recipient will listen from the soul self with love and compassion. Write down all your feelings. You can't forgive if you have denied your feelings.

> Dear _____ ,
>
> I am angry because _____ .
>
> I am sad because _____ .
>
> I am hurt because _____ .
>
> I feel guilty because _____ .
>
> I regret that _____ .
>
> I am fearful that _____ .
>
> Signed,
> [Your name]

Step 2: Write a return letter from their soul self to you.

Imagine that the person or entity you wrote to will now respond with a letter from their soul self. Have them begin it "Dear [Your name]." They will then say what you most want to hear. Sign it with their name.

Step 3: Write a forgiveness letter back to them.

Think about whether you're ready for this step: it comes at a later stage of the forgiveness process. Some people choose to forgive certain things quickly. Others may take one or more lifetimes of repeating their patterns until they finally forgive themselves or others. It may take a long time to reach this stage if the offense was particularly painful to you. If you aren't ready to bring closure to this grievance, simply write to the person and say that you intend to continue to work with forgiveness. Whatever you choose, do it with gentleness and compassion for your process—and it *is* a *process*.

If you are ready to take this step, you can write a letter back (but don't send it), thanking the person or entity for being your learning partner. You might want to say the Forgiveness Prayer with the help of your soul: "I love you, I forgive you, and I thank you for the opportunity to heal my perceptions of you." Some people do the WHEE tapping or use another energy psychology method while saying this (see chapter 5).

The more you have cleared your unconscious blockages, the easier it will be to stay in the moment and let your soul guide the process. Complete healing means knowing that forgiveness of another is ultimately for you: you are really saying this prayer for yourself. (Remember, too, that you are not condoning the other's behavior or reconciling with them unless you are specifically guided to do so.)

Dear _____,

Holding on to my grievance with you only hurts me and makes me suffer. Therefore, I forgive you as a gift to myself. I love you, I forgive you, and I thank you for the opportunity to heal my perceptions of you. You are Spirit, perfect, whole, and complete. You are forgiven, released, and loved unconditionally.

Signed,
[Your name]

A Landlord's Key Unlocks a Soul Lesson

I once learned a soul lesson through a distressing situation with my landlord, a large corporation that was not known as tenant-friendly. The company had jeopardized the security of my office suite by removing the lock on the door leading from the outer hall to where some of my records were kept. I requested that the lock be replaced, but the landlord's response was to minimize and dismiss the problem. Next I sent a letter with a copy to my attorney, explaining further why the problem needed to be resolved. My letter was ignored. I found myself getting angrier and angrier, yet powerless to do anything. I was sending that company a considerable amount of negative energy.

Finally, I realized that I could approach this dilemma differently by taking it to a level beyond my ego. I started saying the Forgiveness Prayer: *I love you, I forgive you, and I thank you for giving me the opportunity to heal my perceptions of you.* The next time I drove by my landlord's office, instead of resenting the company, I blessed it and sent it loving energy. Instead of feeling separate, I remembered my oneness with the people who made up the corporation. I surrendered the impasse to my soul, with the idea that I didn't know the solution, and I had to let it go until I could regain my peace of mind.

I also realized that a part of me unconsciously felt that I deserved to be ignored and disrespected. So guess what—the players in my script had showed up and performed their part on the "stage" of my life. By forgiving the players in my drama, I could forgive myself for my mistaken ideas of who I am and who they are.

The next time I arrived at my office suite, I noticed that the lock was back on the door! I have not had a problem with the landlord since I changed my mind.

The Mother-in-Law and the Mirror

Whenever we notice another person pushing our buttons, it's an opportunity to heal something in ourselves. This story is just one example.

A woman I'll call Tanya once shared with me that she was upset with her son-in-law. She complained that he was cold to her. When she spoke of him, her face became tight with anger. Her ego's view was that her son-in-law was wrong and she was right; he was the cause of her distress and should be punished (by her disapproval and resentment). Of course, she mostly punished herself by feeling that way.

I shared with Tanya the concept that when we are bothered by someone, we have an opportunity to look deeper within ourselves at what is being triggered in us. Because she was motivated to heal herself, I suggested that she use the WHEE tapping method to calm her revengeful thoughts. So she tapped while saying, "Even though I am upset and angry with my son-in-law, I deeply love and accept myself." She tapped a number of times until she was ready to take another step.

Next, I asked how she felt when her son-in-law didn't reciprocate her goodwill. She replied that she felt rejected. I asked whether he reminded her of any other person she felt had rejected her. She promptly answered, "My father and my husband." Her eyes filled with tears as she realized that the wound being activated by her son-in-law dated back to her childhood. She remembered that her father had been emotionally unavailable to her, and that she'd felt she wasn't important.

Tanya's next step was to get in touch with that hurt inner child and to nurture that child from her compassionate Higher Self. She understood that she could now provide the comfort that her inner child needed. She could then choose to see her son-in-law from her soul's perspective.

Now that Tanya could see what was really going on, she also saw the pain that she triggered in her son-in-law. She could see the little child in him that also felt rejected and unlovable. She had the insight that she probably reminded her son-in-law of his own controlling mother, with whom he had a conflicted relationship. By taking responsibility for her own needs, she could move into her heart energy and have more empathy for her son-in-law.

Intuitively, Tanya knew that he was not ready to communicate directly with her about this. She needed to connect with him on a soul level. So her next step was to say from her soul to his soul, "I love you, I forgive you, and I thank you for the opportunity to heal my perceptions of you." Now that she was not attached to changing him, she could see him as his true spiritual being.

Although this would take some practice, and at times she might be tempted to fall back into old ego reactions, she now knows the root cause of her anger toward her son-in-law. This process does not guarantee that he will change, but now she can let go of her attachment to his changing. Either way, she is more at peace.

Advanced Forgiveness Guided Audio Meditation
The Mirrors of Your Mind

Now let's move to an *optional* guided meditation, one that you may be ready for now or later. *Please note: it is not for people in the beginning stages of the forgiveness process.* It is not for those in early recovery from severe trauma or abuse. If you are unsure whether to continue with this meditation, it may be best to wait.

However, if you feel any lack of peace over not doing this exercise at this time, you can even tap on that issue using WHEE or another energy psychology method. You might say, "Even though I believe I am not ready to do this exercise, I deeply love and accept myself."

Before beginning this exercise, select a person in your life who you would like to forgive—someone you disapprove of, or with whom you have a grievance or an annoyance. Don't pick the person who would be the toughest for you to forgive; start with someone easier. Remember, too, that if this exercise becomes too uncomfortable, you can leave it anytime you wish. You might need to do this meditation several times before you feel a shift in your perception, especially if you have a particularly challenging person in mind. You can always return to this exercise later, when you are ready. **Remember: To access the tools you'll need to get the most out of this session, please see "Preparation: Guided Inner Journeys" on page 9.**

ADVANCED FORGIVENESS MEDITATION SCRIPT

Take a couple of deep breaths. Breathe in peace through your heart . . . breathe out the tensions of the day . . . letting go more and more with each inhalation and exhalation. Feel how good it feels to relax and let go . . . feeling so comfortable and at ease. . . . Imagine a bright, white light coming down from above and entering the top of your head with the unlimited light of Love . . . It flows down into your heart and expands out to surround your body with light, balance, and protection.

Now allow your breath to take you to a safe, beautiful place. It can be in nature, such as the ocean, the mountains, a garden, a meadow, or your favorite spot to relax. It can be a place you have visited before, or would like to visit, or it can just be a place you imagine. Go there now and immerse yourself with all of your senses . . . This is your healing sanctuary and you can make it just the way you want it. Notice the beauty of your surroundings . . . You feel the temperature is perfect for you . . . smell the air around you . . . feeling so comfortable, safe, and calm. Feel how good it feels to be here. You can bring in anything or anyone to help you feel supported, such as Jesus, Master Teachers, angels, guides, beloved animals, loved ones, your ideal Future Self, the Holy Spirit, or your Higher Self. (Pause.)

Now I invite you to imagine that there is a comfortable place to sit. Have a seat, and when you are settled, invite into your beautiful place someone that you have not forgiven, someone you disapprove of or with whom you have a grievance or resentment. (Pause.) Have them sit across from you at a comfortable distance. If you need to seat them far away, you can do that . . .

Now, look into their eyes . . . and notice what you see or feel in their presence . . . What thoughts and feelings arise for you? . . . Think about what that person does that upsets you, the behavior you can't stand, just for a moment . . . Then notice that their face becomes a mirror . . . As you look at the image of their face, it begins to go out of focus . . . As the image comes back into focus, you see your own face in the mirror . . .

Now, without judgment, and with your compassionate Higher Self, ask yourself, "Am I like that person in any way? . . . Maybe I don't express it in exactly the same way or to the same degree, but do I express it in a way that is similar?" . . . Do this without judgment of yourself . . . Have the "judge and critic" parts of you step back . . . Just observe what comes up for you objectively . . .

Do you experience them as rejecting or critical? With compassion, ask yourself, "Have I ever been rejecting and critical?" (Pause.)

Do you experience them as controlling? Ask yourself, "Have I ever been controlling?" (Pause.)

Do you experience them as attacking? Ask yourself, "Have I attacked others or myself?" (Pause.)

Do you experience them as insensitive or disrespectful? Ask yourself, "Have I ever been insensitive or disrespectful?" (Pause.)

We usually judge others and ourselves with our ego/personality. Be aware of any part of you that might still judge yourself for your past thoughts, feelings, or behavior. Ask that part to step back. Maybe put that part in another room while you are doing this meditation.

So now, look again in the mirror at yourself and feel your Higher Self—that part of you that is wise, compassionate, unconditionally loving, joyful, and connected to the Divine . . . What does your Higher Self want to say to you? What words of reassurance and encouragement do you hear? (Pause.) Feel the love and acceptance from your Higher Self . . . Say to yourself in the mirror,

"I love you, I forgive you, and I thank you for the opportunity to change my perceptions of you." (Pause.)

Now notice the image fading from the mirror, and see, sense, and feel a beautiful ball of light filling the mirror . . . This light radiates outward, growing larger and larger, dissolving the mirror . . . This light surrounds you both—you and the other person that is sitting across from you—in warmth and love and oneness . . . You realize that this is your soul's vision of you and everyone else. It sees beyond all the personality images to the truth of your spiritual being . . . Now look again into the eyes of the other person and say, "I love you, I forgive you, and I thank you for the opportunity to heal my perceptions of you." (Pause.) Bless them on their way.

Bring your awareness back to the room, and on the count of five, you will be fully awake, refreshed, and feeling wonderful in every way.

1 . . . Feel the life blood returning to your arms and legs . . .

2 . . . Wiggling your toes and fingers . . .

3 . . . Coming out . . .

4 . . . Reenergized . . .

5 . . . Back in the room at the present time and space, feeling fully alert.

Write down any observations and insights that came up during this exercise. If there were resistances to doing any part of this exercise (there usually are), write them down, too. If any limiting beliefs or unresolved feelings emerged, you can tap on those issues using the WHEE or another energy psychology method to help clear them. Above all, be patient and kind with yourself, realizing that forgiveness of oneself and others is a process and takes practice. *You are worth it!* I applaud your efforts and courage to do this work.

A World War II Pilot Practices Forgiveness

Soul forgiveness can bring healing and peace to difficult, real-life situations, as this story shows.

A former World War II transport pilot, William was abandoned by his father at a young age and raised in poverty by his single mother. As this story shows, he had a brush with death that served as a wake-up call for him to dedicate his life to helping others. Even when betrayed by a family member, William was able to forgive. He has lived a soul-guided life, filled with happiness as well as outward success. Rising from poverty to wealth, he always realized that his true abundance came from his relationship with God . . . and what he calls Spirit.

William was eighty-four when I first met him. (He's related to Winston Churchill through his grandmother's lineage.) His mind is sharp and inquisitive, and he continues to ask the meaningful questions about life, death, and purpose. William graciously allowed me to interview him, and he tells his story here.

WILLIAM: I grew up in Chicago in the 1920s. My father abandoned my sister and me when I was two years old. My mother had to work so hard to make enough money. As soon as I was seven, I was able to deliver papers, stock shelves in a grocery store, or do other things to earn a few pennies to put some food on the table. I also became an acolyte at our Episcopal church for three services every Sunday, and I developed a relationship with God. During that period, I was thinking very much of wanting to become a priest.

We were so poor that the rector of the church knew that I didn't have enough money to buy a suit for my high school graduation. One day the rector took me to a local store and I picked out a suit. However, Spirit said to me, "You've got to pay the church back." The walls and ceiling were dirty, so I devoted about a month to cleaning it, washing the walls, the ceiling, and everything. I got it looking very good.

Now that I am as old as I am, I know that God didn't want me to become a priest, that he had something else in mind for me in my later life. World War II came along, and I couldn't wait to enlist. I became a pilot in the Naval Air Corps. I flew out of Santa Ana, California.

A lot of times during the war, there was nobody out there to save pilots in the water. This was before the time of helicopters. I think Spirit said to me, "Why don't you rig up something to drop down so you can save people." I told my commanding officer that I had an idea to rig up an apparatus so airships could drop a ring down to rescue anyone in the water. He said, "Work it out."

One day I told him, "I have it all set, and I think it will work." He said to test it, he would take me out off Catalina Island and put me adrift. So they set me adrift in a raft, the airship dropped the ring, I got in this ring, and it took me up to the airship. I said, "Well, Captain, it worked!" He said, "Congratulations, you can have three days' liberty." That was my pay. This was probably in 1942. They rigged up all the airships on the West Coast and East Coast and saved hundreds of lives. But then helicopters came out, and they rigged the helicopters up with the same type of apparatus, lifting people out of the water with a winch.

I was flying the airship one day and had twelve men on board. We would rendezvous with a convoy leaving the States to go to the South Pacific. We would go back and forth looking for Japanese submarines. I spent all day long with this convoy, pretty much eighteen to twenty-four hours. I thought we'd better turn around because we were running out of fuel. On the way back, we ran into one of the vicious Santa Ana storms, with lightning, thunder, and rain. We were going into the wind, so our air speed was down to only about twenty knots. I got pretty worried. I prayed, "God, let me save my twelve men, and you can have my life anytime." Shortly after that, the coastline of California came up. I radioed ahead and said, "Catch the nose lines on the first pass; we're very low on fuel." I landed the airship, they got the nose lines, and both engines quit.

I said to the men, "Come into town. God saved us, and I'm going to buy you a drink." I went into this tavern with the men, and I told the waitress why we were there. She had to have been an angel, because when she came back, in my change was a shiny new silver dollar. She said, "Keep this with you for the rest of your life. It will bring you good luck." It was brand-new then. Now you can't even read anything on it—it's been in my pocket for sixty years.

All of a sudden my life started to grow. I came back from the war, finished my education. I then started a printing company with a friend of mine. Plus at the same time, I got involved in the banking business and I started putting banks together. The mergers went from smaller banks to merging with Bank One, and then J. P. Morgan Chase.

S: *What happened to your childhood desire to be a priest?*

W: As you get older, you reminisce about your life; you go back and review it. It occurred to me that God didn't want me to go into the priesthood, but got me into the printing business instead, because it started with one employee and ended up with 750 employees. That is 750 families, more than many parishes have. We supported those families by creating jobs and a good working environment for them. I think that was a better choice for me than becoming a priest, because I can't sing!

S: *You had a problem with your brother-in-law at one time, and I remember that it took you about three years to forgive him. Would you share that experience?*

W: My brother-in-law became a salesman with us. Then he bought another printing company, stole some of my employees, and went into competition with me. So I really hated him with a vengeance.

However, I learned from God that you don't hate people—you love them, and you forgive them . . . we have even taken a trip to Europe together. We go out to dinner in the evenings and, inwardly, I don't hate him.

S: *With your attitude, you just knew and believed that everything would be OK?*

W: You have to believe in the love of God and the teachings of God. Like what happened with my father, who dumped us and never gave us a dime all the time that my mother raised us. Then after I came back from the war, he saw me on the street and came up to me, and wanted to become a friend. I said, "It's too late." I cast him off. I have asked to be forgiven for that. In my prayer to God every night, I ask God to bless him. There is no one I really hate.

S: *To come to the later stage of your life and to be able to say that is a true blessing. That is something I think we can all aspire to. Those whom we don't forgive, we often end up having to come back with, and do things over again. That is an incentive to heal those relationships, I would say.*

W: You've got to be careful how you come back.

S: *You have been quite prosperous in your life, not only in your spiritual life but in your outer world. As I listen to you, it seems to come from that deep sense of connection with Source, with God. I don't hear fear and limitation in you. Do you think that is part of your success?*

W: I don't fear death. I do feel that God is around me. I look at God as energy. That energy is all over the Universe. It can be with everyone. I try to do what is right and try to practice his teachings. I also share with other people. God wants us to be helpful to everyone.

William is a deeply spiritual man, one whose life spanned poverty and riches, betrayal and forgiveness. He listened and followed his soul guidance, which brought him a lifetime of joy and purpose. By forgiving himself and others, he found peace of mind.

Right away, the story William told me began to affect others. The transcriptionist who typed this interview shared her impressions with me and gave me permission to share her thoughts:.

> William's story made me realize that what I need is to not wallow in self-pity, to not allow [my troubles] to whittle away at my self-esteem. I need to nurture my Spirit, my soul, and not . . . extinguish my light. Only when I put God in the driver's seat and open myself to guidance by the Divine, will my soul be at peace, will I be on the journey God intended, and will I truly prosper. This is a good story. It motivated me to change my direction. It's never too late . . . it's not over until it's over! And unless I hurry up and get [my perspective right in this lifetime], I'll be back again, trying to get it right the next time.

seven

Real-Life Accounts
of Soul Visioning

This chapter shares the remarkable journeys several courageous people have taken as they connected with their soul's vision. You will learn how they cleared their stumbling blocks and envisioned and manifested their soul's purpose for their life. You will see how people in very different life situations have used the Soul Visioning process, and how their soul's vision manifested later, one to six years down the road.

Some found that changes occurred within forty-eight hours after the Soul Visioning process, while others took several years to manifest their soul's vision for their life. There is no optimal length for this journey; every path is unique. There are timing cycles to each person's life: how quickly can we heal our unconscious limiting beliefs and overcome the barriers to expressing our soul's vision? Some lessons are more challenging than others, but I have found that consistently doing this kind of transformative work speeds up the process.

It also seems that we each have our own challenging life areas. For example, some people find that their soul's vision manifests easily when it comes to their career, whereas they face major obstacles in the arena of intimate relationships. Although the people profiled here were in varying stages when they experienced Soul Visioning, they did have one thing in common: all were highly committed to healing themselves. May their stories inspire you to take your own healing journey and experience the joy of a soul-guided life.

A Soul's Vision in Synchronous Flow

For Roberta and her husband Luke, a series of remarkable changes began within two days of their Soul Visioning weekend. I followed up in an interview about fifteen months later to learn what other benefits had unfolded for this couple. Although Roberta, a social worker and counselor, recalled that she'd had to coax her husband to participate, she reported that the experience had profoundly changed life for both of them.

> ROBERTA: I had known for over two years that I needed help to organize my counseling practice. I was longing to have everything regularly sorted and filed, expenses recorded, and so on. However, I couldn't and didn't take any action to make my situation better.

During Soul Visioning, the "Peak Experiences" guided process helped the couple begin to envision their ideal future by coming up with words to express spiritual purposes and qualities that inspired them. As they proceeded to use the "Applying Your Soul Ideals" worksheet, Roberta's memory of another life experience helped her apply this exercise to her need for organization.

> In the "Applying Your Soul Ideals" worksheets, the purpose of the first column was to determine the soul quality we were seeking. I wrote down "Harmonious Order," because I was focusing on the desire to have my life run more smoothly, be decluttered, and be more organized, especially in my business.

It was suggested that we think of a time when we experienced this quality. Of all things, my wedding popped into my head—how organized I had been and how smoothly it all went. So I used this as a model for the rest of the worksheet. When I planned my wedding, my thoughts, attitudes, and feelings (the second column) had been that I could afford the wedding; it was okay to spend money even if I got into some debt; there were people with expertise who could help me, such as photographers and florists, and that family and friends would also lend their support. With my wedding, I didn't believe I had to do it all myself. I realized that the same thoughts, attitudes, and feelings would also serve me in organizing my business.

What I wrote in the third column (actions, behaviors, and activities) again applied both to my wedding and to my action plan for getting organized. This included asking around for experts, using the Yellow Pages, setting up a budget, deciding on payment methods, asking family and friends to take on certain tasks or roles, and so on. So I realized that "teamwork" (cooperation) was an important soul quality to add.

During the meditation where we went into a garden and connected to our ideal Future Self, I saw myself looking polished and relaxed, going over a to-do list with a female assistant. I could feel this incredible sense of being solid, secure, stable, and grounded, coming from everything being in order and taken care of in timely, efficient ways. And I felt the amazing relief of not being alone with it all—sharing the burden, the responsibilities.

The holographic nature of the Soul Visioning journey into the garden and into the ideal future is a profound experience, because it feels as if you are there. This energy imprints deeply within the unconscious mind and body and is easily remembered.

When I did the energy psychology exercises, I was surprised by the number of negative beliefs that resonated within me. I chose one of those as my primary limiting core belief to work on: that if I attempted to gain control in one area, other areas (especially finances) would get out of control. The positive belief that I installed in its place was that even if an imbalance were to happen initially, it would even out in the end.

The next day, I went to work out at my health club. I spontaneously asked the manager if she knew of anyone who helped with clearing out offices, bookkeeping, and so on. She knew the perfect person, a stay-at-home mom and former accountant who had her own organizing/bookkeeping business. I also knew that my computer was badly in need of an upgrade; I'd had a computer consultant in mind for over a year, yet had never called. After my workout, I went home and, to my surprise, found the computer consultant's business card right away in my messy office. To my further amazement, when I called both places, both personally answered the phone, offered a free hour-long consult, and were available to begin the following Monday. I then ordered a new computer system according to the recommendations I received. Although I was still quite embarrassed to expose my messy office to these two strangers, doing so no longer felt paralyzing.

Just days later, I was sharing this experience with my dearest friend, who is in accounting herself and has great organizational skills. Suddenly we looked at one another in that "Are you thinking what I'm thinking?" kind of way. We arranged for her to begin working at my office during her off time, keeping up with the copying, filing, data entry, shredding, and so on. I had hired three people in less than one week after connecting with the soul quality on which I had focused! Events were unfolding as if the universe was helping me manifest this.

I did get off balance for a while, mostly with cooking and working out. Surprisingly, when I recalled the positive belief that I chose—that any imbalances would be temporary—it all did get back on track, once the initial, heavy work schedule with my helpers was over.

When Roberta's limiting beliefs were cleared, her soul could take charge of the process of creating her ideal future. Her soul's vision could manifest in her life without unconscious fears sabotaging her. She could listen to her inner guidance, which led her to be in the right place, at the right time, with the right people.

Soul Visioning also helped Luke achieve a breakthrough of his own. Roberta continues:

> My husband Luke and I had been struggling with his mother. She had become increasingly intrusive, in a pressuring and critical way, regarding many aspects of our lives. I told Luke that I expected him to set some firm limits with her and to enforce them. Although Luke agreed, he proved unable to set boundaries with her. He had never been able to do that in the six years we had been married, which created tension between us.
>
> During the weekend we did our Soul Visioning, Luke chose to focus on the career area of his life. However, the negative beliefs relating to his work that he tapped on were probably the same beliefs that were blocking him in this situation with his mother. Within forty-eight hours after the weekend, he had a major confrontation with her. Although dealing with his mother was quite painful and scary for Luke, he said what needed to be said. It has now been fifteen months since we've had a problem with her.

It appears that Luke's decision to participate in Soul Visioning with his wife created a big shift in his family relationships. Although reluctant, he was prepared to change. After doing energy psychology tapping exercises to reprocess his limiting core beliefs, his unconscious mind was receptive to reprogramming a more positive perspective.

Desirable changes have also continued to emerge in many areas of Roberta's life.

> For the past nine months or so, we've been working on a major home remodeling project. When it comes to asking for help in my personal life, I used to have even more mental blocks than

I did with my business. I often yearned for a personal assistant (I'm not yet in an income bracket to warrant that) and then the negative beliefs would begin: Who do you think you are? What's wrong with you that you can't manage this on your own? For this project, we needed to pack up and store the majority of our home furnishings.

With much discomfort, I began to ask around for a local stay-at-home mom who could help me. Nothing was quite working out until I happened to be home due to sickness and snow on one of the two days a month that my housekeeper comes; I hadn't seen her in over eighteen months. She asked me how the house project was coming along. I spontaneously asked if she knew of anyone who could help. She informed me that she could help, but only on Mondays, which happens to be my only free day during the week! We began the following Monday and are now two-thirds of the way through the project.

Some portions of Roberta's ideal future have already manifested, while soul qualities in other areas of her life are in the process of unfolding. Still other aspects of her vision are so positively imprinted in her mind and body that she is already beginning to feel what her life will be like when her vision is fully realized.

Although my ideal future has not completely manifested yet, I now know what it feels like to be less bogged down by all the details of life, the responsibilities, the tasks, the clutter and disorganization that used to hold me back. Of course, I long for even more freedom in my daily life. For example, I'm still the one talking to the bookkeeper, whereas an assistant would be more of a buffer between me and these tasks and helpers. Not having this buffer is interfering with my doing the full extent of my life's work, including writing books and doing more teaching.

But I've never lost the image and feeling of my Future Self in the garden, talking with my personal assistant. This really helped to show me how it would look and feel, internally and externally, to have my environment support my Ideal Self. Such a degree of freedom from daily tasks used to be beyond my wildest dreams. I never had this knowledge, this wisdom, before doing the guided meditation. Along with what I wrote in the "Applying Your Soul Ideals" worksheet, this vision is permanently engraved in my mind.

I've had moments of being and feeling this ideal way. When my bookkeeper had the year-end report ready to email to my accountant for taxes, I was like, oh my God! I don't have to manually record, categorize, and calculate hundreds of receipts. Someone else is doing that! I don't have to be an accountant, bookkeeper, computer expert, and office manager, as well as a therapist.

I've somehow embodied my vision—imprinted it in my mind and body—because during the meditation, I was both in the body of my Future Self and was also looking at my Future Self. So now, when I think about or do something that gives me that feeling, I recognize it, and it gives me that extra boost of courage and motivation to follow my vision.

The Soul Visioning process worked very quickly for Roberta and Luke because they were ready to shift their beliefs. When our unconscious blocks are cleared, the soul can fully guide and express in our life. The soul knows the bigger picture and can bring synchronicities into our life, effortlessly and easily.

A Mountaintop View of a Soul's Vision

Deborah, a naturopathic physician, biofeedback therapist, and advanced energy healer, was fifty-one when she came to me seeking clarity in her soul's vision for her life. She described herself as "pretty joyless and disconnected" earlier in her life, until she pursued her spiritual path of healing. Deborah had three Soul Visioning sessions. I interviewed her one year later to find out how her life was unfolding; edited excerpts from that interview follow here. (It is interesting to note that Deborah is predominantly kinesthetic in her perceptions—that is, sensing through bodily feeling rather than visually. The soul's vision can be perceived in many ways.)

SUSAN: *Do you remember why you wanted to do Soul Visioning? Was it about your career, about where to relocate, or was it more general?*
DEBORAH: It was more general, but it did include all of that—the work, relationships, a place to live.

S: *What was it like for you to connect with your soul?*
D: I got a general vibrational knowingness. It was a big smile, a light heart, this feeling of joy and peace. There was a rightness about this.

S: *I think you are describing that feeling of high vibration that happens when you are in the "flow" of soul connection and expression.*
D: And the visual was a white and golden sparkling light. I was basking in it, and I took it in "cellularly." What I remember [about my soul's vision] is not so much a picture; it was a color and an energetic feeling that I identified and integrated into my being.

When I interviewed Deborah one year after her Soul Visioning sessions, positive change had already manifested in at least two areas of her life, and other welcome changes were underway.

S: *Did you picture and feel the kind of partner you would want?*
D: Well, I do want partnership, but it's got to be the right one, and so the Soul Visioning gave me discernment. Not long after I connected with my soul's vision, an old boyfriend from high school emailed me out of the blue. I was curious and had the whole butterflies-in-the-stomach, young-girl feeling about it all. After further emailing and a very brief phone conversation, I realized I want that feeling and partnership, but his energy didn't

resonate with my future visioning. It was all [about the] old us, like how we used to be. He hasn't moved on at all, but I have, and I recognized that.

Her soul's vision for a relationship gave Deborah an inner template for what a healthy relationship would feel and look like.

D: This relationship with an old flame—which wasn't going to work, but maybe I would've [otherwise] stepped into—helped me to not go into some old patterns. I found out that I can still feel excited about the right person coming. But he wasn't it, and this showed me that I know the difference. It really felt good, that I can trust myself!

S: *It's like having an inner compass.*

D: Yes. I can discern much more quickly and easily whether something is part of my soul's purpose or not.

S: *What about the work area of your life? Did you just envision feeling good about going to work, being passionate about what you want to do?*

D: I did Soul Visioning as I was finishing my naturopathy training. I was already doing the work that I wanted to do. My soul confirmed that I'm doing the right thing now, and yet, I'm keeping myself open for other possibilities. Project work and collaboration came up in my vision, and I know that I can shift. I love the work that I do, but it could also look different, if it needs to be.

Deborah was open to letting her soul guide the visioning process. She allowed it to unfold without needing to work out all the specifics in advance. One aspect of her vision was to be part of an intentional community of like-minded people. During her visioning, she experienced how good it would feel to manifest a lifestyle that would fully support this. Less than a year later, what developed out of this vision was a move to Colorado, and an opportunity to do volunteer work at a center where "cultural creatives" gather to share their diverse interests, services, and products.

S: *How did this idea about moving there come to you? Did it come as a flash of insight or as a synchronicity?*

D: Well, it always sounded intriguing to me. Then when I was in energy healing school, my roommate lived in Colorado. I visited her and I just knew; it was a resonance. Part of my vision was the adventure—where am I going, what's the next turn—and not knowing is OK. I have always had a "trusting place" within me since I was little. So the week before I moved here, I still didn't have a place to stay, and it was like, no problem, it'll work, I'll figure it out. The van was already set up, I was mostly packed, and then a friend called and asked, why not stay at her house until I got settled.

S: *So that trust factor is another aspect of Soul Visioning—your higher soul guidance provides the support that you need when you need it. You're in the right place at the right time with the right people. It's not a matter of "C'est la vie"—it's not that whatever will happen will happen, in an irresponsible way. Instead, it is really being open to guidance and trusting it.*

D: Yes, and so I ended up staying at her house for six months. Then I realized it was time for me to have my own place, and she had another little house, so I'm renting that house. It's in an area that I love, a very family and funky place with hardworking people and artists and musicians, a very nice little community with small, family-owned businesses.

Two key aspects of Deborah's vision were to be connected with people of like mind and to be close to nature. Her vision is now unfolding in a way that fulfills her and resonates with her values.

D: The nature that I was seeking is definitely here—a beautiful, nurturing feminine energy, with the mountains and lots of waterfalls and streams. The biodiversity is incredible. Most people here are environmentally conscious, growing organic food. So food growing, and living communally in some way, that's still in the works. A loose, intentional community is very common here, such as multiple generations under one roof. It's very earthy, a real cross-section of society. Soul guidance helped me not only to move here, but to recognize that the move to Colorado was congruent with my soul's vision.

S: *What else was helpful about accessing the wisdom of your soul?*
D: One thing that really helped was asking myself the question, "What is keeping you from experiencing your soul's vision right now?" That helped me to identify in my body where I was holding myself back. Within a minute, the answer was easily identifiable. That led me into feeling as though I had a heavy boulder on my chest. I realized that it was sadness, and when I thought about it more, I recognized that it was my lineage of sadness, mostly. I remember taking on my mother's sorrow and aloneness. She was one of those women who was way ahead of her time, but grew up back when women had to stay at home. So I felt her lack of feeling self-actualized. I took on all that as a young girl, thinking that I'd be safer if I took some of that on. I think it was an unspoken, unconscious contract.

Deborah's "lineage of sadness" also stemmed from both her parents' alcoholism and emotional unavailability. Because Deborah was already deeply relaxed and connected with her soul's guidance, her intuitive wisdom revealed the solution—how to drop the "boulder" of sadness, the weight of her family legacy that she was unconsciously carrying. She reported feeling lighter after doing this work.

D: I think my parents were very unhappy people. They were German, very serious and hardworking. I don't think my mother felt that she could express who she was, at home. My mother drank. My father was always gone, and he would drink too. During my Soul Visioning, I felt the sadness, knowing that a lot of it was not my own. I was able to breathe into it and let it go, and just say that it's not mine. Not all of it left right away, maybe over a couple of months. But when I would feel that sadness, then I could do the breathing again and let it go. I could energetically feel it melting down my limbs into the earth.

S: *Because you're very kinesthetic.*

D: Yes. I know it wants to be transformed; I know that I don't need or want to keep repressing it or holding on to it. So my breath allows the sorrow to leave. Sometimes I send it to the light, but often I'll send it to Mother Earth to be transformed.

S: *And so you were fully supported by your soul's vision and resources so you could go into that place. During the Soul Visioning guided journey, when people first connect with their ideal future, they have support to work through their blocks. When a person envisions that ideal future, they take a "snapshot" of it. Then they frame it, and put a color or colors in the picture frame. Then they run that color through their body, so it imprints. Is that when you felt those white and golden sparkles go through your body?*

D: Yes, that still resides within me. When I framed it and put color to it, I saw the color pouring through the lobes of my brain and then down through my neck and every part of me, and I recall feeling very warm, very loving, very welcome. I still own my soul's vision of my ideal future. It's a part of me. I'm pretty much there right now, and it's a great place. I've come a long way!

There is a palpable energy and feeling of peace, joy, and well-being that often persists after the Soul Visioning experience. These qualities of the soul are embodied and expressed freely when one's ego limitations are forgiven and released.

. . . .

Now you will meet Jeanette and Mary Margaret, both people who needed other work in addition to the Soul Visioning process before they could move ahead in their lives. Soul growth and healing take place on a continuum. Some people have difficulty even beginning to do Soul Visioning. Often, such people become aware of the power of the unconscious mind only when a life event (such as a death, family illness, divorce, or financial loss) triggers the unhealed parts of themselves. This "soul wake-up call" can be the catalyst for looking deeper into the cause of their unhappiness.

In other words, for more entrenched issues, a combination of therapeutic approaches is often necessary before turning to the Soul Visioning process. We can consider various healing strategies to meet our particular needs. In the stories of Jeanette and Mary Margaret, you will learn about several powerful psycho-spiritual methods that I have used in my counseling practice for people who need a stronger sense of control and safety in the initial stages of their process. These two case histories also demonstrate how Soul Visioning can fit into the therapeutic process.

To find out more about these therapies, or to locate certified practitioners in these areas, see the Resources and Notes sections at the end of this book.

Jeanette Finds Gold in the Dark

A psychotherapist and life coach, Jeanette was in her forties when her sister's suicide attempt served as a catalyst for Jeanette to explore her own unhappy life patterns. She was in a deeply depressed state, feeling stuck and not even worthy of having a soul vision. Her agency job was not allowing her to use her full potential, and her relationship history was disastrous. Jeanette had experienced a trauma in her adolescent years and had a family history of being constantly criticized and teased. She had shut down many of her feelings and walled off her Authentic Self to cope with her sense of shame and inadequacy.

Hers is a story of great courage, perseverance, and commitment to her personal and spiritual growth. Jeanette went through many "dark nights of the soul." She wanted to give up numerous times but never did. Through sheer diligence, she discovered her True Self and is now living her soul's purpose and passion.

Jeanette's Story

In our follow-up interview, Jeanette shared the experiences and processes that brought the most healing on her journey of transformation.

SUSAN: *What was the reason you initially began Soul Visioning?*

JEANETTE: I thought it was about processing my trauma around my sister's suicide attempt. It feels profound to me how that was what finally tipped me to be able to get some help. It opened up so many other unhealed traumas for me. It was my own life that I was saving. Back then, I was depressed beyond hope. I had felt resigned to taking antidepressants for the rest of my life. I wasn't good at relationships, and I believed that I wasn't going to have lasting, loving, deep friendships. There was nothing for me to be passionate and excited about. But I wanted to believe that there was something better in store for my life.

S: *Could you talk about how your soul's vision unfolded?*

J: At first I felt that I didn't even have the ability to vision. In some of my earlier visioning sessions, I just kept faking it—a "fake it 'til you make it" sort of thing. But before I knew it, Soul Visioning opened me up to face that A) there was something else possible for me, and that B) maybe there was that voice of God within that could guide me to let my life unfold. But in the beginning, I remember having a really hard time doing the visioning.

S: *Yes, we have to remove the unconscious barriers, the resistances that sabotage and bar us from accessing our soul's vision and our soul guidance.*

J: But just as I would get in touch with one buried feeling or memory and move through it, another one would pop up. Whether I was looking at my family-of-origin stuff, my unhealed interpretations, or the depression, I just couldn't vision.

S: *Those defenses that we develop in childhood to protect us often become our obstacles in adulthood because they no longer serve us.*

J: Yeah, and they were running my life. I think a turning point for me was the Internal Family Systems method (IFS), because the concept that everyone has a True Self meant that I might have one, too. It wasn't too far out for where I was at that point, to grasp the concept of the parts of us, and how some of those parts can be obstacles. Plus with IFS, there was something else that I could do, other than succumb to the part of me that was running the show. I started to take my power back, and to see myself as potentially a powerful person.

The Internal Family Systems (IFS) model of psychotherapy was developed by Richard Schwartz, PhD, based on principles from Psychosynthesis (Roberto Assagioli), Voice Dialogue (Hal and Sidra Stone), and Family Systems theory. The premise of IFS is that our true identity is perfect, whole, and complete, but we develop unconscious coping strategies or "parts" (subpersonalities) that take over to help us survive. For example, we might have a Judge/Critic, a Controller, a Perfectionist, a Pleaser, or an Inner Child running the show. As one analogy puts it, we are like an orchestra of various parts. The goal is to make our True Self or Higher Self the conductor—the part of us that is calm, compassionate, curious, connected, confident, creative, courageous, and clear.

However, if one of our unconscious parts steps up to the podium, we have disharmony and chaos. The parts that are trying to take control aren't bad; they're just trying to protect us. For example, the Perfectionist part says, "If I am perfect, nobody can criticize or reject me." Of course, this is a false premise, because nobody who is in a body is perfect: we all make mistakes.

The IFS method uses a dialoging process between the True Self and the parts that are acting as coping strategies, to help them realize that there is a better alternative to what they are doing. Often these unconscious parts—we might call them defenses—behave in habitual ways, based on outdated thinking. Until they're convinced that we are safe, they won't release their hold. But once they see that the wise, compassionate, and competent True Self (our soul) can take care of us, they are more likely to step back and let that Higher Self take charge.

The problem is that we may be overly identified with these parts. Earlier in her life, Jeanette's Judge and Critic parts were mostly in charge. The IFS process helped her stop identifying with those parts that were no longer serving her, and allowed her Authentic Self to be her guide.

S: *What else helped you to get unstuck?*

J: I also did a lot of work around rescripting, where I would recall a memory from my childhood, and then I'd go in as an adult [and rescript the painful memory].

Here Jeanette is speaking of Holographic Memory Resolution® work. HMR is a powerful body-centered psychotherapy, developed by Brent Baum, an addictions and trauma therapist. It uses a verbal technique that identifies traumatic or troubling memories that are held in the body. Because the unconscious mind doesn't know the difference between reality and metaphor, it is possible to go back into the memory at whatever age(s) a trauma occurred and gently rescript it without retraumatizing the client. This installs a new "resourced" memory and feeling that releases the old emotional pain. The original event can still be remembered, but without the emotional disturbance.

During Jeanette's HMR session, she remembered that even as a four-year-old, when she tried to sing or dance in front of her family, she was teased and humiliated. Her way of coping was to hide under the table.

She learned that it wasn't safe to be herself, and she tried to become "invisible" and hide her talents (a pattern that she carried into adulthood).

During the rescripting phase, I asked, "If your adult self or Higher Self could go back into that scene and change it, what would you like to see happen?" She decided to envision herself as that four-year-old, being accepted by her family, as if it were happening in the moment.

J: HMR rescripting allowed me to see myself not only as that wounded child, but also as a well-resourced adult who can take care of that part of me now. I had to revisit that wounded child— it felt like one hundred times—and I remember thinking in frustration, "We're going to go *there* again? . . . How is this helping if I'm always rescripting the same scene, working with the same part?" But each time I went there, a little more of it got healed. As soon as I was triggered into the wounded child place, I could then say, "Wait! I have a choice in this moment to access my True Self, that part of me that can resource me right now." Whereas before, I was helpless and powerless around it. Over time, I developed a sense of trust in my soul.

S: *Experientially, you got in touch with your Higher Self, which could reclaim those split-off, wounded parts of you. Developing that "muscle" of the Authentic Self empowered you, so that you identify more strongly with your strengths than your weaknesses.*

J: It also offered me a choice. I think that moving through a lot of that serious darkness is what opened me up to even be able to access my soul's vision in the first place. I didn't think I could connect into some realistic vision. So when I understood that I had a choice, when I wasn't feeling like such a victim 99 percent of the time, I had a whole new filter through which to look. If I could feel better—something I didn't think I was ever going to be able to do—then maybe there was something else I could do, something that I couldn't yet see.

S: *So this brought hope?*

J: Yes, and that's where *A Course in Miracles* came in for me.

Part of Jeanette's journey included discovering her spiritual path, *A Course in Miracles* (ACIM), which is a complete, self-study, psycho-spiritual thought system. ACIM teaches that the way to universal love and peace is by undoing guilt in our unconscious mind through for-giving others. The Course thus focuses on healing relationships. It also emphasizes that ACIM is only one of many versions of the universal curriculum. It is a universal spiritual teaching—not a religion—that aims to remove our blocks to the awareness of love's presence, so that we can get in touch with our own inner teacher, which the Course calls the Holy Spirit.

S: *How did spirituality play into your healing process?*

J: Not being raised with a formal religion of any sort meant to me that I was not worthy of God's love, so it never even occurred to me to seek that. So when ACIM came along, for me it just made so much sense. I didn't have to buy into sin or guilt or fear; I didn't have to believe the Noah's Ark story or any of this other stuff that didn't work for me. I didn't have to have faith in something out there. Instead, I could see that it's all inside here, and I think that was the missing piece for me. I was just going to be asking myself to build on the trust that I'd already built with myself, and have faith that everything I see out there is a projection of my internal world. This put me in such a powerful place. I didn't have to turn over that power to something or someone else.

S: *So that helped you to take the next step. When we connect with our soul and experience that Self as more than just a limited, physical body/ego identity, that's where we find true hope, because that's who we really are.*

J: I no longer had to identify myself as a depressed, traumatized nobody who needed to make up for all the things I had done wrong. I felt ACIM was a perfect part of my journey, to get me to see what would most serve me in the long run. Then I noticed that I was having an easier time meditating; I was just going inside and trusting my inner wisdom. I think that's where Soul Visioning came in, because not only could I hear and see what I wanted to hear and see, but it also fit into a realistic piece of my life. Soul Visioning was really concrete for me, in terms of being available to hear what my purpose was.

S: *How did that unfold? How did your soul communicate, and what did it communicate as your soul's vision for your life?*

J: I always knew that I was supposed to be a communicator, but I didn't always know how. I think that it unfolded through my individual clients first—working with them while I was working my own process helped me see that there was something beyond traditional therapy. And I went through the shadow process. It started when you had me read Debbie Ford's book, *The Dark Side of the Light Chasers,* and that's when it hit me: I was supposed to be teaching and raising the consciousness of the planet, and the only way I could do that was through my personal transformation. But I never would have been able to get there, had I not removed a lot of that stuff that was having me identify myself as someone who was unworthy, incapable, and unlovable.

S: *And where has this vision taken you?*

J: It's taken me to great places! I feel that I am a voice of transformation, however that manifests. I am now a national trainer, helping people to do transformational work. I feel much more connected with my purpose; I have no doubt about what I'm here to do, and I don't have an attachment around how I'm here to do it. I feel so clean and clear.

S: *Which was one of your goals when you were visioning your future?*

J: It was. And I remember getting caught up in thinking that I needed to get really creative, and I wasn't creative. I suddenly saw that I didn't need to re-create the wheel. What I needed was to be open to a body of work that spoke to me, so that I could deliver that work unto the world. Shortly thereafter I went through the Shadow Process weekend. And literally, before anyone spoke or anything happened, I just knew [that this was the work I wanted to do]. I would not have known this had I not been able to move out of those limiting beliefs.

The Shadow Process, developed by best-selling author Debbie Ford, is a spiritually based emotional education program designed to uncover and heal the parts of ourselves we have disowned—our shadow. By embracing the shadow (finding our gifts, or the "gold in the dark," as Carl Jung said), we can remove the blocks that prevent us from having the life we want.

S: *Have you experienced that soul guidance works through intuition, through synchronicities?*

J: Yes. Especially now that I have that clean presence and availability, I can hear that intuition. Not only do I hear it, but I follow it now. I trust it. Which ties into that trust-building piece ... Without that, I wouldn't have had experience with trust. Now I find myself looking for opportunities to listen in.

S: *How do you do that?*

J: Each morning when I wake up, I spend ten minutes checking in with myself quietly, asking what kind of day I want to have, and how can I be of service today. Sometimes I set an intention for the day and a word pops into my mind, and I'll revisit it all day. Almost every time, it has some significant relevance to what occurs in my day. It's an interesting way to be present and conscious around how I'm living and the choices that I'm making.

S: *That is what this book is about, how to live a joyful, soul-guided life. You're talking about being in touch with your soul guidance and letting it express through you. What an amazing journey.*

J: You can choose pain if you need to, but it's not a prerequisite for being on this earth. I figure I'm going to be here anyway, I might as well have some choices around it. Even in my worst moments now, when I'm feeling like a victim or going through some challenge, I can ask, "What's going on in me that would have me create this, or why do I need to see it this way?" And it offers me an opportunity to shift my perceptions.

S: *This has not been a quick fix for you. Do you have any words of encouragement or advice for people?*

J: Healing at the core is what's significant. Trying to just heal symptoms like depression, or trying this drug or that drug, or doing breathing exercises four times a day, doesn't really heal anything. I think that healing is about being willing to get at the root and find out, once and for all, what is driving these negative beliefs. It's about healing them, not just curing a symptom that will return later.

S: *Has doing that impacted every area of your life—your relationships, your health, your finances, your spirituality, your work?*

J: Everything. Even though I still don't have a primary relationship, I don't have the devastation around that, the perceived hole in myself. Would I like to have somebody in my life? Absolutely, but I don't feel like something's missing anymore.

It seems that Jeanette has mastered a key lesson concerning her need for a primary relationship. She has learned to stand on her own two feet. She now values her wholeness, rather than needing a special relationship to fill an emptiness or distract her from feelings of unworthiness. Perhaps she wouldn't have been as motivated to change or heal herself if she had anesthetized herself with romantic love. Or perhaps she would have fallen into a pattern of attracting unhealthy relationships until she learned to love herself. Now, either with a relationship or without one, she is fulfilled and happy.

S: *You're such a good example of someone who did their work. Even in the darkest night of the soul, you stuck it out.*

J: I get it that I really hung in there, but I also felt that it was safe for me to go wherever I needed to go, throughout the depths of it. I think that's significant, finding the right person to work with—someone who has done their own work.

S: *And it is important to work with someone who can serve as a cheerleader, someone who can be the mirror of your own soul's perfection until you can remember it for yourself. I am so deeply grateful that you're willing to share your story. I think it's going to inspire many people who are going through the dark night of the soul, and who have asked, how long does this take, and is there any hope and any light? You're an example of a person who hung in there, did the work, and got through it. You came out on the other side, and your life is amazing.*

Jeanette is now a trainer in the field of emotional and spiritual education. This is quite remarkable, considering that she once was in a deeply depressed state of mind, feeling small and invisible. Now she has found her passion and is sharing her considerable talents for the greater good. She has a wonderful community of like-minded friendships, her business is flourishing, and she is fulfilling her soul's vision. It is as though the lampshade has been taken off the light of her soul, so it can radiate to all those who are ready to emerge from their own shadow self.

To learn more about the therapeutic and personal growth methods discussed in this case study, see the Resources section for websites and recommended books.

From High Society to Homelessness

Mary Margaret had hit bottom. In her mid-sixties, she was about to be released from a homeless shelter. She had no family, no job, poor health, and nowhere to go. She was angry at the world and the people she believed had victimized her. But she was motivated to do the work to change her life.

As someone with a deeply entrenched victim script, Mary Margaret needed help to manifest her soul's vision. For over two years, she went through many stages of healing and many methods of therapy with me. In addition to Soul Visioning, I used hypnotherapy (specifically, age regression) to help her to re-parent her own inner child and to rescript difficult childhood scenes. I also used meridian therapies (tapping on pressure points to remove limiting core beliefs), affirmations (to reinforce a more positive view of herself), grief and loss work (mourning and saying goodbye to her mother and her previous therapist, both of whom had died suddenly), forgiveness work (of herself and others), and soul work (reconnecting with a healthy spirituality).

Mary Margaret's persistent efforts paid off. She envisioned her ideal future, reconnected with her spirituality, practiced forgiveness of those she felt had abused her, and rescripted her unconscious self-limiting beliefs. Mary Margaret empowered herself, stepped out of her victim script, and manifested the job of her dreams at the age of sixty-eight. The number of times that she wanted to quit therapy, but didn't, is testimony to her courage in facing herself.

Mary's Margaret's Story

In her story here, excerpted from an interview two years after my therapy with her, Mary Margaret doesn't talk much about her deep sorrow when recalling her childhood wounds. Often, after healing, a person doesn't want to revisit that old energy—or they may even forget about the rut they were in.

Here is her story, in her words.

My name is Mary Margaret. I was the fifth and last child in a family of four older brothers. There was a nine-year gap between my youngest brother and myself.

Both of my parents grew up pretty poor. My mom had always desired a girl, and she wanted me to have "the best of everything." She chose a private Catholic school for me because it offered piano, violin, drama, toe dancing, and art. So I was able to do all the things she never was able to do growing up.

My mother had rheumatic fever as a child. Back then, the treatment for rheumatic fever was to rest, so my mother had her lessons at home and couldn't even go out and play. The fever affected the valves of her heart. After her first baby, her cardiologist advised her not to have any more children. But my mother proceeded to have five more sons—the last were stillborn twins—then she had me many years later.

As a young child, I wasn't consciously aware of how serious my mother's health problems were. But I felt all the stress and strain of her illness. She had episodes of heart trouble and some mini strokes when I was about four or five, but she would always rebound from them. I remember being afraid to be alone with her after the first one, because I didn't know what to do.

My mother told me that she lost her mom when she was about twelve. Ironically, I lost my mom when I was twelve. I will never forget the day she died in front of me. She was talking with neighbors on the sofa. In the middle of a sentence, her head fell back, and she died.

When Mary Margaret talked about her mother's death, she displayed posttraumatic stress responses: her skin grew pale and her eyes glazed over. It was as if she was that child again, frozen in time in those memories. She was eventually able to access her feelings and grieve the loss of her mother. She reclaimed parts of her inner child and provided them with safety and comfort through an age regression process.

Angry and Abandoned

I was a very angry, lonely, abandoned little girl. My mom had died at the end of May, and I had a piano recital coming up the following week. I remember feeling appalled because my family insisted that I play in the recital. When it was my turn to play, somehow I sat down at the piano, and my fingers moved, and everybody clapped, and I walked out. It felt unreal, like a dream.

My father brought my middle brother and his wife and new-born baby to live with us in our house, so that I would have somebody to take care of me during my eighth grade. Nine weeks after my mom died, I was in the kitchen with my oldest sister-in-law, peeling potatoes. I saw my dad's Cadillac pull up. I remember seeing he had a passenger. It was a stranger, and I had no reason to know who this was, but I said to my sister-in-law, "My dad's getting married again." I flew up the stairs, locked my bedroom door, and I started sobbing. It took several requests before I finally came down. What amazed me is that I was right. My father introduced me to a lady who, a year later, became my stepmother. Evidently, my brothers all knew that she existed for at least six or seven years prior to my mom's death.

My future stepmother was very removed from me. She had never been married or been around children. When I would visit her, she would always take me shopping. I was polite, and she was very formal and distant.

The following summer, my father and new stepmother married. A month later, they announced that I was going to boarding school.

Sent Away to School

I had just graduated eighth grade, and I had expected to go to the same school as my entire class for our freshman year. I really felt devastated because those were all my friends. I was told, "You will love this boarding school. Your sister-in-law went there for high school; so did her sister."

After the first year, I acclimated myself to it, and when I would come home in the summer, I couldn't wait to go back to get away from the tension of the "family." I guess my father made my brothers feel obligated to visit me on "Visiting Sunday" at the boarding school. They did not want to do that. My youngest brother, Charlie, never came. He refused to come.

What made me especially angry is that my father gave my stepmother all my mother's jewelry, and she wore it. It broke my heart. I would see her wearing some pin that my father had given to my mom—my mom was so proud of her jewelry. I would see my stepmother throwing her stuff around, and I was angry. But I was too young to speak up and say, "What are you doing?" Besides, I would just be shut down. Anger was not allowed.

Now, I have learned all that anger went inside, and my gut has paid for it with lifelong gastrointestinal trouble since my mom died.

Mary Margaret's coping style was to "stuff" her feelings, which then took the form of intestinal distress. She still needed to acknowledge her feelings and learn to express them. In her sessions with me, I validated the inner-child part of her that had felt rage at her mother "leaving" her and at her father's emotional unavailability. This was not to blame her parents, but rather to acknowledge the younger parts of her that were carrying "frozen emotions" in her body. When she accepted and expressed those disowned feelings, she could resolve them and move on.

Emotional Collapse at College

I wanted to go to Northwestern University in Illinois. If I couldn't go there, then I wanted to go somewhere far away. But the nuns in my boarding school kept pushing for their sister school. They had such influence on me, because I had no other influence. My brothers and their wives were busy raising their children. My father had absolutely no involvement with me except to give me money and charge cards. My stepmother's interaction with me was limited to shopping or lunch. Thus the nuns persuaded me to attend a Catholic college.

At the beginning of my third year, I had an emotional collapse and started having a lot of gastrointestinal trouble. My past had caught up with me. I dropped out of college that year. Our family doctor put me on phenobarbital to "calm my stomach down." It caused me to sleep night and day. After months of this, one of my sisters-in-law got me an appointment with Father Joseph, a Jesuit psychiatrist. Father Joseph encouraged me to go back to school. I transferred my credits to the school where my psychiatrist was teaching. I became very interested in psychology and was good at it.

Father Joseph: Blurring the Boundaries

Father Joseph became the father that I never had. I used to pick him up in the morning and give him a ride, because priests didn't have their own cars. We dined together often. He took me out to dinner for my twenty-first birthday. Sometimes I would invite him—when my parents were gone—over to their house, and cook him dinner.

I didn't know it, but Father Joseph had alcohol problems. I would make him a martini, not knowing that I was enabling his alcoholic behavior. I feel so badly about it now. He was absolutely brilliant. He had patients all over the world. I was using him as a father figure, which probably helped me, but also enabled him in his alcohol problem.

There were definitely times when the boundaries got blurred. But it was when he was drinking. I never connected it; I just didn't realize what was going on. When Father Joseph was not drinking, he was very kind, very compassionate, and totally boundary-appropriate. But if we went out to dinner and he had a couple of drinks, there would be a weakening of the boundaries. Of course, in those days, what I was just dying for was somebody to care about me.

Once, we went to his home. Certain priests lived in an apartment building off campus. We had both been drinking, and we went to dinner, and he invited me to his apartment. It was 2 a.m. Sex was going to be the next step. I was totally willing for this but I had my period, and he said, "Go home, and don't make a sound to wake up any of the other guys in the building." I remember tiptoeing down the back stairs and getting in my car at 3 a.m. Later he said, "I have a priest friend, and I want you to go there, because we're both Catholic and we both need to go to confession." I did.

Our relationship was much more professional after that. But Father Joseph was still very close to my heart, and I was to his.

No Time to Say Goodbye

Whatever medications I was on, I had trouble getting up in the morning. Father Joseph would call me every morning to see how I was doing. I think he realized the state of emotional abandonment I was in. One Sunday morning in January, I expected a call within a certain time range. He was like clockwork. When he didn't call, I phoned the college and asked to speak to him. There was a long pause, and I remember this woman coming back to the switchboard saying, "Father Joseph is dead. We didn't see him this morning for mass, and your call startled us, so we went and knocked on his door and found him dead."

I sobbed the entire day. I told my father, and he must have known how important Father Joseph was to me. When the funeral was held a couple of days later, both my father and my stepmother went with me, which amazed me. I went out to lunch after the funeral with Father Joseph's married sister. She said, "I think he would have left the priesthood for you." On some level I know he was taken with me. But he died. Another loss, just like my mother. No time to say goodbye.

Mary Margaret had repeated losses that were not resolved. She was able to get closure with Father Joseph by writing a letter to him in therapy that expressed what she never got to say when he was alive. A flood of tears that she had held back poured from the depth of her being as she read the letter to me. I asked her to have Father Joseph write a letter back to her, from a soul level, telling her what he would want her to know. This process let Mary Margaret bring release and closure to an important relationship.

I had talked with Father Joseph in therapy about my moving out of the family home and getting my own place, to become my own person. Nine months after he died, I moved out. I was twenty-two.

I continued with my schooling, but dropped out of all the courses that were not psychology. The dean asked me, "How can anybody get straight A's in psychology and fail other subjects?" I just said nothing. He was furious with me. He said, "You know you are wasting your father's money."

My dad was starting to have some health problems. My brother Rick would say to me, "You are the reason that Dad is getting sick. You have given him nothing but grief." The day I moved out of my parents' house, Rick blocked the door. He asked, "Where are you going?" I said, "I'm moving to my apartment." He said, "You're killing your father." I pushed past him. I didn't say a word. I just threw my stuff in my car and drove away.

I remember going into my new apartment. I had all new furniture my father had gotten me, and I lay on the top of the bed, and I just felt at peace. My physical body felt relief and went, "Thank you!"

Becoming a Teacher

During high school summer breaks, my brothers had started working at the family company, learning the business from the ground up. They all knew that once they finished college, they had a career in the family business. However, I was never expected to go into the family business, and when I asked if I could do it, my father told me harshly, "This is a man's business. You go be a teacher. Forget it!"

The Catholic School Board was looking to hire trainees to become teachers. If you qualified, they would put you into a teacher-training program for two or three months. If you passed it, they would find you a position. I sailed through the teacher-training program, and was hired as a full-time teacher for sixth grade. I did that for eleven years.

The money I made as a teacher in the Catholic school system was pitiful. We teachers used to joke that we were donating our time, because the Catholic schools paid so poorly. But I loved teaching, and I would put my own money into it if they didn't have enough books for the classroom or if the children needed anything. When I moved to a new school uptown, the children were very poor. I would buy them all earmuffs, gloves, and things like that. I always figured the money to do that would be there.

Money, Money, Everywhere . . . and Spending Every Bit

My father was very wealthy, so when he died, he left a significant amount of money to all of us. Fifty percent went to my stepmother, and the other half was divided up equally among my four brothers and me.

Whatever money came into my hands . . . I spent. The only way I knew to feel better physically and emotionally was to go shopping. Years later, I remember my first therapist saying, "Well, you didn't do drugs, you didn't do alcohol, and you didn't gamble, so you used shopping as a way to soothe the ache in your soul." This is exactly what my stepmother did as well. The only times my father ever screamed at me were over parking tickets and the bill from my favorite department store, which would sometimes be four pages long. But my stepmother had a part in it too. I remember him screaming at both of us.

I would accumulate a lot of debt, and then I would go running to my brother Rick to be bailed out. I had no concept about saving money. Rick would scream at me when I came to him to pay my bills. I would be so frightened that the bills wouldn't get paid, that I would drive to his home knowing that I would be subjected to hours of horrendous verbal abuse.

Eventually, my brothers sold the family business. They had equal shares, and I had a little bit less. I remember my brothers saying, "We are giving you what you deserve, and don't ask us for more. If you don't take the amount of money that is offered now, there could be a day when you are driving your car and the brakes will just not work for you."

Wandering in the Desert

I never went back to finish college. Then my principal told me, "I'm not renewing your contract." I had not taken the courses for the teaching degree that the school board now required; I hadn't had enough confidence in myself to finish my degree. I was devastated because I loved teaching.

My life fell apart again. Instead of finishing my degree, I spent thirty years wandering in the desert, so to speak, drifting from job to job as an employee of a large retail chain or as an office temp. I also looked for the man of my dreams and the little white picket fence, but never found them. Going from man to man, I hung on for years to relationships that were bad choices. I tried to make them work. I couldn't figure out why they wouldn't work.

Financially, I slowly went down the tubes. I started having difficulty on the job and couldn't pay bills. My workplace had a lot of chemical and environmental problems. I was having severe health problems that were later diagnosed as environmental, chemical, and food allergies. I was getting sicker and sicker.

Spiraling Down Into Homelessness

My life took a tailspin. I woke up on a Christmas morning in a homeless shelter with young women who were victims of domestic violence. I also sabotaged myself out of my job. I did not want my employer to know where I was living or what I was doing. I worked all the time. But they wanted me to work on Thursday nights, and the homeless shelter had a Thursday night counseling group that we had to attend. So I was out of a job. My brothers were furious with me, because the work ethic in our family is huge. In my family, if you are not working, you'd better be dead.

At the same time, the homeless shelter said it was almost time to leave. So here I was. My family had totally abandoned me. I was sick. I had no job, and it was time for me to leave the homeless shelter. I had nowhere to go.

I wanted to find an attorney and go after my brothers. They were all millionaires. They sold the company for millions of dollars. I had been raised a princess, and I felt part of this money was my entitlement. I was angry, resentful, and caught in bitterness—how dare they cheat me?

My soul cried out one day, and I knew I needed help. I asked my allergist to give me the name of somebody I could talk to, and that turned out to be Susan Wisehart, and here I am.

I have found that when we hit bottom, we get our soul's loudest wake-up call. What struck me about Mary Margaret, from a therapist's standpoint, was her willingness to do the work. She had genuinely hit bottom. Her health, money, home, and family were gone. By the time I saw her, she was truly motivated to change her life.

Part of Mary Margaret's personal evolution was to learn that her worth did not depend on her external accomplishments. Even if she was homeless, ill, and without a job, she was still a beautiful soul, a treasured child of God.

One of the first things Mary Margaret did with me was to start envisioning the life that she wanted. The Soul Visioning process helped her connect with her inner guidance, which directed her to a community church. The church placed her with a family that genuinely welcomed her into their home.

I Am Not a Victim!

Initially I was angry at my brothers and accused them of everything, and accepted very little responsibility. Even though I felt like a victim, in my soul I knew this was not what was meant for me. I learned what a victim is and how that identity blocks growth. Something in me said that God did not put me on this earth to fall into a ditch and die. I learned, from Soul Visioning and from going to a community church, that we have a purpose in this life. I thought, there is a Higher Power, and if you believe in that higher power, you are not alone. If you learn how to vision a future for yourself, there is a possibility that you can make it come true. I started to peel away the layers of doubting myself.

When I first began therapy, I felt that I couldn't do anything without my brothers. I was devastated that they wouldn't accept me in their club. It took a couple of years of therapy to realize that theirs wasn't the club that I belonged in. I felt like an emotional orphan and had to come to terms with the loss of my mom. When a child loses a parent, it's something you never get over completely, so you really have to process the loss.

Eventually Mary Margaret started taking responsibility for herself and her own life—but only after a lot of inner work. She was committed to going back and clearing some of those blockages and wounded parts of her inner child. She resolved to deal with her sense of loss and abandonment and rebuild her self-esteem. Gradually she saw that she had choices, that she could create the life she wanted. Once she started to see her options, she started to change her beliefs. "I've got to get this money from my brothers" was replaced by "What do I want from me, from my life, from now on?" At the same time, she also started to heal unfinished business from the past. Eventually there was a big breakthrough—she started to forgive her brothers.

Forgiveness Offers Freedom

At first I could intellectually say that my brothers made their own mistakes, but I had not really forgiven them. When I really started to forgive my brothers, it wasn't just words. I was emotionally ready to let it go. I learned from therapy that they are struggling and suffering in their own lives. They have their own issues to deal with from our family history. They did what they had learned and thought was the best. I released the resentment inside of my gut, and it freed me to start to vision my own future.

Once Mary Margaret began coming from a place of empowerment— her Authentic Self—she was no longer the needy child seeking something to fill her up or someone to take care of her. She was coming from a place of wholeness. Soon after she began the forgiveness process, she started envisioning more of what she wanted, the kind of work environment and lifestyle that would express her soul.

The more centered I got, and my belief in my real self came to the fore, synchronicity started happening.

I began looking for jobs. I got one job that at least carried me through. I revised my resume and started knocking on doors. Somehow, by some Higher Power, I got called for an interview. The job was everything I knew how to do and do well—selling properties and helping seniors move into a retirement building with assisted services. I now enjoy every minute of my day. I get feedback from these eighty- and ninety-year-old people that brings joy to my life. They love me. This job is everything that is meant to be for me. I have won awards for being an example of the company's mission statement, which just made me sob. The residents voted the award to me for creating opportunities for seniors to live meaningful and enriching lives.

During my thirty years of wandering, I stayed out of the church. I had had an abortion; I was dating a married man. I was denied absolution by the Catholic Church, and reminded myself that only God has the right to tell me I'm not forgiven. Now I have come back—not to the Catholic Church, but to a beautiful community church that helps us understand that we are all treasured children of God.

I even went back to school thirty years after I had left, and I got my degree. At sixty-eight years old, I am living proof that you can change your life. You can, with the help of God and a good therapist. You can experience everything you ever hoped for, and become a channel of blessings to this world. It took me three years of therapy to achieve this and to remember my Authentic Self.

Mary Margaret is an example of someone who, growing up, had everything materially but nothing emotionally. Money isn't the key to happiness, and it can't fill up emptiness and hurt. In Mary Margaret's case, shopping became an addiction and an anesthetic, one that almost landed her on the street.

What helped me connect strongly with Mary Margaret was my own childhood in a family that literally took care of homeless people on the streets of Miami. (My grandparents started one of that city's first homeless shelters in the 1930s.) And I know that when it comes to addictions, whether it's alcoholism or shopaholism, the cause is the same: a deep sense of self-loathing and unlovability. But beneath the addict's self-destructive behavior is a pain that invites our compassion. As we just learned in the previous chapter on soul forgiveness, any condemnation that we may feel, for Mary Margaret or any of the other people whose stories are included in this book, reflects in some way how we feel about ourselves.

May these stories provoke, inspire, and challenge you to discover your own soul's vision. If a homeless woman can change her life, think what you can do!

Part Two

Healing through Spiritual Regression Therapy

We carry unconscious memories from the past—including past lives—that continue to affect us both positively and negatively. I have found that recalling and resolving past-life memories is profoundly healing for many people who come from this perspective, as the stories in chapter 9 demonstrate.

A discussion of this nature often brings up the concepts of karma and reincarnation. There are hundreds of books on those subjects, and I don't intend to prove or disprove the existence of multiple lives. My interest as a therapist is in whether these concepts are useful and helpful to some of my clients in their healing process.

Some of my clients have views of karma that I believe can be self-defeating. For example, they may tolerate abusive situations, saying, "Oh, this is just my karma." This may be coming from self-judgment; they may believe they are guilty for past-life actions for which they deserve punishment. At a personality level, we may misunderstand karma by believing that it involves some form of penalty, retribution, or debt that needs to be repaid. These ideas about karma are based on ego thinking, which casts us in the role of a victim acted upon by some external force over which we have little or no control.

I see karma from a different point of view. Rather than punishment and retribution, I look at karma as the lessons we are learning while we are in this classroom called Earth. A useful way to think about karma is that it is simply a matter of memories, patterns, and habits carried over from one incarnation to another. These memories may be in the form of desire patterns, strong beliefs, unconscious urges, and what appear to be unwarranted emotional responses.

Past-life memory is mainly a matter of unconscious feelings that seem to arise from a source other than our current life experience. Some people ask, "Why bother exploring past-life memories?" The answer: it's an opportunity to resolve the repeating karmic patterns, cellular memories, and blockages that can sabotage the fulfillment of our soul's intent.

If we understand that karma is actually memory, then it is the unconscious energy of those memories that is affecting us. However, we were the authors of the experiences and thinking that created those memories. Essentially, we are reading the book of our own mind. No one outside of us wrote any of the words in that book. Put another way, we have sown the seeds of particular desires, urges, and impulses that have later produced the fruits of certain actions.

In one sense, karma is merely a set of habits that we've developed based on the choices that we've made. Our only real choice is whether to become aware of the unconscious past-life patterns that may be influencing our current decisions or behavior.

Innate talents and abilities that we seem to be born with arise not only from genetically inherited patterns, but also from memories of past-life experiences in which we have developed these gifts. Accessing these memories may help us to more fully express these abilities in our present incarnation, to the extent that they are relevant to our current soul purpose.

The power of therapies that involve accessing unconscious memories from other experiences is that we are no longer a victim of our own unconscious. We only need to change the patterns we ourselves have created. Once we become aware of the memories that are still affecting us, we can forgive them and choose a different "script" for our life, one that is more often guided by our soul.

Ultimately, none of our unconscious impulses, desires, or karmic memory patterns can supersede the Will of our soul in any choice that we make. But until we are aware of patterns that are out of harmony with our soul nature, we may not be able to deal with them effectively. Unless we are also aware of our soul ideal and purpose, these unconscious habitual memory patterns compete for control of our personality. Our experiences become an opportunity to learn what unconscious memories we are holding on to that are in conflict with our soul's vision. By choosing the soul's ideal as a standard to govern the quality of our motivation, we can measure our desires and impulses against that standard before allowing them to motivate our actions.

Only by confronting our unconscious fears, doubts, and anger can we begin to discover the sources of those feelings. By allowing our soul to guide the process of changing those patterns, we can accelerate our healing process. The key to our healing is letting go of these unconscious patterns with forgiveness. Soul forgiveness is about recognizing the eternal spiritual nature of others and ourselves. This realization replaces all the mistaken beliefs and ideas we carry in our unconscious memory.

Chapter 8 describes two methods of regression therapy that can assist in this process. Both require the services of qualified professional therapists; please see the Resources section for information on professional organizations that may provide referrals. In chapter 9, we will meet some remarkable people whose experiences with these approaches have enriched their lives and deepened their soul connection.

Past-Life Regression (PLR) therapy is a tool that helps us get in touch with the root causes of repeating, unconscious patterns from previous lives that may be influencing our current life. This approach is often effective when other methods have not worked because, through a form of hypnosis, it goes to the root cause of our unresolved challenges.

The amazing thing about PLR is that we don't have to believe in reincarnation or past lives for it to be effective. The unconscious mind doesn't know the difference between metaphor and reality, so the information that comes forth under hypnosis can be used to resolve underlying blockages. When we heal our unfinished business from the past, we become more aligned with our soul guidance and purpose. I have successfully used this tool in my practice, and you will soon meet several people who healed themselves through this process.

Another life-transforming method is the **Life-Between-Lives Regression (LBL)** process developed by Michael Newton, PhD. These regressions reveal what happens in the spirit realm in *between* incarnations. This experience often involves a meeting with our soul group (those who have incarnated many times with us), our personal spirit guides and mentors, and the Soul Council of Elders (advanced beings and master teachers).

The Soul Council meeting is an unconditionally loving review of our most immediate past life and our current life, so that we may better understand our soul contracts and life purpose and heal repeating karmic patterns. The meeting with our soul group assists us in understanding the roles that various beings play in our life, such as soul mates. This three- to four-hour process connects us more deeply with an awareness of our true nature as a soul.

The stories presented in chapter 9 show how LBL and PLR can heal unconscious blocks from other lifetimes that are affecting our current incarnation. They describe how people have cleared repeating patterns from their past-life unconscious memories and connected with their unlimited soul wisdom. These case histories include excerpts from follow-up interviews that demonstrate the short-term and long-term benefits of the regression sessions, as well as edited transcripts of actual sessions (names have been changed to protect confidentiality).

Through these accounts, we will gain a better understanding of how the soul guides the regression process. Often, the soul may prompt people to experience more than one type of regression or inner work during a single session. For example, during a Soul Visioning session, a past-life memory or a childhood experience that is affecting the current lifetime may surface to be resolved. Sometimes people choose to have a separate follow-up PLR session to focus on a particular issue. The LBL experience helps people make a deeper connection to their soul and to its higher guidance to gain a broader perspective. Soul-directed inner work produces remarkable results, as these personal narratives demonstrate.

eight

Past-Life Regression and Life-Between-Lives Regression

ost of us have barriers in certain areas of our life. We may be sailing along smoothly in our career, but our primary relationship is a disaster. Even if we can easily point to our problem areas, we may need a little help to figure out what's causing them. Some issues are longstanding and deeply buried beneath our conscious awareness. Many of us are oblivious to the "hidden" parts of ourselves that motivate us, the programs running in the background behind the screen of our conscious mind.

Any area of our life is "grist for the mill" of practicing forgiveness and undoing the guilt and/or fear in our unconscious mind. (Some stories of people who have faced and overcome their own unconscious issues will follow in chapter 9.) That is why I would like to introduce you to two other soul-based therapies, past-life regression (PLR) and life-between-lives regression (LBL)—more methods for unblocking and clearing the path to the joy of your soul. Sometimes we need to go beyond what energy psychology methods can do in reprocessing our limiting beliefs and self-sabotaging behaviors. If you have tried the WHEE method, for-giveness practices, and affirming your soul's vision but are still stuck, you might want to consider PLR for a deeper look at what patterns are still affecting you. These regression therapies often work when other approaches don't. An LBL spiritual regression session will give you the benefit of a much-expanded state of soul consciousness with all the sup-port of your "soul team." There are fewer ego filters in this soul realm, and answers to our toughest questions flow with more ease.

Past-Life Regression Therapy

Past-life regression is a process of going back into a previous lifetime through hypnosis, thereby accessing memories to discover unresolved patterns and unfinished business that is still affecting this lifetime. Many years ago, I started incorporating past-life regression therapy into my private practice with clients who were open to these ideas. I am most grateful to Brian Weiss, MD, a Yale-trained psychiatrist and author of *Many Lives, Many Masters,* who has been a major spokesperson for the field of PLR, for having the courage to speak openly about this topic.

While PLR therapy is not yet widely accepted within the mainstream field of psychology, it is practiced by an ever-growing group of licensed and certified professionals. A good regression therapist needs ground-ing in hypnotherapy practices as well as psychological training to deal with the complexities of mental health issues. (A number of organiza-tions conduct professional training at various levels. For more infor-mation or to consult a qualified PLR regression therapist, see the Re-sources portion of this book.)

I do not set out in this book to prove the existence of reincarnation. Rather, our focus here is on the potential healing benefits of past-life regression journeys. People do not need to believe in past lives for the regression process to heal and transform longstanding issues. As a psy-chotherapist, I am interested in whether a therapeutic method is use-ful and helpful. I am convinced that PLR works: many of my clients get better faster, and it seems to get to the "root cause" or origin of repeating patterns. The more we forgive and heal the unconscious guilt in our mind, the more we can access our connection with our soul.

Sometimes it is easier to look at our own repeating patterns by viewing their origin in a past life, as a third-party observer, rather than by squarely confronting uncomfortable themes we have denied within ourselves in this life. During PLR, the past life unfolds as a story—in some ways like a sleeping dream, in which material from our waking life is presented indirectly through symbols and metaphors. This allows our conscious mind to process our beliefs and patterns with more detachment and compassion. Because our unconscious mind can't distinguish between reality and metaphor, it treats our past-life events as if they are happening in the present. In that way, trauma from the past can be healed in the present.

The Past-Life Regression Process

Past-life regression is a two-hour process with hypnosis. The kind of hypnosis used is a deeply relaxed state of focused concentration. This is *not* stage hypnotism—the kind where you are unconscious, squawk like a chicken, reveal your deepest secrets, and remember nothing afterward. During a PLR, you are in control of the process, but you choose to tune out distractions and focus on an inner experience of the past-life memories that come to the surface. You are in a trance—but remember, trance states aren't unusual. For example, have you ever daydreamed while driving down the expressway and missed your exit? That is a light trance. The same thing happens at the movies, when you are so engrossed in what is happening on the screen that you forget that you are in the theatre. The depth of trance you are likely to experience in PLR is deeper than that, but not so deep that you don't remember the experience. Part of your mind still knows that you are in the room, carrying on a conversation.

It is a misconception that people who experience past-life regression only remember famous lives, such as Cleopatra or Ben Franklin. Of the thousands of clients I have "regressed"—guided through PLR—only a few thought they had been well known in a previous life. Many lives people revisit are very mundane and commonplace.

About three-quarters of the people I regress are able to access a past life in their first session. Some people don't get there right away because they need more practice in relaxing and letting go of their left-brain, linear, analytical mindset. Others are a little anxious and are not ready to process certain past-life material. As a result, their unconscious defenses block the information. Usually after some practice with meditation, guided imagery, using the CDs available through my website, or even working with nighttime dreams, most people can access a past-life memory. Dr. Brian Weiss has noted his own challenges with remembering his past lives: it took ninety days of his own regression work before he accessed his first past-life memory.[1] So don't be discouraged if you don't experience a former life on your first try.

Not everyone gets vivid images and details when they recall past lives. Most people process information using all the senses, but with one sense most prominent. If your dominant sense is not visual, you may receive information on a more bodily level, through kinesthetic awareness—having a gut feeling or a felt intuition about the past-life memory. Or if you are hearing-dominant (auditory awareness), you may experience past-life events as an inner conversation.

How do you know which is your dominant sense? Try this: Imagine a beach scene. Notice the beautiful blue colors of the ocean, feel the warm sand under your feet, smell the fresh sea breeze, and hear the waves splashing against the shore. Which instructions were you most easily able to follow? Which sense came through strongest for you? You can also tell by your own language. Do you often say, "I *see* what you mean" (visual) or "I *hear* what you say" (auditory) or "It *feels* right to me" (kinesthetic)? This is another clue to your sensory dominance.

Does PLR entail any risks? I have found the process to be quite safe, although some screening is needed; it is not appropriate for people with severe mental disorders such as schizophrenia. If the memories are intense, the person does not need to relive them at their original intensity. The scenes can be viewed in an observer mode (as if watching a movie) if necessary. Otherwise, for the most part, the person remembers the past life and speaks from a first-person perspective.

Many people turn to PLR because they want to address specific issues, such as phobias, unexplained anxieties, physical symptoms, or other patterns that haven't responded to self-inquiry or conventional intervention. They may feel stuck in their career, relationships, finances, or another life area. Other people don't come seeking help with a specific issue; they just let their unconscious mind take them to the life that is most relevant and helpful. I've found that the soul usually guides people to where they need to go.

The past-life journey begins with various methods of hypnosis, depending on the client's needs: often progressive muscle relaxation is helpful, along with some guided imagery such as imagining a "tunnel of time" through which they travel. After the person is deeply relaxed, the unconscious mind is open to suggestion.

Next, I instruct the person to go back to the root cause of their major issue, or I suggest they go to a lifetime that has relevance to the person's current life. Images and impressions begin to surface in answer to my questions: Is it a bright and sunny day, or is it dark and overcast? Is the temperature warm, cool, or moderate? Are you in a town, a city, or the countryside? Look down at your feet. Feel or notice what you are wearing on your feet, if anything. Are you old, young, or middle-aged?

Once connected with a past life, the client reviews the important events, themes, and interactions with people that are happening in that lifetime.

Then I guide them to the last day of that life to determine what thoughts, feelings, and physical sensations are present at the time of death. These are imprinted into the unconscious mind and are often carried into the next lifetime as core beliefs and symptoms. By bringing these to conscious awareness, the person can potentially reprocess and heal them. I give the client a suggestion to go through the death calmly and without pain or distress.

Then I transition the client from the death scene to the spirit realm, where they connect with their compassionate, nonjudgmental Higher Self. This consciousness is an expanded state of awareness that knows the bigger picture and can answer questions: What lessons were you learning in that lifetime? What beliefs and patterns have you carried into your current lifetime? Did you know anyone in that past life who you also know in this life? Did you leave anything unfinished or unforgiven? This type of review is sometimes assisted by loved ones, guides, or helpers.

What happens next depends on how these and similar questions are answered. Sometimes the person needs to acknowledge and express anger at someone or something. A client who is ready to forgive a person from a prior lifetime can communicate that to the soul of that person; since all minds are joined in the soul realm, the healing work can be done at that level. Or some clients may need to reach out from the Higher Self to forgive, support, and comfort that part of themselves that made mistakes.

Once the lessons have been reviewed and whatever healing that needs to be done is completed (to the extent possible in that session), it is sometimes desirable to go back into the lifetime and rescript it. I give the person this option, asking, "If your soul could go back into that life and change it, what would you like to see happen?" People who choose to do this picture the life as if it is really happening, but this time they play a more empowered role or make whatever changes they are guided to do. This provides clearer choices of how their life can be lived differently in this current incarnation.

To conclude the session, I guide the person back to full alertness in the present moment, with a suggestion to remember what is helpful from that life. We then review the session and discuss possible follow-up steps.

Benefits of Past-Life Regression

I have found PLR to be very effective when other therapies haven't worked. For example, I treated an airline attendant—I'll call her Kate—who had claustrophobia and was about to leave her job. Nothing in her current life could explain this problem. We first tried some traditional forms of therapy; this helped somewhat but didn't eliminate the phobia. Kate believed in reincarnation and asked if I would do a past-life regression.

With hypnosis, I gave her unconscious mind the suggestion to go back to the root cause of her claustrophobia. Kate received a past-life memory: she was trapped in a mineshaft and the walls were caving in on her. As she recalled the event, her breath was short and she displayed visible signs of distress. I did not leave her in the intensity of the moment very long, but progressed her to the next significant event in that lifetime. Ultimately, she had dug her way out of the shaft and had survived. But she had never released the trauma of that experience, and she was still reliving it. Through PLR, once Kate had remembered that life, felt the relief of surviving, and saw that her soul lived on, her phobia was resolved.

Other benefits of regression therapy include relief of physical symptoms and a deeper understanding of the unfinished business that has been carried over into important relationships in this life.

A stay-at-home mom named Dawn came to me because she was concerned about her nine-year-old daughter, Wendy. Whenever Dawn left the house, Wendy clung to her as if she would never return. Nothing could account for this severe level of separation anxiety. Dawn gave appropriate attention to her daughter, and there was no precipitating traumatic event or explanation for her behavior.

In a PLR session, Dawn returned to a previous lifetime where she and Wendy had been in a mother-daughter relationship, but the mother had committed suicide. While this was quite a shock to Dawn, she was able to discover why she had taken her own life. She forgave herself and let go of her feelings of guilt. It also became apparent that Wendy was carrying the unconscious memory of her past-life abandonment.

After our session, Dawn talked to her daughter about their past life (in general terms—not specifically mentioning the suicide, but saying that they had gotten separated). She reassured Wendy that they would never be separated like that again. Surprisingly, Wendy remembered her feelings of abandonment when the past life was discussed, and was able to share her fears. By bringing these memories to the surface and processing them, the daughter released her anxiety.

Through the same PLR session, Dawn also resolved a physical ailment. She had been seeing a chiropractor for two years with a cervical neck problem. After the regression, she no longer had any difficulty with her neck. It is interesting to note that she had hung herself in that past life, and the cellular memory of that experience had seemed to carry over into this lifetime.

Grief and loss issues are sometimes resolved by past-life regression. For example, a few years ago a woman named Clara came to me. Nine years earlier, she had seen her thirty-year-old son drown in an undertow at the beach. This devastated mother was still mourning the loss and had difficulty letting go of a deep sense of guilt about what had happened. She did a PLR with me.

For Clara, a profound healing occurred after she revisited her past-life death scene and I had transitioned her into the spirit realm. Because regression work is done in holographic time, where all experiences exist simultaneously, many people seem to navigate easily between past, present, and potential futures. The state of consciousness that is accessed during hypnosis appears to transcend time and space, as we know it. Therefore, in Clara's case, her soul's Mind knew what healing experiences were needed.

In the spirit realm, Clara became aware of her son's presence there (from her current life). It was a very poignant moment, and she felt a gentle breeze caress her head (even though the windows in the room were closed). Mother and son were able to communicate their feelings to one another. The son reassured Clara that she didn't need to worry about him, that he was right where he needed to be and was fine. Clara also let him know that he didn't need to hang around any more, now that she knew he was OK. It was deeply touching to witness them saying their goodbyes. Communicating what they had needed to say gave them closure and comfort.

While my intent in this book is not to try to "prove" the existence of such states, it's worth noting that some compelling research has been done to investigate the survival of memory from one life to another. Of particular interest is the work of psychiatrist Ian Stevenson, MD, at the University of Virginia. He researched almost 3,000 cases of children who spontaneously recalled past-life memories. These children reported specific and verifiable details of their past lives, such as the towns where they had lived, the names of their former families, and how they died. In some cases, the children spoke in languages to which they had never been exposed. He also documented physical evidence of birthmarks and deformities in the children, which correlated with a significant proportion of the past-life deaths that had been violent. Dr. Stevenson, now deceased, followed up on this information by consulting public records in the places where these children remembered living. He was able to validate a high percentage of the children's reports of details from their past lives. (For more on Dr. Stevenson's research, see the Recommended Books list in the Resources section.)

Now let's turn to another method for accessing the soul realm to help us understand our life purpose; our recurring, dysfunctional patterns of thoughts, feelings, and behavior; and the basis for our soul choices.

Life-Between-Lives Spiritual Regression Therapy

Also known as LBL, life-between-lives regression is another means to accelerate soul growth in a profound way. It is recommended that you have some practice with hypnosis or past-life regression before doing an LBL session, for a greater likelihood of success in connecting with the "between" state.

LBL is a specific hypnotherapy method pioneered by Michael Newton, PhD, counseling psychologist and author of *Journey of Souls* and *Destiny of Souls*. This process allows people to access a state of consciousness in which they can recall their life as a soul in the "between state." The more than 7,000 LBL regressions Dr. Newton has facilitated during his extensive career reveal a fascinating and compelling picture of the spirit world between incarnations. This "superconscious" awareness brings a deep sense of love and compassion and an understanding of our life's purpose and lessons.

Many of my clients, after having a past-life regression (PLR), choose to experience an LBL session. I often recommend it if the person needs to feel a more direct connection with their immortal soul purpose and their loving guides, or if they wish to have a compassionate review of their lessons and progress as a soul.

The PLR is generally a prerequisite because during an LBL, one must sustain a deeper trance state for three to four hours. A PLR usually takes two hours and requires a lighter trance state. The LBL is a form of hypnosis that requires a longer time to access the higher spiritual realms. To experience an LBL, you must be able to maintain an inner focus without being too distracted by the outside world or unrelated thoughts. If you have successfully accessed past-life memories in a regression session, then most likely you will be able to do an LBL session.

Besides its longer length, an LBL journey has a different purpose, too. While the emphasis in a PLR is on reviewing the events of a previous incarnation, an LBL session focuses mostly on the spirit realm after death. The experience varies with the person and what their soul guides them to do. But an LBL session often includes an extended opportunity to meet and communicate with the Council of Elders (advanced beings and master teachers), soul group members, and one's personal spirit guides (mentors). It can also include a trip to the "Library," where one can gain further information about their other past lives and patterns. Some people also report going to "classrooms" for further learning in specialty areas.

Experiencing an LBL Session

What might you experience during a life-between-lives hypnotic regression? Let's imagine a typical session. It begins with a long period of relaxation and guided imagery to lead you into a deep trance state. Next, the process takes you to your immediate past life for a brief review of what happened—the people, the themes, and major events in that life. You are then taken to the last day of that lifetime to gain insight into the circumstances surrounding your death. There is no need to relive any trauma involved in your passing; you can observe it from a distance if needed.

You are then transitioned through the death scene into the spirit realm. The between-lives experience is highly individualized, of course; it cannot be predicted exactly, as it depends on the person's needs. But your primary spirit guide is likely to greet you and orient you to the spirit world. After a period of rest and recuperation and review of your past life with your guide, you might reunite with your primary soul group—those who have incarnated many times with you. There is often a happy welcoming. Meeting with your soul group can help you understand the roles various people play in your life and the lessons that you and these others have chosen to learn together.

A highlight of the between-life visit is a meeting with your soul Council of Elders (advanced teachers). This is an unconditionally loving review of your most immediate past life (or lives), and of your current life. This review is not punitive or judgmental. On the contrary, its intent is to support, encourage, and guide you. Meeting with your Soul Council can help you become more aware of your purpose and soul progress in this lifetime. It may help you heal repeating karmic patterns. It is also an opportunity to ask questions about soul contracts and other areas of interest related to soul growth. The degree of clarity and insight that occurs in these meetings is far beyond the limited vantage point of our ego/personality.

To gain a more in-depth understanding of the amazing things that occur in the life-between-lives regression process, you may wish to read

Dr. Newton's books. His website and training program are listed in the Resources section of this book.

Some Benefits of the Life-Between-Lives Experience

There are many benefits to this kind of soul work. First, many people overcome their fear of death when they experience their immortal, unlimited soul. Some people discover their spiritual selves in a near-death experience, but the LBL process allows us to connect with our soul self without the trauma of dying.

Second, the expansive state of deep peace and love is truly an unforgettable experience, one that we rarely feel in day-to-day life because we are so out of touch with our True Self. The LBL journey is a profound reminder of who we are as eternal, spiritual beings, and the lessons we learn while in our physical incarnation. People often comment after a session that they will not "sweat the small stuff" as much, now that their life purpose has been put into perspective.

Third, healing issues from past lives and progressing in our lessons is so much easier when we can view ourselves from the expanded state of love that is the soul's point of view. The LBL experience also brings greater access to information about our past lives and soul lessons. We can better understand why we chose certain family members and soul companions, and we grow in self-acceptance and compassion for the role that others play in our life. We blame less often, knowing that we chose the people in our life for a purpose.

When we stand at the top of a mountain, our view is vaster than if we stand at the bottom, where we can only see what is right in front of us. From the spirit realm, we can see the bigger picture.

When we forget this, we become so mired in the dense physical dimension that we believe that all we are is a body that gets sick, dies, and is forever gone. I have observed that we heal faster and move forward with renewed energy and purpose when we have experienced our Essence, our true identity as a spiritual being. Reminded of who we really are, we often become less identified with our everyday ego persona.

The LBL journey is a sort of wake-up call by the soul, telling us, "Hey, you are so much more than you think you are. You have forgotten your origin as a soul, but you are one with the Divine."

The beauty of the life-between-lives process is that we actually experience that state. The between-lives state is so expansive and extraordinary that words can seldom convey its beauty and radiance. There are moments during the regression process where there is a state of "beingness," a palpable energy of deep peace, a sense of well-being, unlimited love, and oneness. Have you ever felt that you were in the "zone," so to speak, of profound joy, creativity, balance, and harmony? This is what is often experienced in the between state.

Fourth, the soul realm reminds us that we are not alone—we have guides and master teachers who encourage, challenge, instruct, and support us with our soul growth. Why not take advantage of this loving energy as a resource and a reminder when we need it? This is not meant to foster dependency. Rather, our caring spiritual mentors are there for us until we don't need training wheels anymore, until we are listening more consistently to our own soul guidance. I have found that the LBL process helps people to open up not only to their spirit guides, but to trust their own wisdom as well.

Again, my purpose here is to introduce you to this remarkable healing method, not to prove the existence of the spirit world. Coming from the perspective of spiritual psychotherapy, I find LBL work to be very valuable. This experience helps people to see themselves differently, as more than their limited ego selves, and to compassionately learn from and forgive karmic, repeating patterns in themselves and others.

I am most grateful to Dr. Newton for teaching therapists a highly effective process for helping people to access the soul realm between lives. For me, it is a deep honor to facilitate these journeys; they are a welcome reminder of my own soul identity.

nine

Spiritual Regression: Case Histories and Follow-up Interviews

I'd like to introduce you to a few of the people whose spiritual-growth sessions I've had the privilege to facilitate. Some of the people you'll meet had all three kinds of sessions described in this book, including Soul Visioning, past-life regression, and life-between-lives regression, while others participated in one or two of these inner journeys. (Their names and identities have been changed to protect confidentiality, and the transcripts have been edited and condensed for space considerations and readability.)

To find out what impact these experiences had on them, I followed up by interviewing each person from one to ten years after their sessions. Did this inner work make a difference in their life? In most cases, it was a turning point and a catalyst for positive change.

Some reported that for the first time, they understood why they chose this lifetime and the challenges that came with it—a knowledge that provided a measure of comfort. Many people reported that the LBL meeting with their Soul Council was a spiritual shot in the arm, so to speak. It validated that they were on the right track and doing what they came here to do.

Often, people have found that periodically listening again to the session recordings helps tremendously in bringing back feelings of well-being and connection to their soul purpose. It is also helpful to write down the highlights of the experience and the guidance received from the Spirit realm to reinforce the insights that spiritual regression can bring.

Physician, Heal Thyself

This case history includes Anne's Soul Visioning session (during which some past-life trauma surfaced for healing), a life-between-lives session, and a follow-up interview one year later.

Anne is a surgeon in her early fifties. She came to me feeling "stuck"; she had done a lot of her own personal growth work but needed some individual facilitation. The work one can do on one's own is often like peeling the layers of an onion, leading to a readiness to get to the core issues.

Anne has a highly successful traditional practice and extensive training in energy healing. However, she said, "I feel like I am on the gerbil wheel of doing medicine, thinking that there must be more but not knowing how to get there." She wanted to open an integrative medicine practice and incorporate more energy healing into her work, but she felt that something was holding her back.

Anne knew she was repeating some patterns in her life. She felt disempowered, held hostage to other people's expectations in her professional and personal relationships. "In my group medical practice," she said, "there is a lot of pressure to do things a certain way, to be a good team player, and there is a lot of overwork." In her personal life, Anne was living with a workaholic, controlling husband, trying to make him happy and meet his demands. Anne wanted to change all these patterns. She wanted to discover what was blocking her and to heal that. She also wanted more clarity as to her soul's vision for her future.

Anne Takes a Soul Visioning Journey

In her Soul Visioning session, with hypnosis, I guided Anne into a beautiful garden scene, where she met and merged with her wise, intuitive, empowered, joyful Future Self. This Ideal Self, with the guidance of her higher soul wisdom, envisioned her future as if it were happening right at that moment. She experienced herself writing self-help books, designing an integrative medicine curriculum for medical students, and opening an energy healing center.

"What I really want is freedom and a safe space to come into my own," Anne said. When I asked if there was anything saying no to this ideal future, she replied, "What has held me back is not seeing what's good for me and trying to make it right for everybody else."

At this point I transitioned Anne to the root cause of this limiting pattern of thought. By shifting her focus to where the issue was stored in her body, we brought up the cellular memories connected with those beliefs. (I used elements of Holographic Memory Resolution to access the blocks.[1])

SUSAN: *That feeling of not seeing what's good for you, and trying to make it right for everyone else, where do you feel that in your body? [Throughout this session, I matched Anne's language.]*
ANNE: My solar plexus.

S: *That feeling in your solar plexus, is it inside, outside, or both?*
A: It's like a disconnect inside.

S: *Does it have a size, a shape, or a color, this feeling in your solar plexus, the disconnect?*
A: It's like a lack, empty, the size of my fist.

S: *And does it have a texture, a weight, or a temperature?*
A: It's a bulky, heavy thing.

S: *Anything else you can describe about that feeling?*
A: It's just not very alive.

S: *And is there an emotion that goes with the feeling in your solar plexus?*

A: I'd say it's anger.

S: *Is there an age that comes to mind when you first feel a feeling like this?*

A: Well, I am thirteen, that's when it was strong.

S: *And where are you when you're thirteen and you're feeling this?*

A: I'm arguing with my mom. That was a time when I decided to stop fighting and arguing, and just play the game until I could do what I wanted to do.

Anne learned at a young age to "go along," to make everybody happy, with the hope that her parents would then pay attention to her and meet her emotional needs.

S: *And what are you feeling when you're thirteen and you decide to just play the game?*

A: I'm always superior, and that's my solar plexus.

S: *If you could go back into that scene as your Higher Self and change it, what does this thirteen-year-old part of you need?*

A: To really be seen, and emotionally to be in my mastery, and to be mothered.

S: *How would you like to see this? Would you like to see your mother being more emotionally responsive and nurturing?*

A: Yes, I'd like her to be more open-minded, trusting and encouraging my process.

S: *Take all the time you need to picture your mother being more open-minded, giving you what you need. Can you picture that?*

A: It's hard. (Chuckles.) She needs to be more mature then, too.

S: *Yes, and sometimes mothers just don't know how to do it. Not to blame her, but that's where she was at the time. Is there another resource you could bring to nurture your younger self? Would you like your compassionate adult self to be there for that part of you?*

A: Probably.

S: *That nurturing, mothering part of you being present to this precious thirteen-year-old, who wants to be seen. Take all the time you need to picture that. And when it's just the way you want it, let me know. (Long pause.)*

A: OK.

S: *Is there anything else that needs to happen for this thirteen-year-old?*

A: No, I think that it can continue to happen now, and we can be together.

S: *So do you need to take your thirteen-year-old self out of that energy and bring her back here with you? Maybe placing her in the rose room of your own heart, a special place, and you can just reassure her that you're going to be there for her. (Pause.)* [The rose room is a metaphor for a safe, nurturing place in her heart where her inner child can be loved and cared for.] *And where are you placing her?*

A: She's in my heart.

S: *Is there some beautiful healing color that you can send to her?*

A: I see her and me in a deep purple.

S: *Running deep purple throughout your body, especially to your solar plexus. When that has gone throughout your body, let me know.*

A: OK.

I now ask Anne to scan her body, checking to see if anything else might be blocking her from fully expressing her soul's vision. When there are unresolved memories or traumas from one's past (from this life and/or a past life), they are registered in the body. When we track these "body memories" we see where they were originally imprinted.

> S: *And now scanning your body from head to toe, is there any tightness, tension, or discomfort anywhere right now?*
>
> A: Something around my hands, almost like gloves.

Past-Life Memories Surface for Healing

At this point Anne flashed back to a past-life memory. If the root cause of a blockage is in a past life, people often bring up a past-life memory in answer to the question, "When do you first feel a feeling like that in your body?"

> S: *Is that feeling inside, outside, or both, that feeling in your hands, glovelike?*
>
> A: They're almost heavy or numb, like something from outside.
>
> S: *Does it have a size, shape, or color, that feeling?*
>
> A: Like boxing gloves.
>
> S: *If your hands could do whatever they wanted, what would they do right now?*
>
> A: Take them off, because it's like they're being confined.
>
> S: *Is there anything else you can describe about that feeling in your hands?*
>
> A: They're starting to feel tingly.
>
> S: *Is there an emotion that goes with that feeling?*
>
> A: No, but there's something else, like a numbness. Now there is some pain.

S: *Does it have a temperature, texture, or weight?*
A: It's hot.

S: *Any emotion that goes with that feeling?*
A: It's like something disgusting.

S: *Is there an age that comes to mind when you first feel this hot, disgusting feeling in your hands?*
A: I feel like I am mutilated, like this isn't even this lifetime.

Anne immediately jumped to another lifetime: she was accused of being a witch and was imprisoned.

S: *Where are you?*
A: Hung up but not afraid.

S: *You can float above it and see it at a distance, if that helps. You can get the information but you can detach from it.*

Detaching from the painful memory helped Anne process it without becoming overwhelmed, and understand what happened to her.

A: I don't think they cut my hands off, but I think they tied them off, and I can't see who it is.

S: *And what happens?*
A: I think that they're going to burn me. I don't want to go into this.

It wasn't necessary for Anne to relive the trauma of this scene. But it was important to go back into that frozen memory, that "freeze frame" of terror, to rescript it and reclaim that disowned part of herself. Since the unconscious mind doesn't know the difference between reality and metaphor, it takes the rescripted scene as truth.

S: *OK, you don't have to go into this. Now connect with your Higher Self. Go back into that scene and change it. What would you like to see happen there?*

A: I'd like to run the movie back in my mind to before I was imprisoned, and not be afraid. And I want to speak to the men who imprisoned me and gently say, "Wait," in the name of the Light. I want to say, "It's for you too, it's for God," and to help ease their fear. It's the power of gentle speech.

Anne wanted to speak to her persecutors from a place of peace, and have them hear her message. Each person's inner wisdom knows the best way to rescript a memory. It is important that a practitioner doesn't impose their own ideas on what would be right for the client.

S: *Is there anything else that needs to happen?*

A: No, it's OK.

S: *Now take a snapshot of the scene the way you want to remember it. What scene are you snapshotting?*

A: I'm speaking to these men, but calmly.

S: *How does that feel?*

A: Really nice.

S: *Put a picture frame with color or colors around that scene. What colors are in the picture frame?*

A: Violet and green.

S: *And running the violet and green throughout your body everywhere it will go, especially to your hands. Once you've done that, let me know.*

A: OK.

Taking a snapshot of the scene the way we want to remember the event, and running color throughout the body, anchors the experience into the unconscious mind. In other words, this process imprints a new resourced memory in the body-mind memory. This powerful image and feeling then stays with us. When we think about the framed picture, the good memories are easily recalled mentally, emotionally, and physically.

S: *Scanning your body from head to toes, is there any tightness, tension, or discomfort anywhere in your body?*

This question tests to see if any other unresolved issues or memories are being held in the body, and whether the process is complete.

A: No, it's good.

When Anne said that there was no resistance left in her body, I knew that the energy had cleared around that blockage and we could return to her ideal future.

Anne's Soul Visioning Concludes

S: *Connecting again with your ideal future, three to five years out, under higher soul wisdom, in its most expanded, most ideal vision, is there anything you want to change about it, anything that would make it even more magnificent?*
A: No.

S: *And how does it feel when you connect with this ideal future?*
A: It feels really nice, like an opening for me.

S: *Take a snapshot of this ideal future, something that will immediately take you right back to this good feeling.*
A: I'm in my room, writing things down.

S: *Now put a picture frame of color around that scene.*

A: There's glittery gold around it.

S: *Beautiful. And running glittering gold all throughout your body everywhere it will go.*

Anne's Life-Between-Lives Experience

Anne participated in a life-between-lives session a few months later. She wanted a more direct connection with her spirit guides and Soul Council to assist with her healing work. She also wanted to improve her intuitive abilities to access guidance in her healing practice.

I directed Anne back to her immediate past life. She was a male doctor living in a small Irish town during the 1800s, working in a hospital and teaching students. He was able to see auras, and had written a book about his work integrating energy with science. However, the authorities of the time were threatened by what he was teaching and writing. They tried him and sentenced him to death for writing what they saw as dangerous blasphemy.

The executioners tied the doctor's hands and hung him. It is interesting to note that Anne in this current life has had cervical neck and laryngitis problems. Sometimes past-life traumas show up as physical symptoms. Perhaps there is a correlation between Anne's past-life hanging and the physical manifestations in her throat/neck area in this life. She is extremely healthy otherwise. (As we noted earlier, Dr. Ian Stevenson has studied spontaneous past-life memories in children, observing correlations between their means of death in a past life and certain physical manifestations in this life, such as birthmarks and scars.)

I then transitioned Anne from the death scene into the spirit dimension.

SUSAN: *Detaching yourself from that scene, feel yourself rising above what is happening to you, comfortably and easily slipping out of the body. You've been through the experience of death many times before. And you will be able to talk with me and easily answer my questions, because you are in touch with your inner True Self. Feel your mind expanding into the highest levels of your being as you float out of your body.*

Anne leaves her body quickly and enters the spirit realm. At first Anne sees a "yellow light, a door, a threshold."

ANNE: I'm afraid there's nothing there, or that I can't handle it or I can't go there.

I asked if there was someone who could assist her with this. A figure appeared to her that was robed in white. She was still getting her bearings and was taken to a riverbank.

A: I'm climbing up moist dirt, up a hill. I see my dog Anja. I don't know why I am here.

S: *Ask why you are here.*
A: I see Galiel. That is my guide. He looks like he is in native dress, feathers, and jewelry. He is strong, very muscular, and he just glows luminescent, subtly. He's by the dog. *[Anne's dog Anja is there to help her feel more comfortable.]* I feel better. I feel like Galiel is my gentle other half. He balances out the masculine to my feminine. I'm getting that this is a good way for him to appear to me.

S: *Is there anything Galiel would like to communicate to you?*
A: He says to relax, be still, be present, and it will help to have a more direct connection with him.

At this point it was clear to me that Anne was resisting going further and hearing what her guide had to say.

A: I don't know where I am, but it's like I've got something over my head and I can't see anymore. It's muffled; I can't hear him.

S: *Where do you hold that feeling in your body?*
A: It's like there's something tied over my head.

S: *Go to the root cause of where this energy comes from. Where are you, and what is happening?*
A: I am seeing someone tied up with a sack over their head. It's like a campfire.

S: *What time period is this?*
A: Nomadic. Primitive. I feel numb.

S: *Go to the events that led up to this, so you get more informa-tion about yourself and what is happening.*
A: I'm walking down a path. I think I have a child, too. *[Anne later said that she felt this was her daughter in her current lifetime.]* Someone's coming up behind and then they're grabbing me. They capture me. I don't know where my child goes . . . not with me.

Anne now feels that this may explain why her daughter in this life has always been clingy, needing to be close to her mother. Anne started to feel some anxiety. I had her float above the scene and see it at a distance.

A: They are doing this for someone else who is afraid of me.

Anne went on to describe herself in that lifetime as a simple woman who cared for the women and children of the community.

A: I'm doing healing and easing pain and easing lives, but the people are empowered. They feel like they are in the presence of something powerful, and that's threatening to the authorities. But the authorities don't know me, or they wouldn't be afraid. They are cut off from the Light. I stop doing the healing work because my life is completely interrupted.

I guided Anne back into the spirit realm and asked what needed to be healed from that lifetime. She was taken by Galiel to a place in the outdoors where she could "recuperate" from that difficult lifetime. She received a healing session from her spirit guides (one of whom is her spiritual teacher in this current incarnation).

A: They are working on me, the grids, and all the blocks along my head and neck.

Her guides reassured Anne that she will be able to "remove the grid-locks around me, and I will be able to connect in the Spirit world more deeply." They advised her to set her intention at night, before she goes to sleep, to connect to the spirit realm for rebalancing and recharging.

A: I am asking if I can talk to my [Soul] Council.

S: *Where are you?*
A: It looks like a boardroom. Only it's not so stark, it's warm. I feel so timid, I don't know why I can't know who they are.

S: *Allow yourself to be fully receptive, knowing that they are there to support and empower you even more in your soul growth and purpose . . . that they are fully aligned with you.*

More support figures come in to be with Anne, including her spirit guide Galiel, her father (from this lifetime, who was deceased), and the four or five members of her Soul Council.

A: [I feel] a holiness, a very clear energy. I feel like they know me more than I do in this lifetime. There are no walls in all of these rooms; they are very open and fluid, but there is some structure there for me, because I'm in a physical form.

Anne wanted to know how to get her life and her work to where she wanted them. The answer she was given was to be a "thought leader, just go for it with confidence. Don't get limited by other people's limitations."

At one point during the Soul Council meeting, Anne found herself leaving the scene with one of them.

A: I was taken to a very high perspective, showing me doing a healing [in this current incarnation] way down below. Way below I'm seeing a light connection, and I'm connected all the way up, forever. It's incredible light. I can remember and feel this when I am doing a healing.

Words are inadequate to describe the experience of being in the spirit realm, where there is no time and space as we know it. Clearly, Anne was having a "light bulb moment" on how she could tap into what it felt like to be in her "light body" in the spirit dimension, and on how she could bring that into the physical dimension in doing her healing work. The Soul Council then gave Anne encouragement for her current lifetime.

A: I was told this lifetime is going fine, and there's a lot of opportunity and joy ahead, so don't make it hard. My life is a gradual awakening; it's not like the shade [to my medical intuition] is going to go up all of a sudden.

Anne's spiritual mentors showed her how to access their guidance more directly. They explained that they communicate in thought forms, and that she didn't need to go through a big procedure to connect with them. Their message to her was to "lighten up."

To summarize what Anne realized from her LBL experience, she had a repeating pattern of being persecuted or put to death in other lifetimes for sharing her truth and her healing abilities. In her current lifetime, as a result, a part of her mind was "protecting" her from moving forward, from using her healing abilities and opening her intuitive channels again. Thus, it was difficult for her to connect with the "between state" and "hear" what her guides and Soul Council wanted to share. She had a deep unconscious fear that she could be blindsided and put in danger again by opening up those channels.

Fortunately, Anne released those traumatic past lifetimes, let go of fear, and remembered the truth of who she is. By directly experiencing her immortal spirit, she realized that she can choose to do things differently this time. There is no true failure in a soul-guided life.

Anne's One-Year Follow-up

One year later, I interviewed Anne to determine the longer-term impact of her Soul Visioning and LBL experiences. Anne was a more confident woman who was acting on her soul guidance. She said that Soul Visioning gave her clarity, and added, "I feel incredibly more relaxed and able to trust myself. I think when you are an overachiever doctor-type, you don't develop that sense of listening to your inner guidance. Since I did the visioning and life-between-lives sessions, I can listen to that guidance, trust, and act on it. I feel more empowered."

Once those childhood and past-life blocks were cleared, Anne could more easily access the spirit realm. Her LBL experience helped her to be more directly in touch with her guides in a conscious way. She was shown ways to connect with the healing light, and she uses this "felt memory" in her healing sessions.

Anne has also become more assertive in her professional and personal life. She speaks up more in her work setting; she feels more "equal and adult" and at ease in her relationship with her husband. She is feeling more secure in honoring her own vision and needs. As a result, Anne has opened her integrative medicine center with a staff of practitioners that do energetic healing. She is doing amazing work using energy medicine with her patients, and she shared some of her success stories with me. One case, said Anne, involved a woman of twenty who had had migraine headaches for years.

> On her left side, she had lost both her vision and her hearing, eight months before she saw me. No one could do anything for her. She couldn't sleep through the night; the pain never went

away. After three healing sessions, she regained her hearing. I did some of this energy work from a distance, since she lived far away from my office. She also had prayer circles praying for her and me. To this day, her sight and hearing are restored, and she is a normal young adult who is going to college now.

A side note to this story shows how Anne is fulfilling part of her soul's vision as bridge builder. The person who referred the migraine case to Anne was a mainstream minister who had heard about her healing abilities. Anne is also bridging the gap between traditional and nontraditional medicine. Part of her vision is to write and to teach a curriculum that can be incorporated into integrative medicine programs in medical schools. Anne has also begun to write the self-help books she envisioned.

A Social Worker Discovers Her Life Purpose

Roberta, the social worker you met in chapter 7 as she shared her successes with the Soul Visioning process, now tells of the benefits she received from doing spiritual regression work. She had experienced a past-life regression many years before I met her; it is summarized here because it has relevance to her general spiritual growth. I facilitated a life-between-lives session with Roberta, and then interviewed her nineteen months later to find out if her PLR and LBL sessions had made a difference in her life.

Recollections of an Earlier Past-Life Regression

ROBERTA: I had been married for four years to David, and essential parts of me had been withering away. Meanwhile, I was quite drawn to Luke, a man I had worked with for years. Although we were beginning to realize that our soul vision was to be united, he was reluctant to injure David.

During my regression, it became clear that Luke and I had a "karmic debt" to David. In a past lifetime, David and I were brothers, and Luke [a woman in that lifetime!] was married to David.

Although David realized that Luke and I were in love, he allowed me to live on his land with his wife [Luke] and their three children, while he went away to battle.

Understanding and separating that [prior lifetime] from the present made it possible for Luke and me to be *free to choose* to be together in this lifetime. I could finally see the difference between living a life aligned with our soul's purpose and a life that was no longer aligned. I have now been happily married to Luke for seven years, and we have a beautiful child. We thank God that we had the courage to not only see the path more clearly, but to remove the obstacles in the way with the help of the regression.

This is another benefit of regression work: it permits a longer view of relationships from one lifetime to the next. Sometimes people feel strong attractions to certain others, attractions they can't account for on a conscious level. We repeat the patterns of our past lives until we become more conscious and heal that unfinished business. Spiritual regression work helps us understand how these issues play out over many lifetimes with our soul "partners" until the lessons are learned. By filling in the missing pieces of the puzzle of our relationships, we can more effectively sort through the complexities of our choices. When our motives are revealed, we can consciously begin to learn the lessons of these relationships.

Follow-up Insights into the Life-Between-Lives Session

ROBERTA: The LBL was as powerful as the PLR, only in a different way. First I experienced the lifetime right before my present one, in which I was a very free-spirited, adventurous woman who lived a nomadic life with no roots or true relationships.

When Roberta went into the "between state" after her death in that past life, she experienced a life review.

In no time, I reviewed that lifetime's purpose: realization of the possibility to not conform, to take risks, to have incredible aliveness and freedom. However, there was an underlying emptiness where true attachments were concerned.

Roberta then had a meeting with her Soul Council.

There were beings giving their opinions on what my next lifetime [this current life] would be about—what my soul most needed to evolve.

Roberta was told that she needed to master the challenges of relationships in this current lifetime. To that end, she had chosen a career as a social worker with a specialty in marriage and family therapy. Above all, her lesson for her current life was to experience true "oneness," with empathy being the greatest way to heal the illusion of separateness.

They advise me to bring to others this relationship wisdom and this truth of oneness. This knowing has impacted me greatly. It reduces the limiting beliefs that get in the way [such as a sense of inferiority] and enables me to get refocused much more quickly on my soul vision. For example, when any painful or difficult situation arises, I remember: I'm to learn, to share, and to empathize in the spirit of that oneness.

Looking back to all the ways this has occurred, Roberta says, has helped her recover from many issues that would have interfered with the manifestation of her soul vision.

For example, in this current lifetime, I am a minority in that my parents are both from countries where Spanish is the primary language. Because of their heavy accents, I experienced many incidents of prejudice. However, because we are Caucasian, the degree of prejudice was far less than that experienced by those who are not only in the minority ethnically, but also racially.

Such mitigating circumstances, Roberta observes, are part of a pattern that has unfolded in her current lifetime, according to the guidance from her Soul Council.

> In this current life, there is the need to experience enough of most things to really "get" them and to deeply empathize with others— but not so much that I am consumed or over-identified with any one thing.

In a summary she wrote about the spiritual work she has done, Roberta's words reflected her newfound clarity.

> My husband and I are thankful for the many tools, including Soul Visioning and spiritual regression, and the people who have played such an essential role in our life's journey, in helping us to continue realizing all aspects of our soul's purpose and vision.

A Hypnotherapist Reclaims Her Life Purpose and Passion

Linda's case history describes her life-between-lives spiritual regression and presents excerpts from a follow-up interview three years later.

Linda, a hypnotherapist and lifestyle consultant, was fifty-five when she did an LBL regression with me. In the usual LBL pattern, she returned to her most recent past life and death, then transitioned to the between state. Her immediate past life took place during America's pioneer period. She remembered being in her mother's womb, feeling very resistant to coming into that lifetime. Her parents were homesteaders, and Linda was going to be their third child. This would be a hard life. She felt that there was no reason to be in a body and wanted to stay in the spirit realm, where everything was much "easier." Linda chose to end that life in the womb and return to the "between state." After her death, Linda "hung around awhile to pour love down" on her parents.

In her life review with her guides and Soul Council, Linda was told that she needed to learn the many forms of love in the earth realm, forms that could only be experienced in a body. If she truly wanted to help other people, it was not enough merely to believe in love and compassion here in the Spirit realm; she needed to experience this in the physical dimension. The LBL session had a profound impact on Linda, and she now embraces her life purpose for being on earth.

Linda's Life-Between-Lives Session

In this excerpt from Linda's meeting with her Soul Council, she relays her conversation, and speaks alternately from the Council's perspective and her own.

LINDA: I'm in front of a Council. They are shadows, abstract, not in human form, exactly. I am pleading. I don't want to go into the physical realm.

COUNCIL: YOU NEED TO GO INTO THE PHYSICAL, TO LEARN NOT TO FEEL TRAPPED IN THE BODY. YOUR PURPOSE IS TO WORK OUT THIS RESISTANCE, TO FEEL AS FREE IN THE BODY AS YOU DO WHEN YOU ARE NOT IN IT. IT IS JUST A VEHICLE.

LINDA: It's so easy to stay here in the spirit realm. Why do I have to go back into the physical?

COUNCIL: SO YOU CAN HELP OTHERS. YOU CAN'T HELP OTHERS UNTIL YOU LEARN IT YOURSELF.

LINDA: I want to know why there is so much *hate*?

COUNCIL: PEOPLE HATE BECAUSE THEY DON'T KNOW. THEY HAVE THE FREEDOM WITHIN THEM TO LET GO, BUT THEY DON'T KNOW THAT.

LINDA: I argue that if people didn't have to be in their bodies, they'd know. I'm giving the Council a hard time. I never liked going through other guides. I always thought the best way was going straight to the Source.

By this time, Linda was in a very deep trance, and there was a palpable presence of peace in the room. It becomes very difficult to speak in these "higher vibrations." Often there are long pauses before the next words emerge. Words seem to interrupt the flow at times. I was in a deep trance also, and very much a part of that energy. (It is well known among hypnotherapists that the facilitator is also in an altered state during such sessions; the mind is aware of the present moment, but another part is engaged in another dimension.) At that point, I asked Linda what the Source had to say about all of this.

LINDA: The Source says I'm energy, a storehouse of non-ending radiance. When I stop resisting the human experience, I won't need to experience it anymore. Without it, I can't experience all the different forms of energy, so I can *know* them.

SOURCE: IF YOU LIFT YOUR HEART AND YOUR MIND, YOUR WHOLE BEING, FROM THE SOUL OF PURE LOVE, THERE WOULD BE NO HATE. SO WE NEED THE BODY TO LEARN WHAT IS REALLY MEANT BY PURE LOVE AND RADIANT ENERGY. IT'S LIKE A TEST TUBE OR BEAKER. YOU HAVE TO KEEP PUTTING DIFFERENT INGREDIENTS IN IT, TO COME UP WITH THE PERFECT FORMULA FOR PURE LOVE. WE CAN ONLY LEARN THAT IN THE BODY.

Linda finally seemed to get the idea and was beginning to feel a sense of relief.

LINDA: Each lifetime gives us more tools. Sometimes we never figure out how to use them, but they are still there for us. And each lifetime is really a splendid journey, even if it's only a journey into the womb. Nothing is really a form at all; it just appears to be. It doesn't matter how many journeys I take. Each journey is just a blending of different elements that creates different experiences.

After Linda embraced the need to experience life in a body, she received another realization.

LINDA: We don't know the kind of impact we have on one another, but we need to know just how interrelated we are. So I'll keep reminding myself—*re-Mind-ing,* because that means I already *know* it. Thoughts are very powerful. That's why we need to learn to use our thoughts with purity. The Mind is how we "mind" the soul. Source reminds me that I can experience this anytime I choose, that I never have been restricted.

Afterward, Linda said, "I needed a guide to go into that deep a state, but I was almost more alert, more lucid and aware, than normal."

Because the LBL experience takes place while the client is in a deep superconscious state, it offers a more direct experience of the immortal soul. But we tend to forget very quickly. Our personality or ego mind takes over and distracts us. We need reminders and a commitment to our spiritual path—whatever that is for us—to undo our blocks and heal the resistances to what is always there in us.

Follow-up Interview

I interviewed Linda by phone three and a half years later to find out the impact that the LBL session had on her over the long term. We began by talking about the energy that she had felt during the session. Then, as she shared how her life has unfolded since then, she gained even more insights. Here are some excerpts from our conversation.

Linda began by recalling what she felt in the between-life state.

LINDA: The energy within me was vibrating at such a high force; the feeling inside me was amazingly love-filled and expansive. So long as I choose to keep it pure and let the energy flow, it's unending. I was feeling that this energy was filling me and overflowing. I felt so connected. The guides are there to act like a transformer, because to go directly to Source is very powerful, almost too much for us.

SUSAN: *That's an excellent point. It can be difficult to experience Source directly, while we are in dense physical form. We need help to step up our vibration, our state of consciousness, to be able to experience it in its purity.*

LINDA: This is such a surprising concept for me. I haven't spent any time or energy worrying about guides; that has not resonated with me. That's why the between-life state seems credible to me, because it's so outside of what my conscious expectation would have been.

I then asked Linda what short-term and long-term benefits, if any, the LBL session had for her.

LINDA: Short-term, it was profound, and very surprising. I arrived without expectations. I'd never experienced anything like that before. It was like nothing I would have ever anticipated from myself. The idea that I was resisting the human experience was startling, because I feel like I have always embraced life and been open to it. But as a result, I realized that I needed to learn how to be in the physical realm. I picked up key information that helped me to understand how valuable being in a physical form is to our development.

Long-term, I feel like the experience will always be with me, throughout this life and many more lifetimes. Although after the LBL, I got distracted by life—getting married, moving, and dealing with an aging mother and children—I did have the strong sense of needing to go back to my passion with hypnotherapy and with helping other people.

Linda recalled how strongly she had resisted the Council's assertion that she needed to experience life in the human form.

LINDA: I didn't understand why we can't all just be free from this physical realm. But the Council was saying that we already are free, we just don't know it. They really emphasized this: You have to *know* you are free, you can't just believe it. You can't teach what you don't know. That was profound for me. It showed me that I couldn't help others if I didn't know through my own experience.

From a broader perspective, Linda realized that resistance in general had been a major aspect of her personality.

LINDA: Another thing that I'm really seeing is a part of my personality—that there is resistance in me, in a lot of different ways. Resistance was a key element of this [LBL] experience. I was resisting entering physical form. I was resisting the information that the Council was giving me. I was resisting their guidance.

Then you asked, "What does Source say?" Source said that when I stop resisting the human experience, I won't need to experience it anymore. So many times in my life, I have had desires for what I want to accomplish, and when something came along and tried to kick me into a new trajectory, oftentimes I would put up resistance, and I would feel frustrated. The concept that I got from Source is that this is true of anything in life: when we resist it, we actually make it more powerful.

I started to see this right away in several different areas of my life when I tried to work hard for something. I'm not opposed to goals, but I think that goals need to be directed with flexibility, with the ability to adjust to the experience as it presents itself, and then you won't run up against so many resistances; they will just dissolve. I think of it like aikido: when you put a resistance up, if you allow the resistance to flow right through you, it disperses that energy, and you no longer allow it to have power over you.

SUSAN: *Did you get a sense of what it was in the physical that you did need to experience?*

LINDA: Many, many forms of experience. The guides told me my purpose was, when I go into the physical, to learn to not feel trapped in the body. My purpose is to work out that resistance. It's to feel free of the body, to realize it's just another form of energy, and to control and reorganize that energy.

That was another big theme from the Source—pure love and energy, and learning how to direct that energy, because it is totally under my control. Because it radiates out from me, it impresses upon other people in my sphere of influence, and helps them to feel more whole, more expanded, freer, more empowered. So that led me back to having to experience these things to know them, to help teach them . . . and part of my purpose is to help other people.

So that comes full circle from how everything started. I resisted going into life. It was my choice to die in the womb. And with the Source, I'm being reminded how to work with my energy, so that I never have to feel restricted again.

There is something I've decided from all this. I am going to make a list of areas of constriction/resistance and anything associated with it that I'm experiencing now, and maybe anything from the past that I've been carrying with me. I have resolved to play with that resistant energy, and to have fun with it. Then I will determine how I'm going to redirect that energy, or to let go of it. I will use my own hypnotic techniques—anchoring, triggers, that sort of thing—so that I can consciously and unconsciously let go of it. The idea is to experience transformation of that energy, and a sense of freedom. You'll have to follow up with me again in six months or a year; I'm having fun now!

SUSAN: *How much of a boost did that give you to move back into the passion for your work, like with hypnotherapy?*

LINDA: On an inner level, it's been in the background—not a gnawing, but a yearning that I need to get back to my passion. But in the past three years, what with getting married, moving, moving Mom out of a house she was in for fifty-four years, and issues with my kids, I just didn't feel I could put the energy into it. Yet I think that I was getting on track. The road ahead just had a few boulders on it and some major obstacles I had to work through. There were also some wonderful things: to be in a position where I was free to move wherever I wanted; to find the love of my life and be married after eighteen years of thinking that I never would marry again. A lot of things were actively moving me the way that I needed to move in the physical realm. That finally led me to feel that this is something that I need to bring back into my life.

SUSAN: *What strikes me is that you were living what they were advising you to do while you were in the physical realm. Look at all the various forms of love that you were participating in. In physical, nitty-gritty life, caring for your mother, having your primary relationship in marriage, and dealing with your kids—those are all different forms of love, all manifested in the physical body. You were living it!*

LINDA: Through hypnotherapy, I discovered that life was a wondrous journey, and I was relieved when I learned from the Source that it didn't matter how many times I took this journey. Each lifetime is like opening a gift. It's just the blending of different elements to create whole new experiences.

SUSAN: *I could feel that you were in a very high state of connection with Source, and you were receiving that love, that vibration, that information. Because as I listened to my own voice patterns as I was talking to you, I was in a very deep state of trance also. That's what happens in these LBL sessions sometimes. When that energy gets so high, you're in a state that's beyond words, because it is timeless. It goes beyond form, it goes to pure experience.*

LINDA: Here's the other thing I gained from it, though. My LBL session was so profound, I'm asking myself: how could I forget this experience? If I can't remember something this profound from three years ago, how do any of us really expect to remember what happened in another lifetime? While we're going through all of the stuff that's thrown at us in life, all the distractions, is it any wonder that we forget?

SUSAN: *Yes, and I think that's what the LBL process does, it is a reminder.*

LINDA: I think that is where I came up with this concept that the Mind is how we "mind" our soul. I kept being told that I have control, not the ego; I control my life in this physical form. If I'm in touch with that energy, through that Mind, then I'm going to get the information I need from the soul level; that's the same thing as being connected to Source.

SUSAN: *To me, that's the spiritual path—mindfulness, the spiritual discipline of staying conscious, and not going back into a sleep state of disconnection from Source.*

LINDA: That's what I was getting out of learning how to use my energy. I can learn how to change it, and transform it, by becoming aware—mindful of these different energetic patterns of experience we carry with us. With my work with other people, I think it's going to be amazingly helpful, because there isn't anyone who comes to me for help who isn't feeling areas of resistance in their life. So I'm feeling very strongly that this is something that I really needed to get a handle on, and experience, and know, so that I can help people even better. When they come to a hypnotherapist to help them with some form of inner issue that is making them feel like less than who they are—which to me is one of the restrictions—they are in that state, and they are ready to move beyond it. I just needed to know that myself, first and foremost. So I made this whole exercise up that I am going to be working with, and I'll keep you posted on that.

The follow-up review of Linda's session resulted in a reinvigoration of her soul's purpose. She is more determined to live her life by being in a body, joyfully experiencing and expressing love. She has reconnected with her passion for hypnotherapy, and her soul is now more in charge of charting her life course.

Stepping Out of the Dance of Dysfunction

This case history includes portions of a life-between-lives regression I facilitated with Judy, and a follow-up interview with her two years later.

Judy, a holistic healing practitioner with a business degree, was thirty-nine when she did a life-between-lives session with me. She was participating in a research trial for the National Center for Complementary and Alternative Medicine (funded by the National Institutes of Health), studying the effects of energy medicine on certain kinds of cancer survivors. She wanted an LBL session to get answers to some questions about her relationships and her progress as a soul.

I guided Judy into a deep state of relaxation and gave her a suggestion to go to her immediate past life. (It is easier to transition into the spirit realm from the death scene in the past life.) She immediately returned to a World War II lifetime as a Filipino man who had died when the Japanese bombed Manila.

> Judy: I never felt connected to my family in that lifetime, and just hung out with the other men in the village. The planes were bombing and shooting, generally creating an uproar. My village was destroyed. I remember having a sharp pain in my head, and then it was all over for me. It was so chaotic, so much of a surprise, and there was so much pain from being hit in the head, I just wanted out of there. I went quickly into the spirit dimension.

Judy was met by two guides, a male named Marmon and a female named Josephine.

J: The guides "cleansed" me with light energy. *[This is sometimes done to help clear the pain and trauma of a violent death.]* I felt so loved and nurtured that I started crying. There was a feeling that everything was all right. I felt like I had a new outfit on, a light body. My spirit guides told me that I had gossiped and complained too much in the lifetime just ended, but that I was a hard worker. I contributed to my family but not to the community. I griped about things without trying to make things better. Part of my lesson is to learn the destructive power of words. This is also true of my present life. I need to take action and not just sit on the sidelines and complain.

Her guides then took Judy "upstairs" to a round room for a visit with the Soul Council.

J: I sit on a chair and there are other beings sitting around the perimeter of the room, and there are nine sitting behind a counter or desk. They appear androgynous, dressed in blue robes. The tone of the meeting is quiet, solemn, and serious.

Her Soul Council helps Judy to plan her next incarnation. These wise beings are loving but firm. They discuss the lessons that she needs to learn, and present her with two options for her next [current] lifetime.

J: They point out that I need to find the joy in all things. I was shown a [potential] lifetime as a female with a chauvinistic, domineering father. I would have a family that stressed education, and I would have to work through issues of feeling inadequate or inferior as a female. I could choose a lifetime in Asia or in the USA; the themes would be the same. I actually saw those lifetimes very clearly, and I chose the USA.

The next passage reveals where Judy was taken after her Soul Council meeting. There seem to be classrooms and schools that some souls experience in the "between state," where their learning continues in various specialty areas, in preparation for their next incarnation. Judy described her lessons in healing methods.

> J: I just saw a picture showing how to set a broken bone [energetically]. They are talking about different vibrational levels and how to get them into coherence—how to hold the frequency and bring [the person being healed] into resonance with that vibration. It's easy. I see it, feel it, and bring that vibration into the person's body. Then it can shift them. They are also showing me that I have different energetic instruments in my hands. It's like I have crystals embedded in my fingers, in my palms. If I need a scalpel, it's there. It's about bringing through such a charge that there's no way but for the coherence to set in. It's like electric . . . like a lightning bolt, a charge to set it.

Judy seemed to be speaking metaphorically, and it all made sense to her during the experience.

During her LBL, Judy had another meeting with what she called her "wisdom keepers" (her Soul Council, sometimes called the Council of Elders). She asked for clarity about the purpose of different relationships that she had chosen for her current lifetime.

Among other things, the Council helped Judy look at the dynamics of her current-lifetime relationship with one of her sisters, with whom she has had many lifetimes of difficulty. Judy often experiences manipulation and one-upmanship from this sister; there has been a lot of jealousy and jostling for position between them. The sisters do a "dance" with each other, each wanting acceptance but not getting it. From the soul perspective, Judy came to see that she had "called" her sister into her life so that she could learn to disengage from negativity.

> J: If I don't like something, then I should work to change it, and not just sit back and complain about it.

Judy's last comment echoed one of her lessons from her Filipino lifetime. Judy then asked the Council about another challenging relationship she is having with her boyfriend, who will not commit to her. She was shown a lifetime they shared about two centuries ago.

> J: I had an older sister and our parents wanted to marry us off. This fellow came along as a suitor, and I fell in love. But our parents said that he had to marry the older daughter. He married her and I was heartbroken. I always loved him, and he loved me, but he had his status quo and he wasn't going to change.

Today, this same man is her boyfriend, and her older sister in the earlier incarnation is his daughter from this present lifetime. Once again, he won't "upset the apple cart" with his children to be with her. She wanted him to take a stand in that lifetime as well as this one, but she could see that it wasn't going to happen. The situation requires her to value herself enough to move on.

Questioning her Council members further, Judy wanted to know how she was doing in her soul progress and how to improve. They encouraged her, saying that she is not blocked, just impatient; she is on the right track and needs to let go of her high expectations for herself.

Judy also asked how to connect more with her guidance when working with her clients. The Elders explained that she needed to learn to trust herself and let go of the need to know everything. (Judy tends to feel not good enough if she doesn't know it all.) They reminded her that she is worthy of nurturing, love, and reverence.

Follow-up Interview

In my phone interview with Judy two years after her LBL regression, she reported a number of ways that the session has impacted her life.

Judy had suffered from chronic headaches for many years, and they lessened after her LBL. She saw a possible connection between those headaches and her death as a Filipino man, which had involved a sharp pain in her head, and felt it significant that in the between state, her guides had "cleansed" her with light energy to clear the trauma of the death.

Her life review with her Soul Council helped Judy develop more compassion for herself and others. She realized that we are all interconnected, and we can't judge another without judging ourselves. Recalling that her Soul Council gave her options for the location of her next lifetime, Judy shared how she arrived at some of these major insights. "Seeing the option of an Asian lifetime helped me to be less judgmental, because I know I could have easily chosen the life path of any person I was judging. It also helped me to see how interconnected we are. I chose the USA because I felt there would be more support to get through my lessons. I could have been over in Asia learning these same lessons. I'm really no different from anyone else."

I asked Judy whether her studies in healing while attending "school" in the between state had proved useful in her work. She attributes a greater understanding of her healing abilities to her experiences in the spirit realm. She also reclaimed some of the healing abilities in her hands after the session. Her work in the NIH-funded research study for cancer survivors has continued, and she is contributing her enhanced skills. "I've connected with having energetic healing tools embedded in my hands," she said. "I use them when I work with people. By my holding a higher vibration for people, they can get into resonance with me and with that vibration, and then the shift in their life happens very quickly."

Since her LBL, Judy has learned to value and empower herself in her relationships. She has freed herself from self-defeating patterns involving other people. For instance, she stepped out of the "dance of dysfunction" with her sister. Because she is now conscious of how she used to get drawn into that negative dynamic, she no longer chooses to participate in that. I also asked about the longtime boyfriend who would not commit to her, who had married her sister in a prior lifetime. Going by her insights in the spirit realm, she did indeed leave him.

Judy recognized a pattern of being unavailable to her family in her past life as a Filipino man. The reverse had happened to her in this current incarnation, starting with a dominating father who was disempowering toward women. Having been a judgmental and abandoning male in her previous life, she understands that she came into this life to feel that same insensitivity mirrored back to her. She realizes that she "invited" all the players in her drama to help her learn to have more compassion for herself and others. With this deeper insight into her patterns, she is now breaking that cycle and creating a more joyful life.

Judy's memories of the "clearing and washing of the old dreck" after her last lifetime, and the love she received in the between state, have stayed with her. The experience has reminded Judy of her value as an eternal soul. Despite the dramas, lessons, and transitional circumstances of life, all of which bring growth, she realizes that her essence as a perfect spiritual being, worthy of love, never changes.

"I'm at a place where I am pretty happy with who I am," she concludes. "Other people tell me that I just glow. My energy field is clearer and brighter now."

A Journalist Builds Bridges of Understanding

Betty is a public relations consultant for nonprofit organizations. She has a master's degree in religious studies and writes a column for a metaphysical magazine. To learn more about her life purpose and progress as a soul, she did a series of sessions beginning with two past-life regressions, a life-between-lives regression, and a Soul Visioning session. We had a follow-up interview about a year and a half after her sessions.

Past-Life Insights

Betty's first past-life regression revealed some of her motivations for choosing her husband in this lifetime. During the French Revolution, she was a peasant girl, cleaning a priest's house. (The priest in that past life is her ex-husband in this life.) She was attracted to the handsome priest, but he was "forbidden fruit." He was sent away (perhaps reassigned), never to be seen again by Betty in that lifetime, much to her disappointment. Betty married another man who loved her. He eventually marched off to fight for Napoleon and was apparently killed in battle. This left Betty sad, alone, and disillusioned with the "politics" of war.

Betty came into this current lifetime with a soul agreement to be with the priest from the former lifetime. The intent was to help him open up to Spirit. However, her best efforts to assist him were of no avail, and the marriage ended after many years. Betty admits that she wouldn't face the reality of her stagnant marriage. She again was encountering loss and learning to create a different script for herself in this lifetime. Part of her lesson is feeling worthy of a spiritually intimate relationship and trusting that one is possible for her.

The Quality of a Royal Presence

Betty's second PLR brought up another encounter with political upheaval, but this time, she experienced the futility of war while in the role of a royal leader.

> BETTY: I was both a spiritual and a temporal leader, a princess or a queen of some sort on this large island *(Betty feels this may have been Ireland).* The king—my father and my mentor—died, and the power passed on to me. It was a very peaceful kingdom until the Vikings arrived. I had to send my people to develop a new life in the mountains and secret valleys, with new leaders. I stayed behind with a few core people to meet with the Viking leader and their priest. They were surprised that we were not fighting. The priest wanted us killed. He saw it as our gods against their gods. The Vikings were fearful because they couldn't control us. They placed us in a small temple. They didn't know that we had the power to be taken up to the other side. *(This statement made sense to Betty while she was experiencing this past life.)* When they came to find us, we were gone. I was sad because I was too trusting—in terms of using the power of persuasion to change them and have peace—and it didn't work, because they were too much into their way of doing things.

Sometimes a past-life "character" brings out a part of ourselves that we need to acknowledge. Betty's prior lifetime as a ruler helped her to reclaim some of the presence and feeling of the quality of royalty in her present life. That quality emerged very strongly during the session, as she commented upon hearing her voice on tape.

> B: I hadn't noticed how different my voice was. The way I spoke was very regal, which amazed me, because I don't talk that way.

Having the quality of royalty can mean that we have a sense of our own authority, and that we are worthy to be heard, and to receive good things from others. Other people respond to that. After her session, Betty realized that she needs to own the quality of royalty in her current lifetime.

> B: I am always the one who tells people what's going to happen, but nobody listens. I especially feel that way with people that I am closest to. With the royal presence, you are very accepting of gifts and compliments, like you deserve them. The royal presence is something that I want to bring more of into my life.

Journey to the Life Between Lives

An LBL session further helped to clarify some of the issues that Betty has carried into this current life and to illuminate her soul purpose here. Once in a very deep trance, Betty was regressed to the last day of her most recent past life.

> BETTY: For me it was a surprisingly emotional event. I was a young woman dying in childbirth. I was observing this woman from the perspective of my current existence. Yet at the same time, I was there, feeling intense sadness at leaving my family, especially my husband. I started sobbing, "It seems unfair!"

Betty's young husband in this past life was the same young man who had left her in another past life to follow Napoleon into battle. Now she was the one leaving him behind.

It appears that Betty had carried over unfinished business—some fears of giving birth—to her current life. She filled in some missing pieces when we talked after her LBL session.

B: The past-life death experience that led into my LBL gave me a deeper understanding of one of the out-of-synch pieces in my current life. As a child, I loved my Barbies, but I never enjoyed playing with baby dolls. As for real children, it's not that I didn't like kids. I did, as long as they were over two years old. It's the babies that I couldn't handle. As I got older, I just couldn't see myself with a baby. Every time I thought about it, the words would flash through my mind, "You will die." I am now in my fifties. While I have wonderful stepchildren, I have never wanted my own biological children.

If I had known earlier in life about the Soul Visioning process, I could have healed those fears. This would have allowed me to make childbearing decisions with a clearer vision, no longer obscured by unconscious fear and dread.

It should be noted that Betty is now "birthing" many worthy projects and using her nurturing capacities in other endeavors.

After her death experience, I eased Betty out of her body in that life and into Spirit.

B: After what seemed like a ride on a bullet train of pure energy, I ended up in front of a large library with majestic pillars. My guide told me that I was brought here first because of the questions that I had when I died. A very tall being showed me two books on a balance beam, indicating that the events in the life I just left were meant to balance things that happened in a previous life.

Now her guide took Betty to the "Hall of Mirrors."

B: My guide takes me there so I can see myself as I really am. I am in front of a shiny building. There are several corridors, and various entities like myself are entering them. At the end of the corridor that I enter is an enormous mirror. At first the mirror is cloudy. Then it clears and I come face to face with a huge blue light, so much bigger than this self that has just made her transition. I am not only seeing my Higher Self, I am feeling it, being it. I *am* my Higher Self. The self that has just made her transition is part of my Higher Self, but my Higher Self is the essence of who I really am. I realize that each separate life is like a thread in a magnificent tapestry. Up close, you are apt to focus on the individual threads, but then you are only seeing a section of the whole. To get the bigger picture, you have to stand back. Then it makes sense.

During her visit to the Hall of Mirrors, her Higher Self told Betty that we live many lives. Some are "detour" lives, in which we coast along without fulfilling what we came back to do. Her immediate past life was one of these, she was told, and it was time for her to get back on track.

Betty's next stop was a visit with her soul group. In a happy reunion, she recognized entities there as being close friends in her present life. She was surprised to find her mother in this group, who is quite traditional in her religious beliefs, and to hear her mother say, "I'm more advanced than you think."

Betty then experienced two visits with her Council of Elders.

B: In the last visit, I asked them about progress in my present life. Their message: I am a bridge builder, building bridges of understanding between people. They told me I am doing a good job. As the publisher of a bilingual community newspaper, I built bridges of understanding between Hispanic and non-Hispanic residents.

With my PhD studies, I am building bridges between science and theology, and between traditional Christianity and alternative spirituality. In a column I write, I also try to build bridges by showing that there are many paths to the Divine, and that we are richer by exploring and appreciating them. Sometimes I get frustrated about this soul path stuff—the "What am I doing here?" type of thing. The visit to my Council of Elders provided a measure of comfort.

Soul Visioning Session

In her Soul Visioning, I guided Betty into her ideal future in her current lifetime, where she envisioned a soul-guided life of service as a bridge builder between different cultures and ethnicities. Her vision also included earning her PhD in theology and experiencing a deeply loving, connected primary relationship. It was clear that there were some blocks to her belief that she could have a wonderful life partner after coming out of a difficult divorce.

> BETTY: When I started Soul Visioning, I was freshly and difficultly divorced. The process revealed that I had made a contract with my ex-spouse and now the contract was complete for me. I am now free to invite a soul mate who truly resonates with me into my vibration. My soul vision is an amalgam that integrates the bridge-building aspects of my life with a soul mate. It took me a while—and another PLR—to internalize that vision, but I am feeling it now. I expect it. I am in the flow.

Follow-up Interview

I interviewed Betty eighteen months after her past-life regressions, life-between-lives session, and Soul Visioning.

> BETTY: During my Soul Visioning process, I asked what my soul path should be now. I was told that everything I had done and was doing was part of that path. As I have learned, that doesn't

mean that you don't set your intent. You do. But in Soul Visioning, rather than setting that intent from the ego's "I want X, Y, Z" perspective, you are setting your intent in concert with the full orchestra of your Higher Self, of your soul. It was from the expanded perspective of my soul that the vision for my future emerged.

The message was that I should not get so focused on specific pieces of the soul path. The bigger picture is what counts. I shouldn't obsess over the details so much. I should let myself be guided [by the larger themes of bridging] and let it flow. One of the deep values of Soul Visioning is the recognition that the process is ongoing—that it takes time and dedication to accomplish. This is not the promise of a one-minute miracle. It is the promise of a continuous evolutionary spiral, a living dynamic that leads toward greater soul awareness.

Looking back on the past lives she accessed has given Betty a clearer focus on the role she wants to play in serving the world.

B: My past lives as ruler of an island that was besieged by the Vikings, and as a peasant girl during the French Revolution, have given me the perspective that grandiose political schemes are more likely to muck up the world than fix it.

Betty's past-life experiences confirm her belief that soul-based solutions are needed to solve the world's problems, and are aligned with her current career and the direction in which she is moving.

B: Presently, I am a public relations consultant for non-profits, specializing in youth and family issues. I am working toward my PhD in theology and human sciences, with a focus on the idea that ecstatic experiences with the Divine can transform and deepen our capacity for love, compassion, and altruism.

The visit to the "between state" in the life-between-lives process gave Betty a direct experience of being her Higher Self. This has had a profound impact on her, given that she had died in childbirth and was still feeling, at a deep level, the loss of her family, her child, and her life. And as she said earlier, Betty now realizes that dying in childbirth impacted her decision in this current lifetime not to have children.

The meeting with her Council of Elders validated that Betty is doing well on her soul path, and that there are many paths to the Divine. It was an important lesson that we are so much more than just the roles and dramas that we play out on the stage of life.

I'll let Betty have the last word, sharing her view on how all three processes work in harmony to foster a deeper soul connection.

B: Soul Visioning allows you to experience the individual threads of the tapestry of your Higher Self—and to see how those threads are woven into the bigger picture. It is a fluid process. Indeed, as the Soul Visioning process unfolds, the tapestry changes. Past-life regressions, life-between-lives regressions, and Soul Visioning create new threads in the tapestry of Higher Self. They are the threads of understanding that add nuance and meaning to current life situations. They are the threads of intent that set the tone of living your current life in joyous synchronicity with your soul path.

A Healer Unblocks Her Healing Abilities

This case history describes one of Gayle's several past-life regressions and includes excerpts from her life-between-lives session. It concludes with highlights from a follow-up interview four years later.

Gayle is a quiet, humble, middle-aged nurse at a major university hospital. Though she was often called upon to use her healing and intuitive abilities with doctors and nurses on the hospital staff, and sometimes with patients, Gayle felt apprehensive about using her hands-on healing gifts. She wanted to find out what was holding her back. She didn't trust herself, and carried guilt that she couldn't identify. People would die or get hurt, she feared, if she were put in a position of power. As there was no basis for this belief in Gayle's current life, she wanted to clear any unresolved patterns that she may have carried over from a previous life.

Growing up, Gayle always felt different from others. Beginning when she was five, she saw and spoke with her angels, but her family never accepted or supported her special gifts. At fourteen, she found that she could heal animals. Children often teased her about her psychic abilities and accused her of being a witch. She was also able to talk to deceased relatives. For example, she received specific details about an uncle who had died much earlier and about whom she knew very little. The information that came through about him proved to be accurate. Although Gayle had grown up feeling loved and wanted by her parents, she always wondered if she could fulfill what she was supposed to do in this current life.

Past-Life Insights

At the beginning of Gayle's first PLR, I gave her the suggestion under hypnosis to go to the root cause of her blocks to using her healing gifts in this incarnation. (In regression work, it is not necessary to go into all of the lifetimes that contributed to a particular limiting belief. I give the unconscious mind a suggestion to return to the origin of the issue, and it takes the person wherever they need to go.)

Gayle went back to a lifetime as a Civil War officer named Samuel Smith, who fought in 1862 on the Union side in Virginia. Sergeant Smith was born in Illinois, and was twenty-two when she returned to that lifetime. Gayle later validated this information. Using the Internet to research Civil War casualties, she discovered that a Sgt. Samuel Smith, born in Illinois, had indeed died in 1862.

During Gayle's past-life memory as Sgt. Smith, she recalled being mortally wounded in the back. As Smith lay dying on the battlefield, he felt regret and remorse that many of his men had died under his command.

Journey to the Life Between Lives

In a later life-between-lives session, Gayle visited the spirit realm, between her last lifetime and this current life, to review what she had learned. (Remember, an LBL experience consists of going back to one's most immediate past life, going through the death, and then transitioning into the between state.) Gayle returned to her most immediate past life, during the Civil War. After she briefly reviewed that life, she left her body and easily transitioned into the spirit realm. She passed through a tunnel, heard a loud humming sound, and followed a bright white light. The feeling of returning "home" was overwhelmingly beautiful. But she needed a respite after going through so much fighting in that past life. Helpers were there to assist her.

Soon, Gayle said, Jesus appeared to her as a figure glowing with a brilliant white-gold light. He told her, "You won't be in any more wars," and that she would not return to Earth for a while. According to Gayle, Jesus then said, "I will leave you in the hands of these three"—referring to spirit guides.

Gayle feels a close relationship to Jesus in this current lifetime, so it wasn't surprising that this reassuring figure appeared to her in the transitional period. When a client encounters religious or spiritual figures during an LBL session, I don't make judgments about whether they are "real" or a client's projection. I feel that in the spirit realm we experience whatever makes us comfortable until we can go beyond the form to the Essence of who we are. Just as we have teachers and mentors here in the physical dimension, I believe that we also have nonphysical helpers in the spirit dimension who assist with our soul growth. The degree of their knowledge varies, just as it does on the earth plane. My standpoint is therapeutic. If the guides or teachers act as compassionate helpers, then this is useful. Many people have reported great comfort and direction from them—as Gayle did from her vision of Jesus. Ultimately, we need to learn that higher wisdom is already within us. Until we do, external sources of help (symbolic or not) can be of great value.

One of the three spirit guides who appeared to Gayle was a Native American named Nahanewana, appearing with a golden hue. He has been with her the longest, she says, and "takes care of me the most," usually speaking words of comfort or guidance.

Gayle began to speak in an unfamiliar language for a brief time during this segment of the regression. She later took the recording to a language specialist, who identified the language as a Native American dialect. According to Gayle, Nahanewana talks to her and through her in waking life, spontaneously and frequently, both in English and in his Native American language. Gayle usually understands what he is saying when he speaks in his own language, and speculates that she may have been a Native American in another lifetime.

Another of Gayle's guides, named Rebecca, appeared in a young female body, and her color was pink and mauve. Her third spirit guide was Shaunessy, an Irish fellow who spoke with a brogue and had a blue hue. They communicated telepathically and individually with her.

As a facilitator of Gayle's soul journey in the spirit realm, I was sometimes guided to ask questions to assist in her understanding. I am not sure whether the answers to my questions below were coming from Gayle or the guides. At that point she was connected with her soul guidance, and the answers flowed from her. Again, just who is speaking is not the focus, because the quality of the guidance is more important than the specific form or source of knowledge.

In this brief excerpt from Gayle's LBL session, she spoke in a vernacular that seemed to fit a Civil War soldier of limited education.

GAYLE: I didn't want to fight. Waste of my time. I didn't marry. I wasn't a bad person, but this war thing . . . I wanted to go to school to become a doctor, but I couldn't leave my ma. Next time I want to be a woman. *[After the session, Gayle realized that she chose nursing to fulfill the medical career she didn't pursue in that past life.]*

SUSAN: *And how will that help you?*

G: I won't be in no mo' wars *[sic].*

S: *What do you need to learn by being in a woman's body?*

G: Love. To feel.

S: *Are there any beliefs or patterns or unfinished business from that life that you've carried over into this current life?*

G: Holding grudges.

S: *Anything else from your last life that your guides are talking to you about?*

G: I was unkind. I would fight. Fistfights. Mostly in the tavern. They didn't really believe that I was any good at anything I did.

S: *Can you change that in the life that you are now living?*

G: The grudge part, I'm still doing that. I know it's wrong and I know I shouldn't do it, but it's so hard.

S: *Is that what you're here to learn?*

G: How to forgive people. *[Upon further discussing this with her guides, Gayle recognized that she chose a female identity for this present lifetime so that she could learn to love and to forgive more easily.]*

S: *Anything else your spirit guides want you to do?*

G: To do healing work. Let it flow through me, and I don't do the healing. It comes from the power, the God force. Also, I have to work on my fear.

S: *What is the source of your fear?*

G: I'm not really afraid. I'm doing what I'm supposed to be doing. Sometimes I'd like to be just like everyone else. Because I killed so many.

Gayle is carrying guilt from many lifetimes in which she felt responsible for the death of others.

S: *What will this healing work teach you?*

G: That I am Spirit.

S: *What are the roots of your fears that are holding you back from fully using your healing ability?*

G: That people won't be healed. It's their [choice] whether they are healed, it's not up to me.

S: *Have you carried over any other beliefs, blocks, or errors that hold you back from using your gifts?*

G: I was burnt as a witch. When I was in school in this life, I was called a witch all the time, even though I didn't do anything. So I said to a girl that I wished she'd break her arm. Well, she fell down the school stairs that afternoon and broke her arm, but I didn't do it. They were always calling me a witch, even in this lifetime.

S: *What needs to be done to heal that?*

G: I need to believe in myself. When Spirit speaks to me, I need to trust it.

At this point Gayle's guides told her the session was finished. I facilitated her return from the spirit dimension. Apparently she did not need to explore other aspects of the between state that are typical in an LBL session, because she had received the information she needed.

Gayle's Follow-up Interview

I did a phone interview with Gayle four years later. Gayle has had significant shifts in her life because of her regression experiences. She has let go of grudges related to her personal life: her spiritual growth is more important to her than hanging on to petty resentments, and she is working on releasing grudges in her professional relationships as well.

She has also forgiven herself for the lifetimes in which she felt guilty over people dying under her power or command. She realized that we all choose our earthly curriculum, and that she could not be responsible for the lessons others chose for themselves. Now that Gayle has released this pattern of guilt, I am thrilled to say that she has unblocked her healing ability. Today she uses her hands for healing rather than killing. "I am Spirit. Spirit works through me," she says.

Nowadays, Gayle is an extraordinary hands-on healer in a large hospital and has enjoyed many successes. For example, when a fellow nurse was diagnosed with Stage 3 breast cancer, Gayle gave her weekly hands-on healing treatments for several weeks before she began chemotherapy and radiation. The woman felt very calm and reassured by receiving the healing energy, and the guidance Gayle received was that she would be OK. The woman never got sick from the chemotherapy and, after two years, she has had no recurrence of cancer.

Another nurse suffered an aneurysm and was told she needed surgery, but had only a fifty-fifty chance of survival. When Gayle placed her hands on her, the voice that she calls the Holy Spirit told her that the woman would be all right. The nurse came through the surgery fine with no negative aftereffects. What was most healing, she said, was the reassurance and peace that came over her when Gayle worked on her. This allowed her to go through the process without fear.

Recently, Gayle described a remarkable healing that took place with her mother. While they were on vacation together, her mother stumbled and fell. Gayle took her to the emergency room of a local hospital, where the staff X-rayed her ankle and found a broken bone. Gayle elected to take her to a larger hospital to have her foot and ankle put in a cast. On the way to the other hospital, she did some "hands-on" healing to relieve her mother's pain. When the larger hospital took new X-rays, no break was found.

Gayle also related another interesting consequence of her regressions. She used to have leg pain when working with certain patients, so much so that at times it was hard for her to walk. She realized that this was related to another past life in which she had been wounded in a war. Even though our regressions didn't touch on this other lifetime, her leg pain went away after our sessions and has not returned. When the root of a problem is healed, this often has a ripple effect relating to other lives. I believe that when Gayle forgave herself for that Civil War lifetime, it generalized to similar lifetimes in which she felt guilty. She no longer needed to identify with the pain of those lifetimes.

People often report that their channels of communication with spiritual guides are more open after a PLR or LBL session. Gayle was already in touch with her spirit guides before her regressions, but she feels that they helped her to realize that she isn't "crazy," to be more open to her guidance, and to put more trust in her clairvoyant abilities. Her veils—blocks—were lifted, and she now receives messages from deceased people who want to communicate with loved ones. For example, a deceased mother came through to Gayle, wanting to help her daughter to let go of an issue with which she was struggling. Gayle passed on the message. The daughter was grateful because it gave her clarity about the problem that she previously did not have.

Gayle now can predict when someone is going to get pregnant, and the sex of the child. One of her nursing coworkers had tried unsuccessfully to get pregnant, and was quite discouraged. Gayle intuitively "saw" the soul waiting to come in and the sex of the child. She relayed the message to her colleague. Two weeks later, the woman came to her in tears of joy having learned she was pregnant!

It is important to note that Gayle's sessions are not typical. She has some clairvoyant ability, which allowed her to access very specific names, dates, and places in her past lives that could be independently verified. Of the thousands of people I have regressed, only a few have spoken in another language while in the altered state.

Although these phenomena are interesting, what is most important is that Gayle became unblocked through forgiveness and reconnected with her worth and essence as a soul. This has allowed her to use her talents and gifts to their fullest expression.

A Wise Woman Shares Her Regression Journeys

Rose is seventy-two as of this writing. A retired counseling psychologist and hospice pioneer, she did two past-life journeys with me over a ten-year period and a life-between-lives session four years ago. In a recent follow-up interview she shared how her life has unfolded since then.

I am grateful to Rose for writing her story and sharing it with me (re-grettably, in a shortened form here). Although I have met few people who can recall their sessions in such depth and rich detail, I believe that writing and journaling, as Rose has, helps anyone gain insight from a regression experience.

Like Rose, many women over fifty are working through "wisdom years" transitional issues, including menopause, aging, the empty nest, rene-gotiating their relationships with their husbands, their waning role as mother and/or career woman, and retirement. Who am I? Where am I going? Of what use am I now? Questions like these come up often in my practice. I also find that, like Rose, many people seek out regression work when their Spirit is calling them to find answers through transitions or crises.

I can see why Rose has been a midwife to the dying. She brings such gentleness and dignity to her discussion of aging, death, and loss, which are still taboo subjects in our society.

As a person who has consulted her soul's guidance and the spiritual realm to make the transition into her "wise woman" years, Rose is a wonderful role model. She exemplifies what is possible when an elder places an emphasis on her soul and on using her wisdom to help others.

Rose's Current Lifetime: Some Background

Rose began her story with some background on her current life up to the point when she experienced her first past-life regression (PLR).

As a Western woman, I came of age in a time of advanced educa-tion and job opportunities opening our world. I helped to pioneer many of these changes as a psychologist in private practice, and as a counselor at a large hospice. I helped others develop new plans for personal and professional lives. Women's lives, hospice, loss, and unresolved grief called to me, and I found rewarding work in these areas for many years.

Nearly a decade ago, I moved with my husband, away from the demanding, urban professional life I had experienced for thirty years. We retired to the Meadow, twenty acres in rural Wisconsin. This would be a giant transition for me. Not only were my dreams and meditations opening the vision of how to make this move happen, but Spirit was telling me that this move was necessary. My body was beginning to break down.

I concluded all work except for the women's spiritual retreats that I had begun in Wisconsin ten years before. Like other deeply intuitive and introverted people, I had been "extroverting" for a long time and was weary.

A big challenge would be to let go of my therapist, healer, and teacher roles. At the retreats, I had facilitated lasting growth and new ways of choosing life for many others. Now I desired clarity for myself.

My life has been filled with connections and symbolic experiences that have led to a rich inner reality. I have used meditation, visualization, stories, and dream work both for clients and myself. Because I have memories of other times and places, I intuitively felt that a past-life regression would give me a guideline for the changes I faced in the next year.

Rose was one year into her own retirement and confronting the inner challenges of moving from a fast-paced, stressful life to a quieter, contemplative existence when she had her first past-life regression.

Rose's First PLR Session: A Past Life in Scotland

This past life takes place in Scotland, probably in the late 1600s or early 1700s. I love being this woman. I am struck by her strength and determination to be a good wife, mother, and helper. She learns with an open mind and cheerful attitude. I see and feel her connection to the light of Spirit throughout her lifetime.

Seemingly, this woman has always understood the process of death and transition. Recognizing the need for comfort, distraction, pain relief, and reassurance, she is a steady light in the midst of what was then unknown and fearful to many. I am reminded of C. G. Jung, who suggested that life is not what we want it to be; it is what it calls upon us to be and how we respond to the call. That is where we evolve.

Practical yet imaginative, energetic yet quiet, she is somewhat educated, but learns more from her gardens and the natural world than from books. (I interpret this as a message to put down the books for a while.) She is aware of Spirit every day as she communes with the herbs and flowers. Knowing how to be happy, she follows her understanding of the natural world and sees it all as "One."

As her past-life experience began, Rose was unsure at first whether she was barefoot and standing in a tropical forest, or clad in a wooden clog over wool socks, standing on grass. Sometimes the unconscious mind takes its time to settle on which life to review.

I cannot choose, then I simply step out and find that I step with the firm touch of the clog. I am wearing a heavy tan cotton skirt, blouse, shawl, and scarf. I am looking out over an incredible sunrise, coming up over a lake that stretches for miles down below the hilly terrain, which is wild with flowers.

In my twenties, I have two sons. My husband William is older than I am by ten or twelve years. I lived in England until this marriage. Now I am in Scotland, and William owns a good farm. He travels and teaches others how to farm.

Ours is a strong home with a thatched roof, kitchen/sitting room, and two bedrooms. William uses a small area at one end for his writing and reading. I believe that William came to talk to farmers in northern England where my family lived. He fell in love with me and was pleased that I knew so much about plants and how to read and write. He had been married before, but his wife had died of the chest sickness and they had no children. She was fragile, but I am strong, young, and healthy. I delivered both sons well. They run by my knees all day long.

I have flower and herbal gardens outside the kitchen door. I have learned a great deal about the medicinal use of herbs. The leaves dry in the sun, hanging from the kitchen rafters, and then I store them in clay containers with cork or wooden tops. These are about four or five inches high and hold a piece of wool to absorb dampness. I make teas, and poultices for sore limbs and chest pain. I know how to bandage limbs. William encourages me to learn all I can and be helpful to people.

William is happy with me and I with him. There is kindness between us, enough food and clothing, and a proud home to tend. William travels around the countryside and I don't mind, as I am busy with the boys and the herbs.

I become skilled in caring for the very ill and the dying. I give them teas and potions, and work with a doctor who calls upon me when someone is very ill. Sometimes I stay at their home a few days as they try to reach into the darkness of the night and prepare for death. I do not fear death. It is the passageway of sickness that is difficult for many, and I ease their way with sleeping herbs.

I see myself caring for a woman in her fifties who has the sores sometimes called cancer on her chest. I tend to her wounds, give her tea, bring her flowers, and tell her stories. I know she will die in the next few days. Some people are frightened of the death spirits, but I understand it is a natural part of life. I am older now, and when I care for others, I wear an apron over my dress. I take this off when I go home, believing it carries sickness on it that I don't want in my home.

I see my sons grow to be tall men. One works a great deal with his father, traveling and learning from him. Both of our sons read and write. I read and write better now after William's lessons with his sons, but I still prefer the gardens, home, the care of others, and the light.

When William is in his late fifties, he gets the wasting sickness where he cannot eat and keep the food inside of him. He dies quickly and I use all the knowledge and skills I have to help him die peacefully. We have been married nearly thirty years, and we have had a good life together. He still believed he loved me when he died. I do not understand love as William used the word. But I cared for him deeply.

Our sons are grown and the younger one is one of my sons today. He is a strong man and very good to me. He becomes involved in politics and goes off to lead other men in small battles in Scotland. The older son is married to a woman I know now; it could be my daughter. They have children and their own life.

When my younger son marries, he and his wife live with me and are very good to me. I tell the grandchildren stories of the family history and of fairies and their world of light and healing. I get thinner and my joints move more stiffly now. I still go outside and bathe in the light. Even in old age, the light is healing.

Now I talk with the herbs. They have been telling me how to use them and care for them for a long time. We talk now as old friends do, sharing the secrets of the world. I see colors around herbs that tell me different things about them, and in the moonlight, there is a light around each plant and flower. Sometimes, my son lays me on a thick rug beside my garden, so that I might talk to my friends.

As I lay there one day, I feel I am floating and I can see my body lying on the rug. Up I float, into this light that I have always known. I sense great freedom, peace, and joy. I move with all that is above, around, and through the sense of "me." Then I begin to melt and the "I" becomes one with others in the light and energy.

Rose Finds Links Between Her Scottish and Present Lifetimes

This current lifetime feels very familiar; surely our move to rural Wisconsin is similar to my former self's move to Scotland. I am older, and yet I feel younger in this move, anticipating time to be with my husband and restore myself to good health. I sense a need to let go of bits and pieces of the past that still hurt. I know, too, that we both need time to reconnect and to be present with each other.

My current experience reaffirms my love of light, being alone, gardening, and being with my husband and family. Separating from the fast-moving world permits us to get accustomed to each other in a quiet, ordinary way. I am so exhausted at first that it takes several years before I wake up feeling rested and eager for the day. We spend time watching the many wild animals and birds, watching sunsets and stars.

Within two years, my body can no longer sustain itself without major surgery. I locate a fine healer surgeon, healing more steadily than I have in years. We move my aging mother into a nearby nursing home, where we visit her daily. In her late nineties, she has been disappearing through Alzheimer's bit by bit for five years.

This time of illness and Mother's tiptoeing into death is our awakening to the preciousness of our lives together, and we take conscious steps to let go of even more emotional debris. We talk of things we have done together or separately, travels, family, early life experiences, and what our marriage and friendship have meant to us. We learn simply to "let it go." As I heal physically, my soul opens even more to the power of the present.

Perhaps the greatest gift we have received is that our relationship has deepened. We spend much time with each other and we each follow individual artistic endeavors. We complete as much old business as possible when it appears, and now we do it very quickly in a quiet, healthy, and sometimes humorous way.

As a therapist, I used to think that most couples don't know what marriage is about until they have been married twenty or more years. Now as my husband and I begin our seventies and our fiftieth year of marriage, I think that most of us don't truly know what love is all about until we go a long distance together. Perhaps it is why this time is called "golden." I like to think that I will die by my gardens at the Meadow, and when I do, I'll breathe into the light and just let go.

Rose's past life was a reminder of the joy of a quieter lifestyle. It awakened a knowing within her that this stage of her life can be fulfilling and meaningful. Remembering past-life parts of the self is like a "soul retrieval" that helps us reclaim what we have forgotten. The Scottish woman part of Rose gave wisdom from the past that could be used in her life now, to help her flow more easily into the changes that usually come at this stage of life.

Rose's illness and her mother's decline awakened her realization of the preciousness of life. Her retirement brought the gift of a deeper relationship with her husband. Often we must come to terms with the purpose of our primary relationships and rediscover the gems that lie dormant within them. This past-life memory helped to bring more clarity for Rose's transition into the wisdom years.

Second PLR Session: A Past Life in a Desert Community

Rose contacted me four years after her first PLR session. She had been very ill and had a long recuperation from surgery. This prompted her to face her feelings about aging and her own mortality by experiencing another past-life regression.

During her session, she had an emotionally intense and challenging past-life memory, which she felt had taken place in the Middle East. She commented, "Women were chattel and rules were strict for everyone, for the survival of the tribe. For a woman born in this long-ago time, I was fortunate to have had even the small life I lived." Considering her role in the lifetime that she describes below, I find it significant that Rose has spent a good part of her current life helping to empower women, children, and families in her psychotherapy practice, women's circles, and retreats. She has also helped the catastrophically ill, and has assisted the dying to ease their transition into the afterlife. I have no doubt that her connection to this past life contributed to her great empathy, compassion, and ability to care for people.

From my first barefoot step into a land of brown, tan, and cream colors, I am aware of the dryness of the earth and brilliant sunlight. My skin is brown and I am in my twenties. I live with constant fear of attack, death, fire, and loss. We hide in places under the earth, but there are not many places to hide. Riders with knives come in the night, and they torch anything that burns. Houses are destroyed. Sometimes we move away, but we always come back here. This is our home.

My father died fighting. Men grow up quickly in our little place, and go immediately into protecting and fighting. Many men have died, and I don't even know if my brother is alive. He's been gone so long, guarding out in the distance. My mother was killed. Women and children are stolen and women are raped. I've not been raped; I'm fortunate.

I had two children. I don't know if the father is alive or dead. I don't think I was married. One child was born early and very tiny. He lived a little bit of time and then one day, he left. I was told not to cry, because he was happier in the world of ghosts. I was told I could talk to him and he could hear me. He's no longer a baby, so I don't talk to him the same way. He would have been ten, eleven, twelve years old now.

My other son was killed by soldiers, people we'd never seen before. He was playing at the edge of this place where they were. He was five or six years old. Many were killed. I feel numb talking about it.

Quiet time alone is when I walk to the water hole to irrigate plants I raise to feed the community. It is very dry and dusty here. Some things grow only with great care.

I find another time of quiet when I go out on a mound under the stars, where I watch a tribal leader. He sits at night and learns from the stars. He seems to know when people come to hurt us, and keeps us safe. Before things happen, he knows they will happen. I think if I sit near this special man, I'll learn something. Women in the tribe are not allowed to learn in the way of a man. I am not important enough to ask questions of him.

The man is my friend now. We are not lovers, just friends. I learn to see stars raining light downwards, and I learn a small bit of how stars change through the different moons. I teach him how to see stars and he teaches me how to listen to stars. (I have tears and sigh deeply.) The stars tell him when there will be danger, and they tell me the time to plant and to harvest. I learn how to help our people by listening, seeing, and sharing. I receive the birth of personal consciousness here, learning I am more than I thought. It is an epiphany, a gift of self-knowledge.

After I become more conscious, I teach children how to care for the plants, and how to hide when we are attacked. I wish I had known how to do this with my son who was killed many years before. I feel safer than when I was young, because now I know what is happening and to prepare those I love to be careful.

I'm now in my late thirties. In this desert lifetime, I learn the concept of "letting go." Sometimes two or three seasons go by and there is some peace, and then darkness comes again and many are killed. The stars teach us when to leave, usually soon enough. People who are killed and hurt are those who do not believe the warnings, and stay in their homes to hold on to what they have.

I help to bury our dead. There are prayers for those who have died to have a safe passage. We know that they go to the stars to continue their journey. The most important part of dying and transition is to go beyond the pain, freeing oneself. And those who live need to let go of the pain as well.

When I recall in the session that I will die by fire, I gasp with shock. One family doesn't leave at this time of danger, and they have three children. I love these children dearly, and so I decide to stay. I cover them and myself with a blanket and dirt, and I hold on to them. We're on fire and the little ones, I give them kisses (sigh).

Then the stars begin to rain light. When the starlight enters our bodies, it is like a sparkling light. We detach from those bodies, moving into Spirit. I am with the children and our spirit bodies are holding hands; we're dancing and we're happy. And their mother is there and we go to her to help. She is bent, and we move the light around her for a while. The one girl spirit wraps her arms around the mother and then she becomes straighter.

We stay together for a while, and then we walk into this huge golden light. Then we each become just light. I feel no separation and I feel free from the fear I experienced on earth. Later (I don't know what time means here) I sense a connection to the man who taught me about stars. I tell him all he "knows" is true, and that I'll talk to him again.

I spend a lot of time healing, learning, and being happy. I feel a sense of Self even though I'm not a Self. From this place, you can see there are other worlds. I can visit them as well as Earth, and I do. You just go there, and you can share learning in a faster way in some places. It's instant communication, clear messages, and when that exchange is completed, you can leave through the same way. I see Spirit moving, and we become vehicles of that energy and move quickly with it.

I asked Rose to describe how it felt to be in Spirit.

Whole . . . Great freedom . . . Space . . . Love . . . No fear. The Earth life I've come from seems very slow, thick, dense, like fog. The experience of Spirit is so clear. Transforming, pure light. Nothing is hidden.

At this point, Rose had what she later described as a "soul-shaking experience, a numinous moment."

Then I am overcome, in tears, and with shaking emotion I say, "I'm feeling Jesus." Every life has its crucifixion and its transition. I feel "union." I am touched by the deep love Jesus has for all of us. In the moments that follow, I receive personal direction, affirmation, and a sense of healing, unconditional love.

I have no words to express the palpable presence that was in the room as Rose experienced this deep state of unconditional love. Tears ran down our faces. I can only describe it as a joyful recognition of Divine Love and a direct experience of our soul essence. Rose chose not to write the personal communication she had from Jesus. (Although Rose is not particularly religious, she is deeply spiritual.)

I believe one significance of this life is that when one learns to live with their intuition and their native senses, they are safer in the world. Moreover, the awareness of Spirit is union and a sense of oneness, and it is there for anyone who can be still, listen, feel, and see into the light. In this lifetime, this happened through the stars. Though life can be abominable, Spirit is always present. Even in the driest desert of our soul, Spirit is available.

As in the lifetime in Scotland, once again I have touched the life of a woman of strength and courage, open to learning from life experiences. In this desert lifetime, I risk being different from others. I again work in gardens where I learn to love the light.

I understand from this the need to let go of past pains, and of the connection to pain, if I am to continue healing well in this lifetime. The experience opens me to deep intuitive knowledge of love, spirit, and health that I seem to have lost touch with in the post-surgery cloud of healing. After the visceral sense of this desert lifetime, I determine to follow my own path more fully at the Meadow, and continue to heal myself on as many levels as possible.

It is a good decision, as four months later my mother, who at ninety-seven has suffered with Alzheimer's for six years, makes her transition peacefully, with my husband and me by her side. Six weeks after that, my dear husband is diagnosed with cancer, and will have a long year of treatment before he turns the corner and begins to heal. My husband and I move through this time *not* clinging to pain, but looking for the light in each day.

This past-life experience helped Rose to face the challenges of her own health issues, her mother's Alzheimer's and transition, and her husband's cancer diagnosis. That past-life part of her was a reminder of her deep connection with Spirit despite the difficulties of her outer world. Rose knows to go past pain to her quiet center of Spirit, which is always available even when she is confronted with the darkest storm clouds of life.

Rose's Life-Between-Lives Session

About two years later, I felt guided to invite Rose to do an LBL session. I regressed her back through her present life, back to her birth, then further back to her most recent past life. Her written account of the session reflects her experience of being present, as if all events are happening in the moment.

Slowly, my husband and I find ourselves more connected than ever before and knowing the Spirit light of our union has led us to a good place. We continue to work at healing over the next two years, when Susan invites me to experience a life-between-lives session.

Rose's Most Recent Past-Life Memory

I am Neenah, a healthy, brown-skinned woman who lives in the Southwestern land of North America. It is the late 1700s or early 1800s. Once again I am a healer. We believe that the whole person needs to heal, and often people are not well because of not following their path in the right way. Fevers, diseases, and injuries are treated with herbs, poultices, and drinks. Dreams are sometimes interpreted.

This is during the time when the black-robed priests come to our area and build the first churches. These men are from the Franciscan order, and the priest who comes to our area is kind. I believe there is only one Spirit, one light. The priests don't seem to understand this the way that I do, but it doesn't matter. All healing comes from this one Great Spirit. The priest helps us to hear the words of Jesu [*sic*] and Mary. When he understands our beliefs of Mother Earth, Father Sky, and the help we get for the hunt and for growing corn and beans in a dry area, he helps us to combine these thoughts together. Our little church has pictures painted of Mary/Mother Earth and Jesu/the Father God.

My husband is a hunter, and he makes music well. The black-robed men like him and he plays often for them. He is a good man and kind. We create a happy family with three children.

Again, I sit with those who are dying, giving them support and comfort. I talk to Jesu and Mary and ask that they comfort these souls. I have no fear of death. Our community has always believed in an afterlife, and that people travel on to a happier existence.

When I am an adult, many in our community are very ill. I do not get this illness, nor does anyone in my family. I dreamed I should wash myself whenever I would be with those who are ill. I believe in the messages sent to me in dreams, and I taught my family this as well. Sometimes there is a hunting accident. Without washing the wounds quickly, a bleeding sickness and high fevers begin. We use herbs and plants to help the body heal and help stop the pain. The medicine man chants and offers prayers to the old believers and the priest comes to the new believers. I think that whatever a person believes will be of the most help to them.

We can see that in this lifetime, Neenah demonstrates both intuition and advanced thought.

Neenah's husband dies before her, and though her aging years are good ones as she lives with her daughter, she misses him. She seems to have had a considerably closer relationship with her husband than what she experienced in the Scottish life. She also seems more connected with a larger community.

I know that I will soon die. I am well, but my spirit is weakening, and I think that my heart is getting too old to be here anymore. One night, as my daughter sits by my side, I simply stop breathing and go on. I lift right out of my body. I check to see if she is all right and then I go very fast like the wind, and I'm in Spirit.

Rose's Transition from Death in the Spirit Realm

Pastel rainbows are all around me like wind music. I think some of this color is spirits taking me with them. Then I see my mother and father spirits. They walk with me to a garden. I see many spirits working around the plants and smiling. Some seem familiar and raise their hands in greeting. I have never seen some of the plants before. My parents walk with me to a garden that looks much like the one I have at home, except that it is brighter and healthier.

My parents tell me that someone is waiting for me here. I turn and see a tall man, my spirit guide as I have known him forever, Lothar. He looks younger than he has appeared to me before in my current life. My parents leave. Lothar leads me to a stone bench. He says they have brought me to this garden because it would be familiar to me, while I accustom myself to being in pure Spirit again. I find myself breathing slowly, as if I am very tired or weak right now. He says he will leave me here for a while, but when I am ready, I can call or think of him, and he will return immediately. I marvel at this form of communication. It isn't as if we are really talking, but simply sending messages to each other silently, and it feels completely right.

I don't know how long I sit, gathering my strength. Time is very different here. I begin to review my own life, what I learned from it, what I regretted, and what I enjoyed. I think about how I learned healing from two major sources: from my own community of healers and elders, and from the black-robed priests. They are from the same source of healing and love. Jesu brought the words of love to us, and my husband and I used that thought throughout our lives. I learned about sitting with those who are dying, and I know in my heart that there is truly a transformation and transition at death. In my older years, I was a teacher. I regret not having more time with my children, but they are both strong adults. Not knowing what happened to my oldest son, my heart hurts thinking of him. But I feel grateful for my life and what I learned about family, healing, teaching, Jesu, Mary, and about it all being one.

Then Lothar is walking towards me. He asks if there is anything I wish to know about my life on Earth, and I tell him it hurts me not to know what happened to my son. He points to his right. Then I see my son at age twelve, on a horse, riding with other boys. My son and another boy go off on their own. They ride a long way and are laughing and talking, not paying attention to what they are doing. They are attacked by men from another community. These men take them to their community a long way off towards the setting sun. The boys are adopted.

Lothar presses my hand as if to say, "It is all in the past now. You could only block the memory. But look." Then I see a man in his thirties, who looks so much like my husband that he could only be my son. He is strong and well, happy and content with a family and children, and he lives off to the west in California. He was not mistreated, just stolen. He had to overcome deep grief to go on with his life. The foundation he received in our life together gave him the strength to make a good life. I am so happy for him. I look at Lothar and say, "I do not need to hold on to him. I just needed to know where he is and how he is now. Thank you."

Meeting with the Council of Elders

Lothar waits for me to take this in, and then he says, "Come, there are some people who want to be with you." As if time has turned very quickly, we are now in a place like no other that I have ever seen.

In front of us is a beautiful building with white columns. The building material looks like the brightest marble in the universe. It is closed in and yet open. There are many doors going into this building. It is filled with light. We walk to a doorway as if I had done this dozens of times before. I know what it will look like inside, and it does. There is a circular room and a small pond in the center. There are low curved benches around it. Lothar and I sit. I feel apprehensive and excited at the same time.

Four figures appear and I stand out of respect. First to appear is a tall woman with brown eyes and a long black braid. She is beautiful in a regal, noble way. She is wearing a floor-length, beige-white gown. She smiles at me with compassion and deep interest.

Next to her is a man not quite six feet in height, with brown hair and gray-blue eyes, wearing a light-brown robe. I know him right away. He is my brother guide. He greets me with a hug and a big "Hello, little sister." We have shared many Earth lives together.

Next to him is the archetypal wise old man with a rounded belly and full face. He has white hair and a short white beard. He wears a dark-brown robe. His twinkling eyes are bright blue, and he takes my hand. I feel his warmth and sense of humor. I don't think I know him and yet I feel as if I do.

The last figure astounds me. He is nearly seven feet tall with black hair and smooth, slightly tan skin, and wears a dark-blue robe. He has the dark, piercing eyes of someone from the Far East. I know immediately that he is a seer, and as soon as this thought enters my mind, he nods. He has an intelligent presence, and is powerfully regal.

Rose is unable to remember what the Council of Elders conveyed to her. When she reviewed the recording, it was full of static. (I have found that occasionally, when the energy of the session is high, the tape either has static or is erased.) Her journal writing of her session was interrupted at this juncture, and she never completed it. It seems that certain things were not meant to be remembered until the appropriate time, despite my posthypnotic suggestion to remember everything.

A few months after this session, Rose wrote the following:

Now it is difficult to remember what they wanted me to know. But I do remember that I thought these four spirits were a part of myself. The woman, noble and caring; the brother, warm and tender; the wise old man whose eyes sparkled, and the seer who could see a long way.

Now I only seem to remember my mother's voice telling me near the end to write my words about death; she would help me.

Post-Session Reflections

Here Rose relates insights that came to her two years after her LBL session.

Returning home from a poetry workshop, I recall the Seer. Aware of his presence, I accept him as a guide in my future. Now I feel ready to meet him. A month later as I sit in meditation, I receive the Seer with his strong presence, calm demeanor, and intelligent vision. I hear these words: "Your time for seeing is now. You are a channel to other knowledge that can be helpful to you, your loved ones, and friends. You see ahead, you see the past, and you see the connections. Channel information from the other side. It is all right now, as you are healthy and strong. You have loving support, and many possibilities to continue life in new ways."

Later, I receive a gift of beautiful moon flowers. As I gaze at them, I hear the Seer in my heart once again: "You are beauty and carry it wherever you are. I am only a moment away from you now, and am here through the last part of your life experiences. I have been waiting for you to reach this place. You have completed everything. Now you move totally into your spiritual life, offering healing to self and others, spreading love wherever you go."

Two years after my LBL, I am aware of subtle changes in my inner and outer life. I am confident again, as I was when younger. At the same time, I am more fragile in my body. Arthritis and spinal stenosis due to a teenage injury create constant pain.

I am concluding my retreat work with the women's circles. I offer my writing as part of my volunteer services to help women, families, and needy children in our community. I am also writing our family stories, adding the wisdom that my husband and I have accrued in this challenging and good life. I believe our soul lives and physical lives are moving in the same rhythm now. No matter where we go, we are at home within ourselves.

We have grown in our roles to become the elders, the anchors of our family. We give ourselves openly to the next generations;

we give of ourselves in our individual ways to our community. By living our spiritual convictions, we believe we are leaving our family a spiritual legacy.

I took the knowledge given in the spiritual regressions and used it consciously to give direction to my life in these transitional years of becoming an elder. The LBL enabled me to visualize the strength, knowledge, and depth of these four wonderful guides. They possess soul dimensions of leadership, compassion, caring, loyalty, honesty, humor, sensitivity, and the gift of vision. As I reflect on these four archetypes found deep within my soul, I feel that I am integrating them within my being. They expand my world and give me great comfort as I move ahead.

If doing the regressions has reaffirmed who I am, meditation and dreams support what I have learned. We are so much more than our bodies, and this is especially helpful to remember after age sixty, as we begin to discover minor or major physical challenges that we have never met before.

Indeed, life-between-lives sessions provide a wonderful reminder of that unlimited and expansive sense of our immortal soul.

Rose Reflects on the Regression Process

After completing this time of contemplation and writing, I found myself thinking that dreams and stories have guided the lives of many people. People have recorded memories that they cannot account for in their ordinary life and yet, the stories come to them in dreams, when traveling, after tragic life events. Having the stories witnessed by another is a powerful healing in itself.

Many therapeutic methods recognize the part of a person that is able to transcend into a different view, experience, or understanding of themselves. We may call it the Higher Self, the id, a piece of the collective unconscious, the soul, or simply the healer self within each of us. It has been debated which concept is more accurate, but I believe they are all of equal importance when a person's process in understanding themselves alleviates their psychic trauma and pain.

The most significant aspect of regression work is the presence of the therapist as "witness" to an evolving and active living-out of another lifetime. Nothing is set up for the participant. Each person chooses the events that take place, and has an opportunity to heal whatever psychic pain exists in that lifetime. One can freely determine what has been important to them in this past life, what they have learned, and how it relates to their current life. A gifted therapist creates an atmosphere of trust and safety as the client takes a courageous step into a former lifetime. They gently guide the client through any difficulties they might encounter. And when the session is completed, the therapist respectfully recognizes the experience this person has shared.

I found it helpful afterwards to talk a bit about the lifetime. This began the process of anchoring the knowledge and experience in my conscious awareness. Being given a recording of the session and writing it out furthered my process. Then, I integrated as much of the information as my unconscious self would permit me to do at the time. A good therapist fully believes in the gift of personal freedom to choose for one's self how their soul will use this newly discovered information.

Follow-up Commentary

Ten years after her first regression and four years since her last one, I did a follow-up interview with Rose. She reported that the sessions helped her to make life transitions and to gain clarity about her direction and purpose. She saw the continuity of her true soul identity and gained information in the Spirit realm from her guides. The themes of those past lives in the desert, Scotland, and the Southwest have repeated in this life. The former selves she connected with were women who went through tough times, but maintained a calm that helped others pass through crises and transitions. Her accumulated gifts from working with the shamans, being a "seer" of dreams, serving as a mid-wife to the dying, and being a healer have again been used in this life-time to bless countless others.

Rose found comfort in her lifetimes spent close to nature and from her experiences of dying peacefully. She was reminded not to fear death, and this helped her when her mother died. As Rose was challenged by retirement and health issues, her guides showed her the beauty of a simpler, less complicated life of meditation, sharing, and reflection. We have so few models to show us how to live in our later years. Rose exemplifies a woman who leads a soul-guided life. She is truly a sage and a model of a wise woman who embraces her golden years with peace, dignity, and soul expression.

Living Your Vision
Daily Choices to Express Your Soul

Now that we're in touch with our soul's vision, how do we live it? This final section is about taking time to nurture and reinforce that soul's vision, to energize its expression in our daily life. It is not enough to make one beautiful journey into our ideal future; we must tend to the garden of our soul's creation. We can weed the garden of our mind by practicing forgiveness and reprocessing limiting beliefs on a daily basis. We may cultivate a state of mind that welcomes new beliefs and attitudes that express our soul ideal. With our consistent patience in planting and tending the seeds of our soul's desires, they will blossom in the light of our loving attention.

To help you connect with and nurture your soul's vision in a way that becomes a natural part of *your* life, read on for ten practical suggestions: choices you can make every day. You will find that these tips reinforce one another. The best approach is whatever works for you. You may also wish to consult the Resources section for further ideas.

Suggestion 1:
Connect with your soul's vision daily (in three steps)

Think back to your soul-guided journey to your ideal future: you took a snapshot of a scene from that future to anchor the vision, to imprint the wonderful feeling of being in the synchronous flow of your soul. I suggest that every day, you intentionally access that feeling.

(FOR EXAMPLE: WHEN I WAS SINGLE, I *ENVISIONED* A LIFE PARTNER WHO WAS LOVING AND RESPECTFUL AND WHOSE SOUL PURPOSE INVOLVED BEING OF SERVICE. I *FELT* AND *BELIEVED* IN MY DEEPEST SELF THAT THIS WOULD UNFOLD: I HAD CLEARED MANY LIMITING BELIEFS AROUND IT, AND I FELT WORTHY OF RECEIVING AND GIVING SUCH LOVE. I LET GO OF ANY ATTACHMENT TO WHEN AND HOW IT WOULD HAPPEN. ALTHOUGH I HOPED FOR A SOUL MATE TO SHARE MY SPIRITUAL JOURNEY, MY FOCUS WAS ON MY OWN FORGIVENESS LESSONS, WHICH LET ME STAY OPEN TO THIS POTENTIAL. WITH OR WITHOUT A LIFE PARTNER, I CHOSE TO BE HAPPY. WITHIN TWO YEARS, I WAS SHARING MY LIFE WITH MY SOUL MATE.)

How you access your vision daily is up to you, but I recommend following these three steps.

A. **Envision and feel.** Bring up in your mind the picture and feeling of a scene or scenes from your "Ideal Future" journey and connect with your Ideal Future Self. (If you are not visually oriented, just bring up the good feeling.) *Feel* your soul's vision as if it is happening right now in whatever areas you want to focus on, such as relationships, career/work, health, finances, personal/spiritual growth, and so on. The key is to *feel* and *believe* it.

B. **Affirm.** Say one or more affirmations that go with that vision or feeling. (FOR EXAMPLE, I COULD SAY, "I FEEL THE JOY OF BEING IN RELATIONSHIP WITH MY IDEAL LIFE PARTNER.")

C. **Install by tapping.** While doing the above steps, do the WHEE bilateral tapping (see chapter 5) or any other energy psychology methods that work for you. Adding the *tapping* to the *feeling* while *saying* the affirmation enhances the power, because you are energetically installing the belief, anchoring it in the body-mind. If you have any resistance, do the WHEE tapping to clear limiting beliefs. For example, if you are having trouble believing you can do this, tap and say, "Even though I don't believe I can do this exercise, I deeply love and accept myself." Continue until your rating drops between zero and 2.

Suggestion 2:
Create images to go with your affirmation

To more fully involve your mind and body in the affirmation, link it with some vivid images and then engage with them mentally. Using pictures and symbols adds a depth that goes beyond just saying or thinking the words. It integrates the left and right brain hemispheres, which makes the affirmation even more powerful.

Draw a picture or a symbol that represents the feelings of your affirmation. One way to do this is with a double-page spread in your journal: on one page you write the affirmation, and opposite it you draw the symbol or picture that accompanies it.

You can also place the affirmation and images on sticky notes or sheets of paper to remind you of the *feeling* of your soul vision and of what you *believe*. Post these in strategic locations such as the refrigerator, the bathroom mirror, or on your computer, to keep this positive feeling active in your mind.

Suggestion 3:
Meditate on your ideals

From your chapter 3 worksheets on soul ideals, choose one or two ideals to focus on. Every morning, if possible, meditate for five to ten minutes on your soul ideal, asking for specific guidance on applying it. Ask, "How can I best be used to express my soul's ideal today?" *Be* the change that you want to see in the world. Be the mirror of your soul ideal to those with whom you come into contact every day.

For example, if your ideal is patience, connect with the energy and feeling of patience. You might think of a time when you were patient with someone, or someone was patient with you, to evoke the feeling of that ideal. Set the intent to express an attitude of patience toward everyone and everything that day.

Suggestion 4:
Keep a daily journal

Journal every day on how you apply your soul ideals, and on your experiences with them. See page 77 for instructions for your Daily Ideal Application Journal and a list of questions to guide your writing process.

Suggestion 5:
Practice mindfulness and cultivate positive self-talk

Stay aware of your thoughts, emotions, and bodily sensations throughout the day. Notice when you are engaging in negative self-talk. Stop and choose more affirming thoughts, using the WHEE tapping to anchor them (see chapter 5). If you are feeling overwhelmed and stressed, do the WHEE tapping to help yourself calm down. ("Even though I am stressed about _____, I deeply love and accept myself.")

You might also take a few minutes and, in your imagination, visit your garden sanctuary as you did on your journey to your ideal future. Immerse yourself with all of your senses in the calming energy of that scene. To help trigger the vision and the feeling, try using the OK sign (putting your thumb and index finger together, as you did at the end of that journey).

Suggestion 6:
Practice forgiveness

With the help of your soul, cultivate the practice of forgiving yourself and others. Remember, everyone is a mirror to us. Everyone gives us an opportunity to heal our own thoughts and perceptions. When we see the light in another—the light beyond the "lampshade" of their outer personality—it is reflected back to us. The more we forgive, the more we let go of our limited self. We can then awaken to joy.

Suggestion 7:
Follow a spiritual path

To reinforce your commitment to your soul growth, engage yourself deeply in your spiritual path or practice. If you don't have such a path, find one that resonates with you and helps you stay focused on your soul's purpose. If you already have a spiritual teaching, stay consistent in your practice. After all, this journey is a lifelong commitment. This book provides some tools that can accelerate your growth process in whatever spiritual path you are on.

Suggestion 8:
Surrender any problems to your soul

If a problem seems too big and you feel stuck, you can *surrender* the problem and release it to your soul to guide the process.

Are you struggling with a problem you just can't solve? Ask your soul to help you sort it out, then quiet your mind. When we're struggling, it's as if we're splashing and thrashing in a body of turbulent water. The answer may be there in front of us, like a rope just out of reach. The more we struggle trying to grasp it, the farther we push it away. Try being still and letting the rope come to you. Relax. When the waves calm, the rope can float within your reach.

Often, when we stop resisting, when we stop trying to control a situation, when we stop insisting on coming up with our own answers, that is when the soul's answer appears. It might not be instantaneous, but if we are patient, trust, and let go, we usually get the guidance or the solution that we need. (For more resistant and deeper issues, you can always ask for help from a qualified professional; some resources are listed in the back of the book.)

Suggestion 9:
Do a daily five-minute energy balancing routine

Doing a daily five-minute energy routine is like taking "energy vitamins" in the morning. Donna Eden describes six techniques in her book *Energy Medicine* (see the Resources section). These can help with stress management and keeping your energies unblocked and flowing on a daily basis. They may also enhance the energy psychology methods discussed in this book.

Suggestion 10:
Participate further in Soul Visioning opportunities

If you wish to deepen your understanding of Soul Visioning or want more ongoing support, consider participating in a Soul Visioning teleconference, workshop, or retreat. For further information, visit *www.soulvisioning.com*.

. . . .

I feel it is a sacred honor to have guided you on this Soul Visioning journey through this book. I hope that you have made some valuable discoveries about yourself and learned some helpful tools that will serve you on your healing path. May your soul's vision awaken in you the joy of knowing your True Self!

Resources

Following Up and Following Through

www.soulvisioning.com/svr

At this website you can download a free MP3 file or order a CD of the various guided journeys and meditations in this book. Worksheets to accompany many of the book's exercises are also available for free download.

The website also provides updates on events such as workshops, retreats, teleconferences, and trainings. Soul Visioning™ workshops offer more instruction and direction with some of the processes discussed in this book. Weekend retreats will provide more intensive experiences for those who wish to expand their soul's vision and learn more tools for self-healing. Teleconferences will be scheduled periodically for those who want added group support to keep their vision alive. Training programs for therapists in Soul Visioning methods will also be offered in the future.

Energy Psychology

Association for Comprehensive Energy Psychology (ACEP)

www.energypsych.org

ACEP provides training, workshops, conferences, and certification in energy psychology; it also conducts research. A member list of licensed/certified practitioners can be found on the website.

International Society for the Study of Subtle Energies and Energy Medicine (ISSSEEM)

www.issseem.org

ISSSEEM is an international nonprofit interdisciplinary organization dedicated to exploring and applying subtle energies as they relate to the experience of consciousness, healing, and human potential.

Daniel Benor, MD, developer of Whole Health—Easily and Effectively (WHEE)®

www.wholistichealingresearch.com/wheearticles.html

Introductory article:
www.wholistichealingresearch.com/selfhealingwheeandother.html

WHEE for children:
www.wholistichealingresearch.com/wheeforchildren.html

Study on effects of WHEE and HeartMath intervention:
www.wholistichealingresearch.com/WHEE_Research.html

Gary Craig, developer of Emotional Freedom Techniques (EFT)

www.emofree.com

This site offers a free manual and stories of people who have benefited from this energy psychology technique.

Tapas Fleming, developer of Tapas Acupressure Technique (TAT)®

www.TATlife.com

The resources here include downloadable, illustrated instructions for this powerful acupressure technique.

Past-Life Regression and Life-Between-Lives Regression

International Association for Regression Research and Therapies (IARRT)

www.iarrt.org

IARRT certifies and provides training in past-life regression at the beginning, middle, and advanced levels, and also conducts workshops and conferences on this topic. The site includes a referral list.

Michael Newton, PhD, developer of Life-Between-Lives (LBL) Regression

www.spiritualregression.org

Dr. Newton offers LBL training and a list of certified practitioners.

Brian Weiss, MD, proponent of Past-Life Regression (PLR)

www.brianweiss.com

This site offers a listing of past-life regression workshops, events, and trainings.

Other Websites of Interest

Association for Research and Enlightenment (ARE)

www.edgarcayce.org

ARE provides programs on holistic health, intuition, and soul growth.

EMDR International Association (EMDRIA)

www.EMDRIA.org

This organization promotes training, research, and a listing of certified practitioners in EMDR (Eye Movement Desensitization and Reprocessing), a process that is approved by the American Psychological Association for treatment of posttraumatic stress disorder and trauma.

Debbie Ford

www.debbieford.com

This site offers Shadow Process workshops, coaching, and training programs.

Foundation for A Course in Miracles

www.facim.org

The Foundation provides workshops and publications based on A Course in Miracles (ACIM).

Holographic Memory Resolution® developed by Brent Baum

www.healingdimensions.com

Training programs and practitioners are listed on this site.

Internal Family Systems training, developed by Richard Schwartz, PhD

www.internalfamilysystems.org

Workshops, training programs, and conferences in the IFS model are included on this site.

Sonia Choquette

www.soniachoquette.com

This site offers workshops, training in intuition, and books.

Recommended Books

Energy Psychology

Benor, Daniel. *Spiritual Healing: Scientific Validation of a Healing Revolution*. Southfield, MI: Vision Publications, 2001.

Eden, Donna, and David Feinstein. *Energy Medicine*. New York: Tarcher/Putnam, 1999.

Feinstein, David. *Energy Psychology Interactive: Rapid Interventions for Lasting Change*. Ashland, OR: Innersource, 2004.

Feinstein, David, Donna Eden, and Gary Craig. *The Promise of Energy Psychology: Revolutionary Tools for Dramatic Personal Change*. New York: Penguin, 2005.

Shealy, C.N. and Dawson Church. *Soul Medicine: Awakening Your Inner Blueprint for Abundant Health and Energy*. Santa Rosa, CA: Elite Books, 2006.

Forgiveness

Borris-Dunchunstang, Eileen. *Finding Forgiveness: A Seven-Step Program for Letting Go of Anger and Bitterness*. New York: McGraw-Hill, 2006.

Foundation for Inner Peace. *A Course in Miracles*, 2nd ed. Mill Valley, CA: Foundation for Inner Peace, 1996.

Renard, Gary R. *The Disappearance of the Universe*. Carlsbad, CA: Hay House, 2004.

Wapnick, Kenneth. *Forgiveness and Jesus*. Temecula, CA: Foundation for A Course in Miracles, 1983.

Past-Life Regression and Life-Between-Lives Regression

Bolduc, Henry Leo. *Life Patterns: Soul Lessons & Forgiveness*. Independence, VA: Adventures Into Time Publishers, 1994.

Bowman, Carol. *Children's Past Lives: How Past Life Memories Affect Your Child*. New York: Bantam, 1997.

———. *Return from Heaven*. New York: HarperCollins, 2001.

Lucas, Winafred. *Regression Therapy: A Handbook for Professionals. Volume I: Past Life Therapy*. Crest Park, CA: Deep Forest Press, 1993.

———. *Regression Therapy: A Handbook for Professionals. Volume II: Special Instances of Altered State Work*. Crest Park, CA: Deep Forest Press, 1993.

Newton, Michael. *Destiny of Souls: New Case Studies of Life Between Lives*. St. Paul, MN: Llewellyn, 2000.

———. *Journey of Souls: Case Studies of Life Between Lives*. St. Paul, MN: Llewellyn, 2001.

Stevenson, Ian. *Twenty Cases Suggestive of Reincarnation*, 2nd ed., revised and enlarged. Charlottesville, VA: University of Virginia Press, 1980.

———. *Children Who Remember Previous Lives: A Question of Reincarnation*. Jefferson, NC: McFarland & Company, 2001.

Todeschi, Kevin J. *Family Karma: The Hidden Ties That Bind*. Virginia Beach, VA: ARE Press, 2005.

Weiss, Brian L. *Many Lives, Many Masters*. New York: Simon & Schuster, 1988.

Woolger, Roger. *Healing Your Past Lives: Exploring the Many Lives of the Soul*. Boulder, CO: Sounds True, 2004.

Personality/Personal Growth

Baum, Brent. *The Healing Dimensions: Resolving Trauma in Body, Mind and Spirit*. Tucson, AZ: Healing Dimensions, A.C.C., 1997.

Nemeth, Maria. *The Energy of Money: A Spiritual Guide to Financial and Personal Fulfillment*. New York: Ballantine Wellspring, 1999.

Norretranders, Tor. *The User Illusion: Cutting Consciousness Down to Size*. New York: Penguin, 1999.

Pascal, Eugene. *Jung to Live By: A Guide to the Practical Application of Jungian Principles for Everyday Life*. New York: Warner, 1992.

Riso, Don Richard and Russ Hudson. *The Wisdom of the Enneagram: The Complete Guide to Psychological and Spiritual Growth for the Nine Personality Types*. New York: Bantam, 1999.

Schwartz, Richard. *Internal Family Systems Therapy*. New York: Guilford, 1995.

Relationships

Grayson, Henry. *Mindful Loving: Ten Practices for Creating Deeper Connections*. New York: Gotham, 2003.

Hendrix, Harville. *Getting the Love You Want*. New York: Harper, 1988.

Soul Growth

Assagioli, Roberto. *The Act of Will*. Baltimore, MD: Penguin Books, 1973.

Choquette, Sonia. *Soul Lessons and Soul Purpose: A Channeled Guide to Why You Are Here*. Carlsbad, CA: Hay House, 2007.

Ford, Debbie. *The Dark Side of the Light Chasers*. Hodder Mobius, 2001.

Reed, Henry. *Channeling Your Higher Self*. Virginia Beach, VA: ARE Press, 2007.

Thurston, Mark. *Soul-Purpose: Discovering and Fulfilling Your Destiny*. New York: Harper & Row, 1989.

Tolle, Eckhart. *A New Earth: Awakening to Your Life's Purpose*. New York: Penguin Group, 2006.

Notes

Introduction

1. The soul, sometimes referred to in this book as the Higher Self, the True Self, the Divine Self, and the Authentic Self, represents an aspect of our Divine nature. As I am using them here, these terms are roughly equivalent. However, for ease of reading, the word *soul* is lowercased throughout this book.

2. Exactly how much of the mind's function is unconscious, and how much is conscious? Research has resulted in varying opinions, but cognitive neuroscientists generally agree that most of the mind operates at an unconscious level.

Chapter Two

1. An overview of a number of such surveys and a summary of their conclusions can be found in Martin Seligman's *Authentic Happiness: Using the New Positive Psychology to Realize Your Potential for Lasting Fulfillment* (New York: Free Press/Simon & Schuster, 2002), p. 61.

2. Edgar Cayce Readings, 254–42 (case number/reading number). Edgar Cayce was considered the "father of holistic health." The complete collection of his medical and life intuitive readings can be found at the Association for Research and Enlightenment in Virginia Beach, Virginia.

Chapter Four

1. According to the concept of the "inner child," there are parts of us that carry hurts from our past, hurts that become repressed into the unconscious mind. Children cope with painful experiences as well as they can, given their environment and resources at the time. A child may not have many options to escape painful situations, so these "cellular memories" are stored away until the person is more capable of dealing with the unresolved emotions. Inner-child work gets in touch with those split-off memories and feelings, so that the needs that were not met earlier can be provided by the nurturing adult's Higher Self. Hypnosis allows the client to access those deeper memories and, from a place of compassion, care for and acknowledge those unmet needs. Once these memories are healed, the child is no longer running the show, and the Higher Self can take charge.

Chapter Five

1. The WHEE method is not EMDR or EFT, but it includes elements of both: bilateral tapping combined with the EFT affirmation statement.

Chapter Six

1. Foundation for Inner Peace, *A Course in Miracles*, 2nd ed. (Mill Valley, CA: Foundation for Inner Peace, 1996), Text, p. 562.

2. Thanks to Judith Perlman, LCSW, for permission to use her adapted template for the Forgiveness Letter. It is modified here using the language of Soul Visioning.

Chapter Eight

1. Dr. Weiss has made this statement in workshops and on his website, *www.brianweiss.com:* "It took me three months of daily meditation before I had my first regression experience" (text retrieved in July 2008).

Chapter Nine

1. I have integrated many modalities into the work that I do. In Anne's case, I used my Soul Visioning guided process, hypnotherapy, age regression, and Holographic Memory Resolution® (HMR). Some of the questions I asked Anne were based in part on HMR. For example, I asked her where she felt certain feelings in her body: "Does it have a size, shape, color, or a temperature, weight, or texture? Is there a number or age that comes to mind when you first feel a feeling like that?" Other techniques, such as framing the rescripted picture and running colors, serve to anchor the new resourced memory and feeling into the body-mind.

Journey of Souls

Case Studies of Life Between Lives

Michael Newton, Ph.D.

This remarkable book uncovers—for the first time—the mystery of life in the spirit world after death on earth. Dr. Michael Newton, a hypnotherapist in private practice, has developed his own hypnosis technique to reach his subjects' hidden memories of the hereafter. The narrative is woven as a progressive travel log around the accounts of twenty-nine people who were placed in a state of super-consciousness. While in deep hypnosis, these subjects describe what has happened to them between their former reincarnations on earth. They reveal graphic details about how it feels to die, who meets us right after death, what the spirit world is really like, where we go and what we do as souls, and why we choose to come back in certain bodies.

After reading *Journey of Souls*, you will acquire a better understanding of the immortality of the human soul. Plus, you will meet day-to-day personal challenges with a greater sense of purpose as you begin to understand the reasons behind events in your own life.

978-1-56718-485-3
288 pp., 6 x 9 $16.95

Destiny of Souls
New Case Studies of Life Between Lives

MICHAEL NEWTON, PH.D.

A pioneer in uncovering the secrets of life, internationally recognized spiritual hypnotherapist Dr. Michael Newton takes you once again into the heart of the spirit world. His groundbreaking research was first published in the best-selling *Journey of Souls*, the definitive study on the afterlife. Now, in *Destiny of Souls*, the saga continues with seventy case histories of real people who were regressed into their lives between lives. Dr. Newton answers the requests of the thousands of readers of the first book who wanted more details about various aspects of life on the other side. *Destiny of Souls* is also designed for the enjoyment of first-time readers who haven't read *Journey of Souls*.

978-1-56718-499-0
384 pp., 6 x 9 $17.95

To order, call 1-877-NEW-WRLD
Prices subject to change without notice
Order at Llewellyn.com 24 hours a day, 7 days a week!

Life Between Lives

Hypnotherapy for Spiritual Regression

Michael Newton, Ph.D.

A famed hypnotherapist's groundbreaking methods of accessing the spiritual realms.

Dr. Michael Newton is world-famous for his spiritual regression techniques that take subjects back to their time in the spirit world. His two best-selling books of client case studies have left thousands of readers eager to discover their own afterlife adventures, their soul companions, their guides, and their purpose in this lifetime.

Now, for the first time in print, Dr. Newton reveals his step-by-step methods. His experiential approach to the spiritual realms sheds light on the age-old questions of who we are, where we came from, and why we are here.

978-0-7387-0465-4
240 pp., 6 x 9 $15.95

Gifts of the Soul
Experience the Mystical in Everyday Life

CONSTANCE RODRIGUEZ, PH.D.

Personal transformation and spiritual evolution await you in the mystical realms of the universe. Blending ancient mystery traditions, Jungian psychology, and cutting-edge science, this practical guide is your boarding ticket to soul awareness and inner wisdom.

Psychotherapist Constance Rodriguez shares sacred keys for accessing the elemental, physical, astral, imaginal, and cosmic realms. She introduces the subtle energy body—the personal human energy field linked to the soul—that takes you to these gateways of higher consciousness. Through Dr. Rodriguez's psychonoetic or "soul-knowing" exercises, you can seek guidance from past lives, nature spirits, the four directions, spirit guides, and your own body and imagination. The answers and insights found in these inner and outer worlds can help you heal past trauma, resolve everyday problems, develop intuition, grow spiritually, and understand the path of your soul.

978-0-7387-1311-3
216 pp., 6 x 9 $15.95

The Fresh Start Promise

*28 Days to Total Mind, Body,
Spirit Transformation*

EDWIGE GILBERT

Everyone has the impulse for a new beginning—a fresh start. Whether your motivation is weight loss, stress reduction, recovery, or simply a lasting feeling of joie de vivre, this 28-day program can help you change your life . . . permanently.

Transform your mind, body, and spirit in just four weeks! With unique French flair, Edwige Gilbert offers a lasting program for personal change and spiritual growth that requires just twenty minutes twice a day. Dispel fears and negative thoughts that obstruct your vision of change. Tap into the universal healing energy known as Qi (chi) for vitality and enthusiasm to pursue your goal. Discover your talents and gifts and reconnect with your true self. Integrating the body, mind, and spirit, Gilbert's proven techniques and exercises are based on yoga and Taoist traditions, hypnotherapy, and behavior modification principles.

Gilbert's inspiring makeover concludes with a plan to strengthen your new conditioning, achieve future goals, and maintain a life of laughter, love, and peace.

978-0-7387-1322-9
288 pp., 6 x 9 $17.95

Real Steps to Enlightenment
Dynamic Tools to Create Change
Amy Elizabeth Garcia

Connecting with the divine is crucial for spiritual advancement, but choosing a spiritual path is anything but easy.

Amy Elizabeth Garcia simplifies the journey to enlightenment into thirty-three spiritual goals, such as finding your life purpose, developing trust in the universe, relinquishing the need to control, recognizing synchronicity, and fostering peace. Focusing on a specific spiritual lesson, each chapter begins with a divine message from the author's spiritual master that includes stories from his human incarnations. Garcia goes a step further in bringing these concepts to life by sharing her own life experiences. Every chapter includes a prayer inspired by angels and exercises for spiritual growth—the perfect complement to this beginner's guide to enlightenment.

978-0-7387-0896-6
264 pp., 5³⁄₁₆ x 8 $14.95

Bringing Your Soul to Light
Healing Through Past Lives and the Time Between

DR. LINDA BACKMAN

What happens after we die? What is the purpose of my current life? Have I lived before?

In this unique and inspiring guide, Dr. Linda Backman answers these questions with compassion, objectivity, and more than thirty years of experience conducting traditional and past-life regression therapy with clients. *Bringing Your Soul to Light* includes a wealth of first-hand accounts from actual past-life and between-life regression sessions, offering readers a compelling and personal glimpse into the immortality of the soul.

Readers will discover the extraordinary universal connections we all share in this lifetime and beyond. They'll learn how they can use this knowledge to heal and grow, both physically and spiritually, by understanding themselves on a soul level and releasing energetic remnants of past-life trauma

978-0-7387-1321-2
264 pp., 6 x 9 $16.95

Wheels of Life

A User's Guide to the Chakra System

ANODEA JUDITH

An instruction manual for owning and operating the inner gears that run the machinery of our lives. Written in a practical, down-to-earth style, this fully illustrated book will take the reader on a journey through aspects of consciousness, from the bodily instincts of survival to the processing of deep thoughts.

Discover this ancient metaphysical system under the new light of popular Western metaphors: quantum physics, Kabbalah, physical exercises, poetic meditations, and visionary art. Learn how to open these centers in yourself, and see how the chakras shed light on the present world crises we face today. And learn what you can do about it!

This book will be a vital resource for: magicians, witches, pagans, mystics, yoga practitioners, martial arts people, psychologists, medical people, and all those who are concerned with holistic growth techniques.

978-0-87542-320-3
480 pp., 6 x 9, illus. $21.95

Yoga Nidra Meditation
Chakra Theory & Visualization

JONN MUMFORD
NARRATION BY JASMINE RIDDLE

Yoga nidra is a life-changing technique practiced by sages and yogis for thousands of years. Available for the first time as a digitally remastered compact disc, *Yoga Nidra Meditation* can help you achieve a unique state of consciousness conducive to self-healing and spiritual growth.

Dr. Jonn Mumford, a world-renowned authority on Tantra and yoga, and Jasmine Riddle will guide you through Tantric meditation and visualization exercises. Accompanied by music and mantras, your conscious awareness will rotate through your physical body, mental images and sensations, and the chakras—ultimately ending with "psychic sleep." During this special state of consciousness between wakefulness and sleep, you can communicate with your subconscious.

Full relaxation—physical, mental and emotional—is just one of the many benefits of yoga nidra. The enclosed sixteen-page booklet explores how this technique is a catalyst for efficient sleep, deep meditation, healing childhood traumas, awakening the chakras, and spiritual enlightenment.

978-0-7387-1446-2
A digitally-remastered audio CD $16.95
and 16-page four-color booklet

To Write to the Author

If you wish to contact the author or would like more information about this book, please write to the author in care of Llewellyn Worldwide and we will forward your request. Both the author and publisher appreciate hearing from you and learning of your enjoyment of this book and how it has helped you. Llewellyn Worldwide cannot guarantee that every letter written to the author can be answered, but all will be forwarded. Please write to:

Susan Wisehart
c/o Llewellyn Worldwide
2143 Wooddale Drive
Woodbury, MN 55125-2989
Please enclose a self-addressed stamped envelope for reply,
or $1.00 to cover costs. If outside U.S.A., enclose
international postal reply coupon.

Many of Llewellyn's authors have websites with additional information and resources. For more information, please visit our website at:
www.llewellyn.com